MGM
WHEN THE LION ROARS

By Peter Hay

WITH

Woolsey Ackerman ◆ Robert S. Birchard ◆ David Chierichetti

Hiro Clark ◆ Vic Cox ◆ Lee Davis ◆ Daniel Eagan ◆ John Fricke

Timothy Gray ◆ Howard Mandelbaum ◆ Richard P. May

Michele Rubin ◆ Merrill Shindler ◆ Linda Sunshine

Lena Tabori ◆ Marc Wanamaker

Turner Publishing, Inc.

PUBLISHED BY TURNER PUBLISHING, INC.
A Division of Turner Broadcasting System, Inc.
One CNN Center
Atlanta, Georgia 30348

Library of Congress Catalog Card Number: 91-065802

PRODUCED BY WELCOME ENTERPRISES, INC.
164 East 95th Street
New York, New York 10128

PROJECT DIRECTOR: Lena Tabori
PROJECT MANAGER: Hiro Clark
DESIGNER: Mary Tiegreen
EDITOR: Daniel Eagan
PICTURE RESEARCH: Woolsey Ackerman

DISTRIBUTED BY ANDREWS AND McMEEL
A UNIVERSAL PRESS SYNDICATE COMPANY
4900 Main Street
Kansas City, Missouri 64112

PICTURE CREDITS: The majority of the illustrations were provided by Turner Entertainment Company and the MGM Collection at the Academy of Motion Picture Arts and Sciences in Los Angeles. Individual credits [right (r), left (l), center (c), top (t), bottom (b), top left (tl), bottom left (bl), top right (tr), bottom right (br), right center (rc), left center (lc), top center (tc), bottom center (bc)]: Courtesy of Woolsey Ackerman: pages 24-25, 38(bl & br), 63(t), 75, 97(lc), 98(tl), 104(b), 105(tl), 108-9, 112(tl), 118(bl), 122(tl & lc), 139(tl), 146(t & bl), 164(tr), 202(bl), 209(tl, tr, lc, & br), 234(br), 286(b), 289(t), 307(br); Courtesy of Camden House Auctioneers, Inc.: pages 168(tl & tr), 169(tl), 173(tr, rc/top, & rc/bottom), 174(tl & r), 175(t); Courtesy of Ed Carfagno Jr. & Sr.: pages 142-3, 149, 150-1(tl, lc, & r), 173(br) 174(bl & br), 175(bl & br), 186(rc), 318-9(t), 320(tr, c, & b), 321; Courtesy of Bruce Hershenson: pages 15, 40, 49(tl), 73, 97(br), 101(t), 113(br), 114(l), 119(tl), 185; Courtesy of Marge Meisinger: page 208(c & rc); Courtesy of Liza Minnelli (Photos by Geoffrey Clements): pages 235(tr), 240(tl), 241(tr), 296(b); Courtesy of Mrs. Vincente (Lee) Minnelli: pages 218(t), 255(tr); Courtesy of Dorothy Tuttle Nitch: page 238(bl); Courtesy of Marvin Paige, Motion Picture and Television Research Service Archive: pages 8, 41(t), 48(bc), 62, 66(tl), 67(lc & bl), 82, 84, 85, 108(tl), 116(tr & c), 117, 118(t), 120(tl, tr, & bl), 124, 129(br), 139(bl & br), 140(tl), 147, 148, 156(tl & bl), 157, 164(tl), 177, 190(tc & tr), 191, 199, 200, 211, 213(tl & tc), 215(tr, bl & br), 234(t & bl), 235(br), 238-9(l & tr), 242-3(tl & r), 245(bl & br), 253, 268(tl), 287(br); Courtesy of Jay Scarfone and William Stillman Collection (Photos by Tim McGowan): page 208(bl); Courtesy of Lena Tabori: pages 38(br), 311(t); Courtesy of the Thomas Tarr Technicolor Collection: page 172 (tl); Courtesy of Mary Tiegreen: pages 20(tr), 21, 28(t), 33(t), 36(lc), 37(tl), 41(rc), 47(t), 50(tr); Courtesy of Marc Wanamaker/Bison Archives: pages 3, 10, 11, 12, 14(r), 20(tl), 58-59, 61(tr), 66(br), 67(tr), 69(tr), 161(tr), 162(b), 166(tl & bl), 166-7(tc), 167(tr & bl), 251(tr), 256(tl), 281(tl & tr), 302(t), 307(rc), 312(t).

First edition

10 9 8 7 6 5 4 3 2 1

Printed and bound in Japan by Toppan Printing, Co., Inc.

ISBN: 1-878685-04-X

ACKNOWLEDGMENTS

Turner Publishing would like to thank the following people for helping to make the book possible: Ted Turner, Scott Sassa, Ira Miskin, Roger Mayer, Dick May, Woolsey Ackerman, Cathy Manolis, Gerry Clark, Betty Cohen, Sue Kroll, Jed Simmons, Andy Velcoff, Susan Tungate, Barbara Swint, Marshall Orson, Jennifer Falk-Weiss, Dennis Miller, Joni Levin, Keith Clarke, Hazel Newsom, Frank Martin.

—Michael Reagan

Thanks to Lena Tabori for asking and Michael Reagan for having faith; Hiro Clark for sensitivity and editing; Nancy Van Anders for researching; Roger Mayer and Woolsey Ackerman at Turner Entertainment and Ted Hatfield at MGM/UA for sharing information; Point Blank Productions (Frank Martin, Michael Henry Wilson, Joni Levin, Keith Clarke, Mike Loreto) for advice, clippings, and all their taped interviews; Daniel Eagan for saving me from some grievous errors, though I own what heresies remain.

. Thanks to librarians at the Academy of Motion Picture Arts and Sciences, USC Special Collections, American Film Institute, Los Angeles City Public Library, and the Glendale and Pasadena Public Library System.

Thanks to friends for being there: Lia Benedetti, Michael Donaldson, Hermine Fuerst-Garcia, Jacqueline Green, Paul Jarrico, Richard Kahlenberg, Joshua Karton, Miles Kreuger, Eva Nemeth, Marsie Scharlatt, Brad Schreiber, Harold Spector, Eve Siegel Tettemer.

And thanks to my wife Dorthea Atwater and my mother Eva Hay for keeping me going during a difficult period.

—Peter Hay

A few thanks from Welcome:

At Turner: To Ted Turner for falling in love with the MGM library, for buying it, and caring for it; to Michael Reagan for wanting this book, and for wanting us to make it for him; to Ira Miskin and Roger Mayer, for their consistent support; to Dick May, whose professionalism, knowledge, integrity, and savvy rest comfortably with his kindness; and Cathy Manolis, for making the impossible often possible; to Woolsey Ackerman, our picture researcher, our critic if we strayed, our constant source of information, our factchecker, our cheerleader.

At Welcome: No book in Welcome's history has been so fascinating, so seductive, so complex and so elusive as has MGM. In the year that we have worked on it, so have more than seventeen authors responded with speed, talent, and good nature to our endless requests. Most of them are listed on our title page. Some, like my friend John Hart, just pitched in where needed. Hiro Clark, my vice president, saw the forest and the trees at all times. He managed, edited, wrote, cajoled, and cared for everyone—both outside and inside. He is, first and foremost, responsible for seeing this project through. However,we both had solid help: Daniel Eagan edited the running text, Linda Sunshine the sidebars, Michele Rubin the yearbars; Marsha Lloyd, Robin Jacobson, Timothy Gray were all copyeditors; Jennifer Downing aided on all levels; Marc Wanamaker was our second factchecker; Steven Gorney saved us as we struggled through the maze of publishing software on our brilliant but idiosyncratic Apples; and Ellen Mendlow guarded the treasure trove of art and photographs and guided their passage through our impatient hands.

To Mary Tiegreen, the wonderfully gifted designer of this book, with whom I worked hand in hand from the beginning (when there was only a beginning); to her associate, Dianna Russo, whose energy and dedication were indispensable; and to Jennifer Vignone, Scott Park, and Mutsumi Hyuga for their help.

Picture research was complicated by the diversity of sources, which, in turn, gave us the opportunity to make relationships with some impassioned and highly knowledgeable collectors. Particular thanks to Marvin Paige, Marc Wanamaker, Bruce Hershenson, Mrs. Lee Minnelli, and Igor Edelman, without whom we simply would not have gotten started in the right direction. Thanks also to Liza Minnelli, for allowing our photographer to visit her home.

And, finally, to John Hanley at Toppan Printing Co., who saved us from ourselves.

—Lena Tabori

ADDITIONAL PHOTOGRAPHS: *page 1* Grand Hotel *(1932); pages 2-3* Flesh and the Devil *(1926); page 4* Louis B. Mayer; *pages 6-7* Laughing Sinners *(1931); page 8* Lion's Roar *cover; pages 16-17* The Kiss *(1929); pages 58-59* Grand Hotel *(1932); pages 142-43* Marie Antoinette *(1938); pages 248-49* An American in Paris *(1951); page 324* Doctor Zhivago *(1965); page 336* Buster Keaton.

All dates accompanying film titles, with a few exceptions, are based on official theatrical release dates.

CONTENTS

LION'S ROAR

ARS GRATIA ARTIS

The Fourth Issue

INTRODUCTION

"It was *the* great film studio of the world," actress Helen Hayes recently recalled of Metro-Goldwyn-Mayer in the 1930s, "not just of America or of Hollywood, but of the world." When people think of a dream factory, or its typical product, they usually conjure up some of the unerasable images from MGM's golden age and the kingdom where Garbo and Gilbert, Crawford and Gable, Loy and Powell, Tracy and Hepburn, Mickey and Judy—and so many others—once dwelt. Those memories are tripped every time the magnificent head of a lion appears and his menacing but measured roar is heard.

Leo the Lion is still roaring, though he is no longer king of the jungle. Successive heirs have dismantled and auctioned off the treasures of the kingdom; his subjects have moved elsewhere. His former territory has been claimed by new predators. Yet, even in decline, MGM remains a potent combination of letters, not only representing the surviving film company but also lending prestige to hotels and an airline. The roaring lion, one of the best known corporate symbols in the world, is worth almost as much as any of those tangible assets. Most of all, the spirit of MGM survives through some two thousand films, which keep alive the name and the standard of filmmaking that the studio once embodied.

This book is about that past. It attempts to convey how the dreams were born, grew, and became real; how movies were made and promoted; how a great enterprise was built and then destroyed—all in less than the span of a person's working life. We use as markers the two epic productions of *Ben-Hur*, released in 1925 and 1959, to define the period of MGM's greatness, which coincided with the studio era of Hollywood and helped to define it.

During those years practically every major star, director, and writer worked at the studio. Obviously, in this brief history we can only touch upon a few of their names. In showing what went into the making of a fantasy such as *The Wizard of Oz*, or into the launching of Joan Crawford toward stardom, we ask the reader to imagine the vast industrial process by which such creative acts were repeated hundreds of times. Because the pictures tell their own stories, the brief historical narrative is meant to sketch the events and people behind the scenes. But the story is not just about a handful of directors, stars, and executives of soaring ambition; it is also about a family of thousands who worked together for decades, living out their creative years in an institution that became legendary while still at its height.

Inevitably, in a business centered upon the telling of tales, MGM created its own folkways and lore. While a purely historical account might have left out the famous anecdotes spun around the studio and some of its outstanding personalities, we felt that these were an important part of the company's culture. Few of them can be authenticated for source or accuracy, but they often tell us more than the so-called facts. The movies are not about facts either. They are about dreams, illusions, and myth.

There have been film factories before MGM and since, and yet there was something special about the studio, with its own style and way of making films, which made it preeminent. There was no formula, or else it might be more easily articulated and imitated. But we hope that this book might come close to defining the essence of what was once MGM.

PROLOGUE

Metro-Goldwyn-Mayer was the result of a corporate merger made on Wall Street in April 1924. The deal was the crowning achievement of theater magnate Marcus Loew's career. Born in the slums of Manhattan's Lower East Side, this modest, self-made man went to work at the age of nine for thirty-five cents a day and by the time of his death, at the age of fifty-seven, he had built an entertainment empire worth thirty-five million dollars. Loew's personal fortune eclipsed that of all the other movie moguls of his time, except for that of his rival, Adolph Zukor, the founder of Paramount Pictures. Both men were short and slight, and both started in the fur business. Like the Warner brothers, William Fox, Carl Laemmle, and Samuel Goldwyn, most of whom got their start in the clothing trade as well, Loew and Zukor knew their material, whether it was made of fabric, images, or dreams.

Less flamboyant than other pioneers of the film industry, Marcus Loew had a quiet genius for business. He tended to hire people for life and then demanded their total loyalty. Nils T. Granlund, a colorful Scandinavian whom Loew employed as a publicist in 1912 for his growing string of theaters, wrote that the devotion he felt "to this wonderful guy… was to last for the rest of his life and his death was my biggest heartbreak." Throughout its period of preeminence, MGM was owned by Loew's Incorporated and bore the discreet stamp of its founder.

Loew's empire began with The People's Vaudeville Company, which Loew founded in November 1904 to manage his first penny arcade in New York City; within a year he controlled twenty. The working poor—many of them immigrants who had been pouring into the United States at a rate of one million a year, and who were unable to afford or understand mainstream entertainment—flocked to these noisy penny arcades, filled with games of chance. There they were drawn to a particular novelty: moving pictures.

An early picture of the studio, after Louis B. Mayer's name is added to Metro-Goldwyn in 1925. The original indoor film stages use as much glass as possible to exploit the abundant California sunlight.

As early as 1894, Americans had become acquainted with moving images through Thomas Edison's Kinetoscope, a box with a peephole through which the viewer watched a mechanically operated strip of film. These peep shows were ideal for the arcades since they accommodated only one viewer at a time. The next breakthrough involved projecting images onto a screen, a process developed independently by several inventors. On April 23, 1896, the first program of motion pictures in the United States was screened at Koster and Bial's Music Hall in New York. The impact was immediate, but as the technological novelty wore off and the flow of original material proved to be erratic, the sophisticated public grew tired of being shown the same films over and over. Some theater managers even used such movies as "chasers"—a vaudeville term for acts so boring that they would chase the audiences out of the overcrowded amusement palaces to allow more paying customers to enter.

Boredom was certainly not a problem at the penny arcades; they were so crowded with people that entrepreneurs like Marcus Loew sought to satisfy public demand by investing in projection machines, leasing additional empty storefronts, and equipping them with screens and benches. They charged five cents for admission, which is how the "nickelodeons" originally got their name. One of the first of these opened near Pittsburgh in 1905. Within three years, there were thousands of nickelodeons, attracting millions of customers eager to see something new every day. "This resulted in a tremendous consumption of subjects," wrote Terry Ramsaye, an early film historian, "since the subjects were normally just one reel long. The clamorous demand was for film, film, film—regardless of quality or content. The only requirement was that it be new." The early movies developed most of the genres that are in use today: slapstick comedy, western, melodrama, thriller, spectacle, fantasy, and science fiction, with hits such as *The Great Train Robbery*, *The Kiss*, *Rescued from an Eagle's Nest*, and *A Trip to the Moon*.

Profits from the penny arcades allowed Loew and his fellow entrepreneurs to build chains of nickelodeons, then to take over dance halls and vaudeville theaters. Finally, they erected their own luxurious, airy picture palaces, which played continuous programs of motion pictures, often mixed with live acts and music. Vaudeville, which dominated American show business during this period, had undergone an evolution that the motion-picture industry would emulate. The nineteenth-century variety show—a mixture of songs, comic skits, magic, and animal acts—had grown from its humble origins as popular entertainment into a huge business. Big-time vaudeville (so-called to distinguish it from small-time operators such as Loew during his early years) was ruled by rival entertainment tycoons. They competed ruthlessly, controlling exclusive "acts" by thousands of artists, whom they booked on circuits and into gilded palaces across the land. They also hired major stars of the legitimate stage at fantastic salaries, mainly for their publicity value. Vaudeville pampered its audiences with magnificent surroundings, continuous programs running from morning until night, and a mind-boggling array of entertainment offered at a relatively low price.

Although Marcus Loew named his enterprise the People's Vaudeville, he aspired to capture the more affluent and respectable customers of big-time vaudeville. He succeeded with astonishing speed: in 1909, Loew's National was New York City's latest and largest theater, with a capacity of 2,800 and programs combining vaudeville and pictures. Two years later, Loew bought out William Morris, one of the vaudeville kings of the era, and moved into his offices on Forty-second Street, establishing an enduring presence in the heart of the show-business district. As the movie theater moguls appropriated vaudeville's monopolistic practices of booking and distribution, and applied them to the business of exhibiting films, their biggest problem remained the supply of quality films to their huge new audiences.

A nickelodeon in San Francisco (circa 1905), at the beginning of the moving-picture craze that sweeps America. One step up from penny arcades, nickelodeons try to attract a better class of audience. The sign at the entrance reads: "Refined Entertainment for Ladies, Gentlemen & Children."

To solve the problem, they had to take on the Motion Picture Patents Company, organized by Thomas Edison after years of feuding with rival inventors. This monopolistic trust attempted to control film production by granting licenses to studios and producers to use their equipment, and by regulating the length of a film to a single ten-minute reel. The restrictions placed on independent producers left exhibitors, such as Marcus Loew, without a full supply of movies to satisfy their eager audiences. In 1912, Adolph Zukor hired Edwin S. Porter to produce just six pictures a year for his production company, Famous Players. The pioneer filmmaker told the exhibitor, "There isn't that much talent in the world."

Motion-picture producers defied and dodged the Patents Company's spies and bailiffs by moving progressively west, ending up in sunny California. By the time the courts ordered the dissolution of the trust in 1915, the whole world seemed to be in love with movies. "Stars" were being created practically overnight by an adoring public, with a few—Mary Pickford, Charles Chaplin, and later Douglas Fairbanks—commanding astronomical salaries.

That same year, Metro Pictures Corporation was formed by a group of distributors to provide financing for independent films. It became an umbrella organization for a variety of smaller companies, including Quality Pictures, which Richard Rowland and Joseph Engel—Metro's president and treasurer—set up to make dramatic features in partnership with the great matinee idol of the period, Francis X. Bushman. J. Robert Rubin, an ambitious young lawyer who had served as an assistant district attorney and later deputy police commissioner of New York City, became Metro's legal counsel. The most important promise of Metro lay in its announcement that it would start releasing films at the rate of one every week. Although this goal would prove to be elusive, Metro was energetic in pursuing it.

The secretary of the new company,

Louis B. Mayer, was a former salvager of scrap metal who had caught the show-business bug around 1907, after leasing and transforming an old burlesque house into a theater in Haverhill, Massachusetts. A few years later, he combined his experiences as a theatrical producer and exhibitor to become a regional "exchange man," or middleman, between film distributors and exhibitors. In 1915, in addition to his new position with Metro Pictures, Mayer gambled much of his small fortune on securing the New England distribution rights for *The Birth of a Nation*. The D. W. Griffith Civil War epic ushered in a new period in the history of film, establishing it both as art and industry. Incidentally, it also resulted in Mayer's first sizable return on his years invested as a showman and inspired him to make his own pictures. Eventually, Mayer would leave Metro because he signed actress Anita Stewart in a private deal that did not include the company. Mayer's first feature film, *Virtuous Wives*, shot in Brooklyn, was successful enough for him to plan a move to California in 1918, to produce his next movie with the star.

The following year, 1919, was a critical one for Metro. Mayer was not the only distributor to leave the combine. As the company's base of operations diminished, it was unable to compete with the newer and more powerful distributors—First National, Paramount, and Fox. Rowland offered to sell Metro to Adolph Zukor, who frankly told him, "The only reason I'd have to take you in would be to put you out of business." Then Rowland turned to Marcus Loew, who, by this time, was being squeezed by the same market forces. Loew agreed to buy Metro.

The purchase—at just over three million dollars—seemed a shrewd and necessary move. Loew's theaters were concentrated in the New York area; the flagship was the 3,200-seat State Theater in Times Square, which opened in August 1921. But unlike his rivals William Fox and Adolph Zukor, who each amassed a huge number of theaters, Marcus Loew would never own more than 175 theaters.

A view of the Triangle film studios (circa 1917), on the site of what later becames the Metro-Goldwyn-Mayer lot. Formed by three movie pioneers—Thomas H. Ince, Mack Sennett, and D. W. Griffith—the Triangle facility becomes one of the largest and most modern for film production in the world.

With the acquisition of Metro, Loew's intended to be more competitive by producing only top-quality, first-class films for its urban, and urbane, customers.

Despite a few Metro hits, such as *The Four Horsemen of the Apocalypse*, which propelled a handsome young man named Rudolph Valentino to instant stardom, Marcus Loew grew increasingly frustrated over the following three years with the unpredictable nature of a business in which temperamental stars and egomaniacal directors, who were paid extravagant salaries, could hold up production for weeks. Even more disappointing to Loew was Metro's inability to produce anywhere near the fifty to seventy-five quality films he had hoped for each year. Reluctantly, he was forced to turn to independent filmmakers to fulfill the company's promised schedule of prestige features. One of the people he contacted was Louis B. Mayer, who had his own small production company on Mission Road, in unfashionable East Los Angeles.

Amidst deepening management problems, made worse by a periodic downturn in the industry in 1923, Metro's president, Richard Rowland, resigned. At this point, the physically ailing Loew pondered selling the studio, but in January 1924, Joseph Godsol, the president of Goldwyn Pictures, offered to sell him his company, which owned an extensive production facility in Culver City, west of Los Angeles. Ironically, Samuel Goldwyn never had a direct hand in Metro-Goldwyn-Mayer. When the merger with Metro was proposed, he was no longer associated with Goldwyn Pictures, having been ousted from its helm during a power struggle a couple of years earlier. In fact, that dismissal was the third time the former glove salesman had lost control of a film company, and, as a result, he decided to pursue his dreams as an independent producer.

Goldwyn's indirect legacy to MGM, however, was considerable. It was he, not Godsol, who had built up Goldwyn Pictures' impressive roster of stars, writers, and directors. The studio had a number of story properties in various stages of preparation—some of which promised exactly the kind of prestige that Loew sought. *Ben-Hur*, a colossal production, was being filmed in Italy, while Rex Ingram, one of the most respected directors at the time, was shooting *The Arab* in North Africa. And director Erich von Stroheim had recently spent nine months filming *Greed*.

While still in charge, Goldwyn had begun a program of buying theaters, and Marcus Loew was particularly excited by the company's half-interest in New York's 4,500-seat Capitol Theater, the world's largest movie palace and a major competitor to Loew's State Theater. In addition, there were sales offices scattered around the world, which were more a reflection on Sam Goldwyn's ambitions than on his grasp.

Joe Godsol added to the merger's appeal with a distribution deal he set up in early 1924 with Cosmopolitan Pictures, a company created by newspaper magnate William Randolph Hearst to promote his mistress, Marion Davies. In exchange for the distribution of Davies's films to its theaters, Goldwyn Pictures would benefit from the invaluable publicity provided by Hearst's influential chain of newspapers.

The most attractive feature of the proposed merger, however, was the studio in Culver City, which housed some of the best filmmaking facilities on the West Coast. Over its imposing entrance gates was the company's trademark, designed in 1917 by a young lyricist and advertising man, Howard Dietz: a

The Four Horsemen of the Apocalypse (1921) is adapted from a best-selling Spanish novel about World War I. Metro's top scenarist, June Mathis, writes the screenplay and pushes for Valentino (then an obscure bit player) to be given the chance to play a principal role in the film.

majestic lion under the high-sounding if not entirely truthful motto, *Ars Gratia Artis*.

Loew delegated his right-hand man, Nicholas Schenck, to look into Joe Godsol's proposal. As soon as Schenck, a tough businessman, saw the debit side of the company's ledger, he understood why Godsol was keen to sell. The problems at Goldwyn were the same as those at Metro, writ large. Both companies were expending huge sums on stars, literary properties, and overheads. Productions ran behind schedule and over budget. Aware that costs would have to be brought within reasonable and predictable limits, Schenck sought the kind of manager who knew how to deal with creative people, yet understood the need to bring efficiency and discipline to the chaos of film production. The new management team would have to take the lead in anticipating new trends in public tastes, while adhering to the policies and budgets established by the head executives in New York.

In 1924, there were not many candidates in the market for such a job. Either they were already running rival organizations, or they were plagued with similar financial problems. Attorney Robert Rubin suggested Metro's former secretary, Louis B. Mayer, as a candidate to run the Metro-Goldwyn combine on the West Coast. Mayer was known among members of the film colony as a small but successful producer, one who understood and attended to the myriad

MARCUS LOEW AND NICHOLAS SCHENCK

LEFT: *Marcus Loew, the esteemed founder of Metro-Goldwyn-Mayer, inspires the loyalty and stability that become hallmarks of the studio.* RIGHT: *Nicholas Schenck, the trusted right-hand man, is given Loew's crown and wields ultimate power over the MGM studio for thirty years.*

"Sure I'm another Napoleon," Marcus Loew was fond of saying when people compared him to the French emperor. Then he would add, self-deprecatingly: "I'm a little more than five feet tall and I don't weigh much." Indeed, the mogul's pint-sized physique concealed oversized ambition. "You must want a big success and then beat it into submission," he confided to *Theater* magazine in 1914. "You must be as ravenous to reach it as the wolf who licks his teeth behind a fleeing rabbit; you must be as mad to win as the man who, with one hand growing cold on the revolver in his pocket, with the other hand pushes his last gold piece on the 'Double-O' at Monte Carlo."

Loew avoided cards and horses ("I won't bet on anything that eats but can't talk," he explained), but he gambled in a big way by entering show business in 1904. However, his own experiences with economic downturns taught him to place more faith in the prime real estate on which he built his picture palaces than in the pictures themselves. Unlike his friend and rival Adolph Zukor, Loew never quite believed that movies had a solid future; he became involved in producing films out of competitive necessity rather than in pursuit of a dream. And, until his death in 1927, he hedged his bets by keeping vaudeville on the bill at many of his theaters.

Marcus Loew was one of a handful of entrepreneurs who created order out of the chaos of film production and distribution. Combining opportunism with high moral principles, Loew attracted like-minded people, notably Louis B. Mayer, to work for him. Both cultivated a family atmosphere as part of their corporate culture, and believed that loyalty between management and workers was a two-way street. In a business in which strong owners tended to drive out ambitious employees,

Loew's was noted for the stability of its management. In summing up his achievements, *Motion Picture World* likened his operations to "the maneuvers of a crack army division," adding, "The supply of movies is assured and standardized... The public knows what it will get for its money, week after week. Thus the Loew line is held."

The Schenck brothers were operating amusement parks in the New York area in 1911 when they met Marcus Loew. Soon after, they joined Loew's growing organization. Joseph Schenck was a charmer and an extravagant wheeler-dealer, who became a major figure in Hollywood, where he headed United Artists and cofounded Twentieth Century. Nicholas Schenck, on the other hand, remained at the head office of Loew's in New York for forty-four years, rising quickly through the ranks to become president in 1927. Nick was generally regarded as dull, and had few interests in life outside his family, physical fitness, and betting on horses.

Schenck may have seemed the ultimate company man, but, for all his long years of service to Loew's, in 1929 he attempted to sell control of MGM to William Fox, an action that struck Louis B. Mayer and his men as a betrayal. After the sale failed, Schenck resumed his leadership of Loew's, and was content as long as the profits continued to roll in. When they stopped, following World War II, he had no qualms about hiring a successor and easing out Mayer after twenty-seven years as the head of MGM.

Louis B. Mayer may have personified the success and prestige of MGM to the world at large, but insiders knew it was really Nicholas Schenck who controlled the fate of MGM for almost three decades. "Schenck never gets his picture in the papers," director John Huston once said, "and he doesn't go to parties, and he avoids going out in public, but he's the real king of the pack."

details of financing and producing films. Moreover, his commitment to providing audiences with top quality entertainment seemed to mesh with Loew's goals. Loew recalled visiting Mayer's Mission Road studio in 1923 and being impressed by the orderly hum of productive activity on its four stages. It is possible he may have met a young man there whom Mayer had recently hired to oversee production, Irving Thalberg. Only twenty-four years old, Thalberg had already established a solid reputation for himself as an efficient supervisor while at Carl Laemmle's Universal Pictures. Rubin called Mayer, advising his friend and client to hop on a train to New York if he was interested in Marcus Loew's plans.

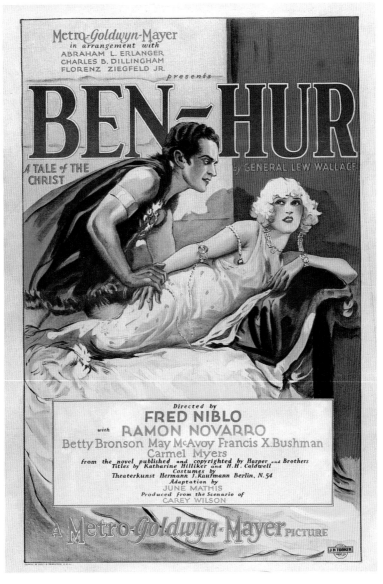

Metro's merger with Goldwyn Pictures was consummated on April 17, 1924. Through a stock swap worth about five million dollars, Loew's Inc. acquired the Goldwyn studio in Culver City, complete with six hundred employees and contract players, as well as the company's theaters and international distribution arm. The new enterprise, to be called Metro-Goldwyn, then bought out Louis B. Mayer Productions, paying $75,000 for its contracts and facilities—less than 2 percent of Goldwyn's price. Mayer became first vice-president and general manager of Loew's West Coast operations at a salary of $1,500 a week. To sweeten the deal, it was agreed that any picture produced and released through Metro-Goldwyn would give a special credit to Louis B. Mayer.

The new studio boss also negotiated the salaries for his small management team, notably Irving Thalberg, who was appointed second vice-president in charge of production

The golden age of MGM begins and ends with an epic production of Ben-Hur *(1925 and 1959), inspired by General Lew Wallace's novel of the same name. While on a train to assume his post as governor of New Mexico, Wallace engaged in a heated discussion about the founder of Christianity with the famous atheist Colonel Ingersoll. This conversation plants the seed for the book in Wallace's mind.*

at a salary of $650 a week. Additional bonuses were promised: up to 20 percent of Metro-Goldwyn's profits to be split among Mayer (53 percent), new corporate secretary Robert Rubin (27 percent), and Irving Thalberg (20 percent). It was a reflection of Mayer's strong paternal affection and confidence in Thalberg, who had worked for him just over a year, that he included the brilliant young man in the profit-sharing arrangement.

Marcus Loew's continuing anxiety over the flow of product to his expanding chain of movie theaters prompted the insertion of a clause in the contract that called for Mayer to produce at least fifteen pictures in the first year. In fact, Loew's hopes and Mayer's ambition soared even higher. On April 20, 1924, *The Film Daily* trumpeted the news that "in all likelihood Metro-Goldwyn will release fifty pictures" during the 1924-25 season. "Of that number, Metro will produce 38 and Goldwyn 12."

So the name Metro-Goldwyn-Mayer represented, in descending order, the relative importance of the component companies at the time of the merger. While final approval over budgets and contracts would reside at the head office of Loew's Inc. in New York City, a great deal of necessary autonomy was given to the executives in charge of production in Culver City. Profound tension would exist between these two centers of power, leading to occasional fireworks and frequent trips back and forth between coasts. The result, however, was prodigious. No Hollywood studio could claim to be greater than Metro-Goldwyn-Mayer, during the thirty-five years when the lion roared.

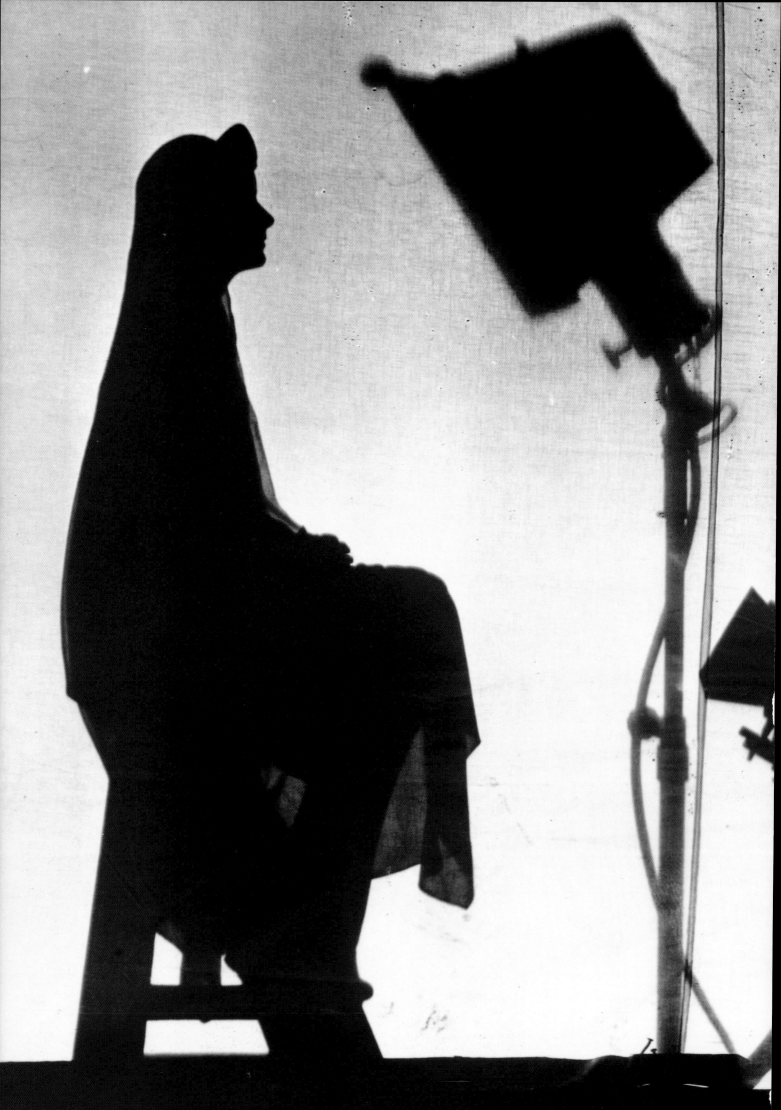

PART ONE

The Kingdom Is Born

Louis B. Mayer's vision for MGM was simple and direct. Early in his career, he had stated his credo in a telegram to director Lois Weber: "My unchanging policy will be great star, great director, great play, great cast. Spare nothing, neither expense, time, nor effort. Results only are what I am after."

With this plan in mind, Mayer officially launched the Metro-Goldwyn enterprise in a public ceremony on April 26, 1924. An array of stars, writers, directors, and local dignitaries gathered at the studio to watch as Abe Lehr, Samuel Goldwyn's former lieutenant and vice-president, handed Mayer a giant key bearing the word "SUCCESS" on it. "This is a great moment for me," said Mayer. "I accept this solemn trust and pledge the best that I have to give." A man who possessed high moral vision, Mayer told the crowd that "each picture should teach a lesson, should have a reason for existence."

The air of solemnity was broken by the late arrival of cowboy star and folk humorist Will Rogers, who presented Irving Thalberg and production supervisor Harry Rapf with smaller keys of their own. Marshall Neilan, a top director with Goldwyn Pictures at the time of the merger, interrupted the ceremonies to order his cast and crew back to the set of

LEFT: *In* Flesh and the Devil *(1926), Garbo tempts John Gilbert in the prelude to their first love scene on screen.*

ABOVE: *A natural showman, L. B. Mayer arranges for a public ceremony to officially launch MGM on April 26, 1924. Hundreds of stars, directors, and other employees assemble on the lawn of the Culver City lot with local dignitaries, including the admiral of the Pacific Fleet. A naval band provides the music, and congratulations are read from telegrams sent by President Calvin Coolidge and Secretary of Commerce Herbert Hoover. Flanked by two of his most important aides, Harry Rapf (left) and Irving Thalberg (right), Mayer accepts the key to the kingdom.*

1924

◆ On April 17, Loew's Incorporated completes the merger of Loew's theater chain, Metro's distribution network, Goldwyn Pictures studio, and Louis B. Mayer Productions.

◆ Goldwyn's trademark, a roaring lion encircled by a banner reading *Ars Gratia Artis* (*Art for Art's Sake*), comes with the $5 million package.

◆ Irving Thalberg is put in charge of all production at age twenty-four.

◆ *He Who Gets Slapped*, starring Lon Chaney, John Gilbert, and Norma Shearer, is MGM's first film, and is a critical and commercial success.

◆ Mayer and Thalberg inherit *Greed*, shot by Erich von Stroheim for Goldwyn in 1923, and cut the forty-two reels to ten. It fails at the box office, but later, film historians will call it a masterpiece.

◆ In its first year, the new studio releases films starring Renée Adorée, Wallace Beery, Eleanor Boardman, Lon Chaney, Ronald Colman, Jackie Coogan, Marion Davies, John Gilbert, Boris Karloff, Buster Keaton, Adolph Menjou, Mae Murray, Ramon Novarro, ZaSu Pitts, Norma Shearer, Blanche Sweet, and Laurette Taylor.

TOP: *Inaugurating its third season in 1926, MGM uses the slogan "More stars than there are in heaven!" From the beginning, the studio emphasizes female stars. (Clockwise from top left) Marion Davies, Lillian Gish, Renée Adorée, Greta Garbo, Mae Murray, and Norma Shearer.*

ABOVE: *A fan letter sent to Norma Shearer. The great director D. W. Griffith once told Shearer that she should seek a career outside motion pictures. "Your eyes are too blue," he said.*

Tess of the D'Urbervilles. Having directed a few of Mayer's earlier independent productions, Neilan was already familiar with the executive's long homilies. In fact, there was a history of mutual dislike between the two men.

When Marshall Neilan finished shooting *Tess of the D'Urbervilles*, in which the young heroine is hanged for murdering a man who had raped her, Mayer decided he did not care for the ending and ordered a happier one in which Tess is reprieved and reunited with her lover. Neilan protested and even tried to enlist the support of Thomas Hardy, the book's author. But Mayer stood his ground, claiming to know best what a mass audience wanted. Above all, the studio chief was determined to send an early and clear signal to independent-minded directors on the lot that management would rule and dictate in all important matters, including artistic ones. As a compromise, however, he showed Neilan's version to the critics and made two endings available to exhibitors for them to choose.

Neilan quit rather than take orders from Mayer, and he was not alone in regarding the new management team with disdain. Erich von Stroheim had been working for a year on *Greed*, based on Frank Norris's realist novel *McTeague*, which told about a San Franciscan dentist whose life is ruined by the lust for gold. The director insisted on total faithfulness to the text, leading to rumors that he was shooting the entire novel, sentence by sentence. Von Stroheim, an actor and director who enjoyed living up to his billing as "The Man You Love to Hate," was infamous for his treatment of actors. "I crush them," he claimed, "beat them until they are ready to quit. That's when I get their real soul. . . ." While in San Francisco, he forced his actors to live and sleep on the

ABOVE: *Appearing opposite almost every female star of the late twenties, John Gilbert is MGM's great lover. Born in Logan, Utah, the actor makes love on the silent screen with his soulful eyes.*

RIGHT: *Mexican-born Ramon Novarro, one of the studio's early candidates to exploit the Valentino craze; his most famous role is* Ben-Hur *(1925).*

LOUIS B. MAYER

ike most of the film pioneers, Louis B. Mayer was a self-made man. He enjoyed making things up about himself: changing his birthdate from 1882 to 1885, shifting his birthplace in imperial Russia from Vilna to Minsk or to a small village between the two. In order to lend dignity to his Anglicized name, he added a middle initial (which he said stood for Burt or Burton). Mayer grew up in Canada, but after becoming an American citizen, he decided to celebrate his birthday on the Fourth of July.

As a boy, he managed his father's marine salvage business. Working among the longshoremen, he developed a powerful upper torso on his small, stocky frame, and picked up a colorful, and sometimes off-color, vocabulary to go with a scrappy, pugnacious personality.

The main influence on Mayer's life was his mother, who sang songs and told stories to him. He worshiped her. After her untimely death in 1913, her favorite son, who was then twenty-eight years old, turned her into an icon. For as long as he lived, a portrait of her hung over his bed. Nothing angered Mayer more than insults to the ideal of motherhood. Once, when director Erich von Stroheim stated his opinion that all women were whores, Mayer asked if he thought of his mother that way, then hit him in the face.

Although Mayer was about the same age as his wife, Margaret, he treated her as if she were another daughter, and did not seem to mind that their marriage produced no sons, a circumstance that

BELOW: Paterfamilias Louis B. Mayer and his first wife, Margaret, stand between daughters Edith (left) and Irene (right), both of whom later marry producers themselves.

might be considered a misfortune in a Jewish family. Mayer enjoyed the role of patriarch most: surrounded by a small brood of adoring females at home, he thought of the whole MGM studio as his family, and threw picnics and invited his top executives to his home every Sunday. Some, such as Judy Garland, came to resent his intrusiveness, but many needed and loved him. "To me," Joan Crawford once said, "L. B. Mayer was my father, my father confessor, the best friend I ever had." He loved giving advice to employees, and cherished the Puritan values of family and hard work which he had absorbed in New England, where he had his first successes as a theatrical producer and a film distributor. Frances Marion recalled that the first time Mayer gave her a writing assignment, the studio chief stressed that his wife and two little girls must never be embarrassed by any of his pictures. "I worship good women, honorable men, and saintly mothers," he stated.

Romantic and sentimental, Mayer's view of American life was reflected most purely in the MGM films made in the decade after producer Irving Thalberg's death in 1936. "The story he wanted to tell," Spencer Tracy said at Mayer's funeral, "was the story of America, the land for which he had an almost furious love, born of gratitude—and of contrast with the hatred in the dark land of his boyhood across the seas. It was this love of America that made him an authority on America. . . ."

ABOVE: *Gibson Gowland as McTeague in the final sequence of* Greed *(1924).*
LEFT: *Director Erich von Stroheim (front row in middle) on location in the desert with the suffering cast and crew.*

ABOVE: *Advertising copy from* Greed's *campaign book gives no hint of the problems that beset this famous picture's production and release.*

location sets so that they would give more authentic performances. He also led a cast and crew of more than forty people into the hellish furnace of Death Valley in the middle of summer and boasted of working in temperatures that hit 140 degrees in the shade. "I believe," he declared, "the results I achieved through the actual heat and physical strain were worth the trouble we had all gone to."

It was not the harsh surroundings endured by the cast that particularly worried the studio but rather the obsessive director's lavish spending—over half a million dollars in a period when an average film could be made for under a hundred thousand. As it turned out, much of the money was wasted. When von Stroheim finished his version of *Greed*, it was reported to be seven hours long. After he managed to cut it to four, the director appealed to Marcus Loew to exhibit his work as a special presentation over two evenings. He was referred back to Mayer, who wanted it to be a standard feature under two hours in length. Anything longer would limit the number of screenings theaters could schedule, decreasing the chance to recoup the film's costs. When von Stroheim balked at cutting it further, Irving Thalberg, who had already clashed with the director when both were at Universal, worked with an editor to make the additional cuts.

Greed was released to generally unfavorable reviews. "Never has there been a more out-and-out box-office flop shown on the screen than this picture," sneered *Variety*. However, since *Variety* and other critics defended von Stroheim's directing, and with the cut footage eventually lost forever, it became a controversial legend that one of the greatest masterpieces of the silent era had been butchered by Thalberg. The new pragmatic masters at MGM appeared

GOLD! GOLD! GOLD!

HISTORY'S PAGES ARE VIVID WITH ITS GLITTERING ALLURE. THE STORY OF A BEAUTY WHO PLACED THE LOVE OF GOLD ABOVE ALL ELSE IN THE WORLD IS ONE OF THE MOST ASTOUNDING STORIES OF REAL LIFE EVER FILMED. THE GREAT FILM MASTERPIECE COMES DIRECT TO YOU FROM ITS BROADWAY WORLD PREMIERE.

OVERLEAF: *A program for the premiere of* Ben-Hur *heralds the Circus Maximus chariot race.*

Goldwyn Pictures
Corporation
469 FIFTH AVENUE
NEW YORK

Rome, July 21, 1924

My dear Mr. Mayer:

. . . Four weeks ago today we all arrived in Rome. I believe Mr. Loew and Mr. Rubin were sick when they saw the existing conditions here. . . .

Imagine a company of Americans coming to Italy with the announcement that they were going to spend millions of dollars—expense meant nothing—and then following it up by calling the Italians lazy idiots and fools. . . .

[Director] Brabin and [writer] Mathis got at swords point the moment they both arrived here, with the result there were two factions . . . pulling against each other. From what I hear they both ran wild in extravagance. They were weeks and weeks in North Africa making a few feet of desert stuff that took up thirty or forty reels of film but cannot be used. . . .

They spent over a month on the water with the galley fleet and hundreds of people but a very few feet of the shots can be used. By the time I got here the boats were about ready to fall apart with wear and tear. . . .

Another thing that got the country down on us was because they came in here boasting about the millions they were going to spend and then ordered all their costumes in Germany. This nearly started violence and I can hardly blame them. . . .

I am expecting to see you, Mrs. Mayer and the girls over here in August and by that time you will find everything running like silk. . . .

Faithfully Yours,

FN/EBN

Best regards to you & Irving

26

ABOVE: *The Roman army marching into Jerusalem in* Ben-Hur *(1925).*
LEFT: *Fred Niblo directing a shot of Ben-Hur (Ramon Novarro) rescuing Arrius (Frank Currier) after the sinking of the Roman fleet.*
FAR LEFT: *Extract from a letter Niblo sent Mayer to explain the production problems.*
OPPOSITE TOP: *Original cast and crew members of* Ben-Hur *pose under the Goldwyn banner in the sands of Egypt.*
BOTTOM: *Roman galleys built on the Italian coast.*

to be more interested in the bottom line and pleasing the masses than in art.

Mayer and Thalberg faced problems of a much greater magnitude with *Ben-Hur*. A bestseller of the nineteenth century, *Ben-Hur* had been staged in spectacular fashion many times during the first two decades of the century. Goldwyn Pictures had formed a partnership with a New York syndicate of theatrical producers to film General Lew Wallace's novel, set in the time of Christ. One unusual aspect of the deal would come to haunt MGM: the syndicate would receive 50 percent of the gross receipts in exchange for the studio's use of the title and story. Before a single frame had been shot, the project promised to be the most expensive motion picture ever made.

June Mathis, who had supervised *The Four Horsemen of the Apocalypse* before leaving Metro, was hired to write the scenario. She insisted that the picture must be made on location, winning out over the quieter voice of reason of J. J. Cohn, then a production manager at Goldwyn.

By the time of the MGM merger, considerable time and almost the entire original budget had been spent filming on locations in Egypt and in various parts of Italy. And when the footage was found to be unusable, the fate of *Ben-Hur* became the subject of intense discussions between New York and Culver City. Thalberg advised that cast and crew be brought back to California. Marcus Loew, however, thought the project might be salvageable if new personnel were dispatched to take it over. He offered to accompany them to Europe, where he could take a firsthand look at the situation.

A few weeks later, Loew set sail with his wife and an entourage that included J. Robert Rubin; Fred Niblo, one of Mayer's contract directors; Ramon Novarro, a Mexican-born star from the Metro stable; and two writers, Bess Meredyth and Carey Wilson, who had been working with Thalberg on revising the scenario. This small expeditionary force landed

THE MAKING OF A SPECTACLE

TOP: *Art from studio promotion book with stylized chariot race and scenes from the picture.*
ABOVE AND RIGHT: *Messala (Francis X. Bushman) glares as Ben-Hur (Ramon Novarro) pulls even in the race.*
BELOW: *Line drawing from stationery used by the* Ben-Hur *production team.*

Before Fred Niblo replaced Charles Brabin as director of *Ben-Hur*, he wrote to Louis B. Mayer: "*Ben-Hur* can be the biggest thing that has ever been done. It can also be the biggest flop."

The chariot race was by far the greatest challenge to the production, its success or failure being crucial to that of the film. In addition to being a major moment in the plot, the race provided the opportunity to create an exhilarating spectacle, the kind that was ideally suited to film, with its ability to cut from one revealing shot—grimacing faces, flashing whips, spinning wheels, and thundering hoofs—to another.

When the day came to begin filming the scene, more than forty cameras—many of them borrowed from other studios—were lined up to photograph every angle of the huge set that recreated the Circus Maximus. More than 3,000 extras appeared as spectators. Production chief Irving Thalberg judged them too sparse, so he demanded that another 300 be recruited from among the curious bystanders and put in makeshift robes.

Word of the spectacle had spread throughout Hollywood, and many a top star—such as Mary Pickford and Douglas Fairbanks—came to watch from a specially erected dais.

Though the script called for a number of staged crashes, at one point during the filming, the wheel of one chariot smashed into another vehicle. A pileup of four chariots and tangled horses and stuntmen threatened to ruin the whole shoot. Miraculously, no one was hurt. The accidental crash—which was faithfully recorded by several cameras—became the most stunning sequence in the chariot race.

INTER-OFFICE COMMUNICATION

To: MR. MAYER
Subject: BEN HUR—CAMERA CAR
           FOR CHARIOT RACE
From: FRED NIBLO
Date: JULY 2ND 1925

Regarding CAMERA CAR for chariot race . . .

I respectfully suggest that as soon as possible, we should get a car in readiness for all our follow shots, close-up shots, and trick shots of the chariot race, horses hooves, etc.

This simply necessitates building platforms on the chassis of any Cadillac or other car that can go 45 or 50 miles an hour. It should be equipped with balloon tires and the platforms made very solid and capable of carrying two to four cameras.

A car of this kind is absolutely essential to get a big smash into the chariot race. In fact, it is so important that I would like to see two cars prepared instead of one.

SECOND CRASH

SCENE: East side of Spina wall. Greek in lead Messala directly behind. Pulls up alongside Greek and crosses him, crowding Greek against wall, causing inside horse and wheel to mount base of Spina. As we get chariot on this angle, we tumble it. In background, we see Ben-Hur coming down hemmed in by two other teams. He leaps over Greek's team just clearing it, possibly having Ben-Hur's chariot hit wrecked chariot, careen a bit, steady itself and away. Team alongside of him runs over leg or head of one of Greek's horses.

METHOD: Greek's chariot is built with breakaway axle and chariot. Messala crosses in front, causing crash. Will build a small runway alongside Spina to get Greek's chariot on an angle before tipping it. This is background for spill. Mat will be Ben-Hur's team coming down from background, jumping over padded wreckage which, in double printing, will be Greek's team. Part of mat will be additional team which runs over head or leg of one of Greek's horses.

—*Production Notes (October 13, 1925)*

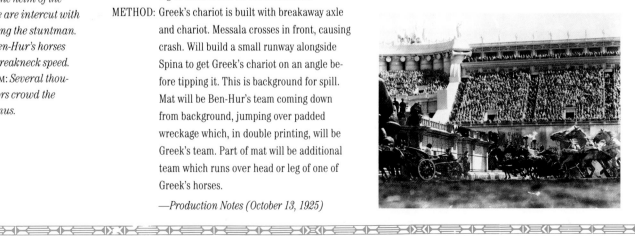

TOP: *Novarro's double drives his chariot over the wreckage of a competitor.*
ABOVE: *Taking close-up shots of Bushman at the helm of the chariot. These are intercut with sequences using the stuntman.*
RIGHT TOP: *Ben-Hur's horses charging at breakneck speed.*
RIGHT BOTTOM: *Several thousand spectators crowd the Circus Maximus.*

The interior of Ben-Hur's residence is similar to the fantasy architecture of many stars' homes in this period.

in Italy, pretending to be on a vacation, but it was not long before they took over the project in a quiet coup. Niblo assumed the directing chores, and Novarro replaced George Walsh as Ben-Hur. During the dog days of summer, the production stood idle, while new sets were built for the revised script. The problems continued: as the weather remained foul, difficulties arose in translating for the Italian cast and crew, and the lack of skilled technicians resulted in constant delays.

By September, Mayer was sufficiently worried to go on location himself to assess the film's progress—or lack of it. He arrived with his family in time to witness Fred Niblo directing a spectacular sea battle off Livorno. Unfortunately, a staged fire set aboard one of the Roman galleys got out of control, and hundreds of Italian extras, some of whom could not swim, were seen diving—in real, rather than pretended, panic—into the Mediterranean. Much of the fleet, already in poor condition, was damaged or had sunk. Mayer concluded that the financial sinkhole had to be plugged. By early 1925, even Marcus Loew agreed that the entire production should return to the States, with Thalberg assuming direct control of the project.

Any other production executive might have conducted the most frugal salvage operation. Thalberg proceeded, instead, to spend $300,000—which was considered a fairly generous budget for a film during this period—to build a replica of the Circus Maximus to be used in the climactic chariot race. He knew that the race would be the centerpiece of any cinematic adaptation of the book: an exhilarating spectacle that film could portray better than any other medium. The chariot race—its filming and editing—became the talk of Hollywood. Thalberg closely supervised every aspect of postproduction. He snatched a resounding triumph from what could have been a disaster. *Ben-Hur* vindicated his contention that directors and their films should be brought under the producer's central control, both financially and artistically.

Loew's publicity machine geared up to exploit every aspect of the mammoth production. Its myriad problems, particularly the cost overruns, now became something to shout about in the campaign book given to exhibitors: "COST A FORTUNE AND WORTH IT!" screamed one headline. The copy continued: *"BEN-HUR* IS THE MOST POWERFUL STORY EVER TOLD IN MOTION PICTURES—IT CONTAINS EVERYTHING THAT EVERY OTHER BIG MOTION PICTURE HAS OFFERED—AND MORE. IT IS BIGGER BY FAR THAN EVEN METRO-GOLDWYN-MAYER HAD DARED HOPE IT WOULD BE, AND AUDIENCES THE WORLD OVER, INCLUDING PEOPLE OF EVERY CREED, HAVE ACCLAIMED IT THE GREATEST TRIBUTE GIVEN TO THE SCREEN SINCE THE BIRTH OF MOTION PICTURES."

The handbook also offered nine practical publicity suggestions based on just one theme: "BY ALL MEANS—GET OVER THE BIGNESS OF THE PICTURE." Additional stories gave advice on how to flash the stars' names on a marquee and how to get churches, libraries, and schools involved. Commercial tie-ins included an illustrated book containing the photoplay (75 cents) and blotters "scented with BEN HUR, the perfume preferred by Carmel Myers," one of the stars of the picture.

All the hoopla worked. *Ben-Hur*, which premiered in New York on December 30, 1925, became a huge critical and box-office success, eventually bringing in over nine million dollars. Unfortunately, after subtracting distribution costs, Loew's would end up losing money since half the receipts went to the syndicate, leading Marcus Loew to comment that it was "a contract I do not want to claim credit for." What the Loew's theater chain did gain, however, was an enhanced image among the public for providing a special kind of movie

The TRAIL of '98

ROBERT W. SERVICE'S
Epic of The Alaskan Gold Quest

ABOVE: *Publicity art for* The Trail of '98 *(1928).*
RIGHT: *Shooting the Klondike gold rush on location, with Colorado standing in for the Yukon.*

ABOVE: *John Gilbert (top) and Norma Shearer (bottom) in* He Who Gets Slapped *(1924). Gilbert, in spite of his matinee-idol status, has deep insecurities about his appearance and his acting ability. When critics carp about Shearer's eyes and legs, Thalberg arranges for a well-known artist to declare publicly that her eyes have a classic beauty, and he orders the costume department to design flowing robes to hide her legs.*

LEFT: *Lon Chaney shows one of his thousand faces in* He Who Gets Slapped.

35

ABOVE: *(Left to right) Constance Bennett, Joan Crawford, and Sally O'Neil in* Sally, Irene and Mary *(1925), the story of three showgirls with different fates. MGM varies this premise in the plots of several films.*

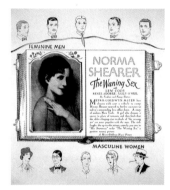

ABOVE: *Norma Shearer chalks up a victory playing an attorney in the eternal battle between the sexes in* The Waning Sex *(1926).*

experience. Although MGM would also produce dozens of ordinary, fairly low-budget pictures, with the launching of spectacles like *Ben-Hur*, MGM laid the foundation for its future reputation as the producer of elite, prestigious films.

The first picture initiated by the new regime at MGM was a more modest film that took less than six months to produce. *He Who Gets Slapped*, a melodrama about a scientist-turned-clown who falls in love with a circus girl, was adapted from a play by the Russian emigré Leonid Andreyev.

Thalberg saw its principal role as a vehicle for Lon Chaney, whom he had previously worked with at Universal in *The Hunchback of Notre Dame*. The producer would always be on the lookout for opportunities to exploit Chaney, known as "the man of a thousand faces." He matched him frequently with Tod Browning, a director with a strong penchant for the bizarre. After playing an assortment of twisted scientists and evil conmen, Chaney triumphed as the neurotic ventriloquist in *The Unholy Three*, which made millions in 1925 and was remade with sound just before Chaney died in 1930.

In *He Who Gets Slapped*, Thalberg teamed Chaney with two of the studio's younger stars, John Gilbert and Norma Shearer. Rounding out the production crew were two experienced individuals from the Goldwyn studio, writer Carey Wilson and Swedish director Victor Seastrom. Unlike *Ben-Hur*, shooting proceeded smoothly, and the film premiered in October 1924, at Loew's Capitol Theater on

Broadway. Despite its somber mood, MGM's first wholly produced film scored a hit. It had cost around $170,000 to make but showed a profit of $350,000—a result that Mayer and Thalberg were to repeat many times more.

For the picture that was to become the follow-up hit to *Ben-Hur*, Thalberg turned to director King Vidor, a Texan who had been with Metro before the merger. Known for his ability to adapt novels and plays to film, Vidor confessed to Thalberg that he was interested in developing his own themes and was growing tired of making movies that played for a week, then disappeared into oblivion. The ambitious director spoke of the three subjects that interested him most: steel, wheat, and war. Thalberg pounced on Vidor's idea for a new kind of realistic war movie. He thought he had found just the right vehicle when he saw a Broadway hit coauthored by Maxwell Anderson and Laurence Stallings, *What Price Glory?* A Marine veteran, Stallings wrote by drawing directly on his World War I combat experiences. When Thalberg found out that the screen rights to the play had already been purchased by a rival studio, he convinced Stallings to return with him to Hollywood and prepare another war story.

The result was *The Big Parade*, a simple but powerful tale, built around antiwar and antiheroic themes, about a World War I soldier who falls in love with a French farm girl. Vidor specifically refrained from having his cast use excessive makeup in an attempt to impart the grim reality of war.

ABOVE: *A watercolor portrait of Mae Murray promotes her appearance in* The Merry Widow *(1925). One of the great stars of the silent era, Murray constantly complains to Irving Thalberg about Erich von Stroheim's behavior while making the picture. Calling him "the dirty Hun," Murray objects that not enough close-ups of her face are made, and that the director has turned his back on her love scene with John Gilbert, leaving instructions to "let me know when it's over."*

◆ *Ben-Hur* finishes production at $3.9 million and is a smash, grossing $9,386,000. Tickets sell for $2.50, but MGM loses money. Distribution and copyright royalties leave MGM $850,000 short of the film's cost. The new studio figures the legend is worth it.

◆ *The Big Parade* runs ninety-six weeks at the Astor in New York, a record that will last for twenty-five years.

◆ Lillian Gish signs a six-picture contract.

◆ *The Merry Widow*, directed by Erich von Stroheim, has more shots of more shoes than Irving Thalberg can stand. Von Stroheim says the character "has a foot fetish." Thalberg says, "And you have a footage fetish!" They part ways, and von Stroheim never directs for MGM again. The picture is a success.

◆ *Pretty Ladies* is Joan Crawford's first movie for MGM and the only movie with her real name, Lucille Le Sueur, on the credits.

◆ Loew's/MGM makes a profit of $4,708,631 in its first year. Only Paramount, in business for eleven years, earns more.

Lon Chaney, playing a ventriloquist, listens to his dummy in the silent version of The Unholy Three.

John Gilbert, the studio's rising matinee idol, at first objected to playing such a role. The son of itinerant actors, Gilbert had begun his movie career as a stagehand at Thomas Ince's studio before becoming a bit player. Insecure about his abilities, Gilbert had once overheard someone comment that he was a terrible actor and that his nose looked too Jewish. "I gazed long into my mirror and burst into tears," he would later recall. "The reflection in the glass before me became a loathsome thing."

Gilbert appealed to Thalberg, who advised him to give it a try. After watching the first rushes, the actor accepted the role, and thereafter developed an unusual rapport with Vidor. Silent-era directors could talk to their actors while the cameras whirred, which led to the constant improvising of a scene. "I didn't have a big voice," King Vidor told film historian Kevin Brownlow in 1962. "I might say, 'More,' 'Now,' 'That's wonderful,' 'That's great' . . . It's like a love affair—you just can't describe it. I actually remember moments when I didn't say a thing. I'd just have a quick thought and Gilbert would react to it."

In preparing the film, Vidor viewed hours of documentary footage shot by the U.S. Army during the war. He became inspired by the slow cadence of a funeral cortege. "I took a metronome into the projection room," Vidor recalled in his autobiography, "and set the tempo to conform with the beat on the screen. When we filmed the march through Belleau Wood in a small forest near Los Angeles, I used the same metronome, and a drummer with a bass drum amplified the metronomic ticks so that all in a range of several hundred yards could hear. I instructed the men that each step must be taken on a drum beat, each turn of the head, lift of a rifle, pull of a trigger, in short, every physical move must occur on the beat of the drum. Those extras who were veterans of the American Expeditionary Force and had served time in France thought I had gone completely daft and

ABOVE: *The piano score played in theaters to accompany* The Big Parade. *The passage introduces the march through Belleau Wood, and gives the accompanist notes on close-ups of the characters' faces.*

TOP: *Reshooting one of the key scenes in the Belleau woods near Los Angeles. Retakes total one third of the overall budget.*

RIGHT CENTER: *King Vidor directs Tim O'Brien (left) and John Gilbert in their World War I dugout, reproduced on the MGM lot.*

RIGHT: *Audiences line up around the block for* The Big Parade, *MGM's first blockbuster picture, which opens simultaneously at the Capitol and the Astor in New York , to huge box-office acclaim and a several-million-dollar gross.*

OPPOSITE AND TOP: *One-sheet posters prominently display the names of King Vidor, the director, and Laurence Stallings, the injured war hero who wrote the original story for* The Big Parade *(1925).*

ABOVE AND RIGHT: *Promotional art is distributed to all the theaters, and illustrated programs, with scenes from the film, are handed out at all the premieres.*

IRVING THALBERG

After watching a preview of the film *Tugboat Annie*, Irving Thalberg asked Mervyn LeRoy if having Wallace Beery's shoes squeak would improve a certain scene. The director agreed, but reminded the producer that shooting had finished, the set had been struck, and the bit players and extras had been dismissed. "Mervyn, I didn't ask you how much it would cost," Thalberg looked at him sternly. "I asked you whether it would help the picture." The scene was reshot, LeRoy recalled, "because Irving Thalberg wanted everything just right."

Perfectionism and total dedication made Thalberg's methods legendary before he was thirty years of age. "Entertainment is Thalberg's God," said his friend the writer Charles MacArthur. "He's content to serve Him without billing, like a priest at an altar or a rabbi under the scrolls." Once, in the middle of a story conference that Thalberg was conducting with director King Vidor and writer Laurence Stallings, a limousine arrived to take them to Mabel Normand's funeral. "We had talked story all the way there," Stallings recalled, "and after we got down on our knees in the chapel, Thalberg had an idea. He turned to us and said, 'Why not kill him before he gets to the hotel?' It was intended *sotto voce*, but the priest's intonation... ended just then and Thalberg's voice sounded titanic."

Among the giant personalities at MGM, nobody, perhaps not even Greta Garbo, projected as great a mystique as did Thalberg. Part of it came from his youthful looks, which were contradicted by his mature and self-assured judgment.

Playing hard: Mayer and Thalberg prepare to choose teams for one of their regular Sunday baseball games.

"The astounding thing about him," observed writer Jim Tully, "is his gentle, dreamy air; his almost placid personality—except in the midst of an argument. A frail boy, he has terrifying energy—enormous vitality."

Thalberg's overwhelming focus may have come from the intimations of mortality that overshadowed his entire life. As a child, he had been sickly and weak. When he contracted rheumatic fever at the age of seventeen, doctors were not hopeful. Thalberg's mother, Henrietta, defied medical opinion and sent her son back to finish high school. Despite his poor health, he began working and, by the age of twenty-one, was running the California studios of Carl Laemmle's Universal Pictures.

Not content merely to crank out films for "Uncle" Carl, Thalberg found in Louis B. Mayer the ideal partner with whom to realize the grandiose vision that became MGM. "I don't think either of them could have created it without the other, " said David O. Selznick, who was close to both. "They were a great team."

For a man with a strong sense of his own mortality, Thalberg expended enormous care and, occasionally, many years preparing his pictures. His physical handicaps seem to have increased his appreciation of life, and he was interested in making movies that reflected his own fascination with the complexity of human nature and relationships. In the final scenes of *Grand Hotel*, for which Irving Thalberg spent a great deal of time polishing the script, Lionel Barrymore utters a line that might have come from Thalberg's own thoughts: "Life is wonderful, but it's very dangerous. If you have the courage to live it, it's marvelous."

Irving Thalberg weds Norma Shearer. (Left to right) director Jack Conway, Isabella Crowdin, Douglas Shearer, Marion Davies, the bride and groom, Sylvia Thalberg, L. B. Mayer, Edith and Irene Mayer, and director King Vidor.

expressed their ridicule most volubly. One British veteran wanted to know if he were performing in 'some bloody ballet.' I did not say so at the time, but that is exactly what it was—a bloody ballet, a ballet of death."

The Big Parade had not been planned as an epic. It was shot on a regular $200,000 budget. Thalberg took a rough cut of the film with him on a vacation he took with his parents in Coronado and tested it before an audience. The reaction was positive, and, as a consequence, Thalberg realized that potentially it could be an even greater success if the film's scope was expanded. The producer told Vidor that, in essence, he had made a war movie without the war. He instructed the director to reshoot some of the battle sequences, and then asked him to return to Texas to restage the now-famous scene of an army column on the march, involving 3,000 soldiers, 200 trucks, and 100 airplanes. After Vidor started work on his next picture, Thalberg brought in director George Hill to provide additional night battle shots. "Movies aren't made," Thalberg often claimed, "they're remade." This practice earned the MGM lot the amusing but respectful moniker, "Retake Valley."

Thalberg had employed this method of retakes when he worked at Universal Pictures, but Carl Laemmle, its founder, had not been particularly disposed to big, expensive productions. Mayer, on the other hand, agreed with his young producer and went directly to Marcus Loew and Nick Schenck, to present Thalberg's arguments. They authorized the added expense despite their fears that exhibitors might refuse to show a film with a strong antiwar stance. Loew's then demonstrated its support for the picture by staging a huge publicity campaign and glittering openings at both the Capitol and Astor theaters.

Here was new thinking. In convincing Loew of the need to increase *The Big Parade*'s budget by as much as a 20 percent stake, Mayer and Thalberg also succeeded in raising the potential payoff to an even higher degree: the extra cost was not meant to rescue a floundering production, as in *Ben-Hur*; rather, the aim was to create the impression of a blockbuster without paying the price for one. In effect, Loew's got another *Ben-Hur* for an extra forty thousand dollars.

The Big Parade was the most profitable film in the early history of MGM, running ninety-six weeks at the Astor alone and grossing almost $5 million within five years, including a broad re-release in 1927. As the dimensions of the hit became evident, the top brass were shocked to find a clause in King Vidor's pre-MGM contract that entitled him to 20 percent of the film's net profits. In negotiations with Vidor, MGM lawyers displayed some creative accounting, playing down the potential success of the film while emphasizing its costs. The director, already busy with another project, unwittingly accepted a small check in exchange for his stake. "I thus spared myself," he recalled wryly, "from becoming a millionaire instead of a struggling young director trying to do something interesting and better with a camera."

Following his successful collaboration with Thalberg, Vidor grew into a versatile director who managed to make the studio system work for him. He capitalized on the respect he had earned to initiate a number of projects that were closer to his own heart than to MGM's. In *The Crowd*, for example, he focused his camera on the average man, but now in a peacetime urban setting that emphasized the grim nature of fate and an individual's inability to battle forces

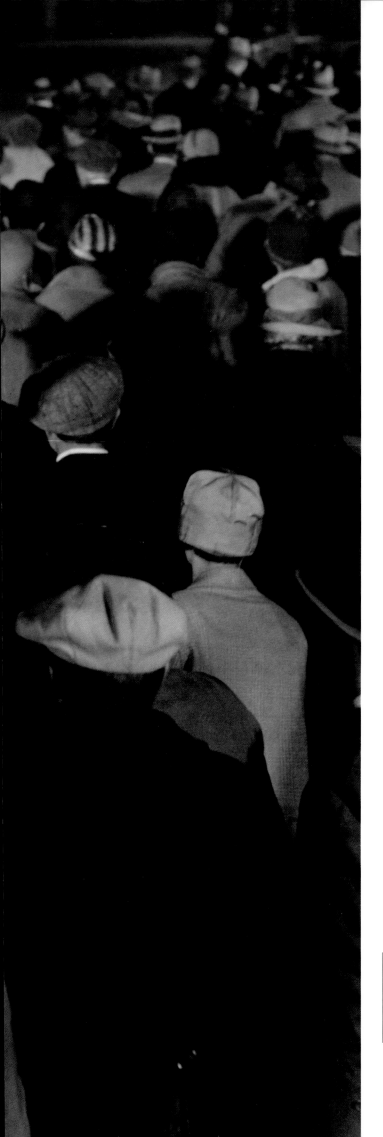

beyond his control. Vidor even cast an unknown, James Murray, in the starring role to underline the anonymous nature of his hero. Mayer objected once again to the film's downbeat ending and offered exhibitors two versions, one with a happier conclusion.

Once they had established control over budgets and directors, Mayer and Thalberg turned their attention to the studio's stable of feature players. In those early days of creation, MGM still had fewer stars than there were in heaven. Most were holdovers from Metro and Goldwyn Pictures, and a few came from Mayer's former production company. Among the more famous were Lon Chaney, Ramon Novarro, William Haines, Marion Davies, Mae Murray, Conrad Nagel, and ZaSu Pitts.

For the most part, Mayer relied on these actors for MGM's films. In 1925, however, Nicholas Schenck signed Lillian Gish to a six-picture deal that cost the studio $800,000 (she would later claim it was one million). Gish, along with her sister Dorothy, had been appearing in motion pictures, notably for D. W. Griffith, since 1912. She insisted on a contract that gave her final approval over projects and casting.

For her first picture at MGM, Gish chose *La Bohème*. After expressing admiration for *The Big Parade*, she

LEFT: *A face in* The Crowd *(1928)—James Murray begs for help for his sick child, in Vidor's powerful film depicting the alienation of modern man in the big city.*

ABOVE: *King Vidor, one of MGM's most versatile directors in the early days.*

Lillian Gish struggles against the relentless elements in The Wind *(1928). Nature provides the desert heat, but machines are used to whip up the wind.*

Lillian Gish goes mad in The Wind, *the film that ends her career at MGM. D. W. Griffith considered Gish the best film actress he knew and thought she had "the best mind of any woman I have ever met."*

picked John Gilbert and Renée Adorée as costars, and Vidor as her director. Meticulous and headstrong, Gish was so critical of the sets and costumes that Erté, the famous Parisian couturier, refused to speak to her. While Vidor indulged her, Thalberg finally decided to step in after viewing rushes of her love scenes with Gilbert. "It seemed to me," Gish stated in her memoirs, "that if we avoided showing the lovers in a physical embrace, the scenes would build up suppressed emotion and be much more effective. But I reckoned without the exploitation MGM had given John Gilbert as the Great Lover." Thalberg insisted on doing the love scenes with passion. For the next two or three days, as she went off to rehearse, Lillian Gish would sigh, "Oh, dear, I've got to go through another day of kissing John Gilbert!"

Gish proved to be far more difficult and expensive than Mayer had anticipated. Her choice of projects was out of touch with public tastes. The failure of two films in particular led to her departure from MGM, despite her strong performances. *The Scarlet Letter*'s adulterous theme caused problems with censors, and MGM had no appetite for dour, Puritanical tracts. *The Wind* was an equally bleak choice. It was a story about a prim woman who is suddenly stranded in a godforsaken dustbowl town. In desperation, she marries a man she does not love, and later is raped by a local lout. Underscoring the heavy drama is the relentless, driving wind that never ceases and eventually drives the woman to the brink of madness. Victor Seastrom shot the film under horrendous conditions in the Mojave Desert, where "film coating melted from its celluloid base," Gish recalled. "Finally the technicians packed it frozen and rushed it to the Culver City laboratories to be thawed out and developed."

ABOVE: *Gish's first film at MGM,* La Bohème *(1926), directed by King Vidor, is based on the novel that Puccini used for his opera.*
RIGHT AND FAR RIGHT: *With Thalberg and Vidor, and in a scene with John Gilbert. The actress goes without food or drink for several days, and practices discreet breathing so she can realistically portray the starvation of Mimi.*

THE TYCOON AND THE COMEDIENNE

When William Randolph Hearst met Marion Davies in 1917, the newspaper magnate could already boast that he had started a war and elected a president. Davies was a chorus girl and a sometime model, whose only real break had been a showcase in the 1916 edition of Florenz Ziegfeld's Broadway *Follies*. Although married (and unable to get a divorce), Hearst had a well-known affair with Davies that lasted until his death in 1950. He also set out to make her the biggest star in Hollywood. In order to do so, he formed Cosmopolitan Pictures, along with a distribution deal through Paramount, and marshaled the forces of his newspaper empire for relentless promotion.

Pretty, vivacious, and a talented comedienne, Davies may have succeeded even without the constant hype from Hearst's newspapers, which were ordered to run at least one story a day on her. Louella Parsons, who would become the most feared gossip columnist in Hollywood, caught Hearst's attention when she praised one of Davies's films. He syndicated Parsons's column, but her predictable references to the actress eventually drew ridicule and parody. The publicity campaign Hearst waged for Davies alienated the public, who found her film vehicles too sticky and sentimental. After he arranged a new distribution deal with Goldwyn Pictures in 1924, Cosmopolitan became an important factor in the MGM merger. It was agreed that Davies would be paid $10,000 a week, the most of any star on the MGM payroll, and that Hearst would be given complete control over her projects. Though these terms seemed steep, in return, Louis B. Mayer and MGM would be receiving the invaluable support of Hearst's media empire.

One of the queens of Hollywood social life, Davies brought a sense of legitimacy to MGM. Her connection with Hearst gave Mayer and the studio access to the highest levels of society and Washington politics. Her fourteen-room bungalow on the MGM lot became the center for parties for visiting celebrities and dignitaries. Hearst also built her a beach house in Santa Monica which had 118 rooms, including 3 dining rooms, 2 bars, swimming pools, tennis courts, a movie theater, and 55 bathrooms. The drawing room, with its ceiling of fourteen-carat gold leaf, came from a castle of the Earl of Essex. Even more astounding in its opulence was San Simeon, Hearst's mountaintop Xanadu some three hours north of Los Angeles. Davies, one of the most genuinely loved personalities in the film colony, entertained her wide circle of friends with boundless generosity. "Her warmth and kindness could have taught many of us a great deal about the art of loving," said Mary Astor, who appeared with Davies in one of her last movies.

Unfortunately, her films rarely found favor with the public. Hearst spent lavish sums on properties, most of which failed to exploit her comic skills. Davies registered strongly as an office worker in *Tillie the Toiler* (1927), which was based on a comic strip that appeared in Hearst newspapers; showed off her skill at impersonations in *The Patsy* (1928), her most profitable vehicle; and was endearing in *Show People* (1928), a sharp satire of Hollywood. But films such as *Marianne* (1929), in which she played a French waif during World War I, and *The Floradora Girl* (1930), a Gay Nineties musical, made Davies seem too artificial and old-fashioned.

She also had to compete for parts against Norma Shearer. Hearst especially wanted Davies to star in *The Barretts of Wimpole Street* (1934) and *Marie Antoinette* (made in 1938), both of which had been planned by Irving Thalberg as star vehicles for his wife. Mayer, who faced the dilemma of upsetting either Hearst or Thalberg, offered Hearst *Marie Antoinette* if Cosmopolitan would pay for it. In better times, Hearst might have accepted the deal, but his cash problems were by then so serious that Davies would soon be putting up her own money to settle his debts. Instead, Hearst moved Cosmopolitan to the Warner Bros. lot in 1934. Davies would make only four more films, retiring in 1937.

ABOVE: *Marion Davies in a publicity photograph for* Peg O' My Heart *(1933).*
BELOW: *An advertisement, with a picture of William Randolph Hearst. Aimed at exhibitors, it touts the lavish promotional campaign backing a new season of films (1930-31) produced by Cosmopolitan Pictures and distributed by MGM.*

MARION **DAVIES**
AND
Robert **MONTGOMERY**

IN

BLONDIE
OF THE
FOLLIES

with

BILLIE DOVE
JIMMY DURANTE
A **MARION DAVIES**
PRODUCTION
DIALOGUE AND CONTINUITY BY FRANCES MARION
Directed by EDMUND
GOULDING

TOP LEFT: *Hearst commanded top MGM talent for his mistress, Marion Davies, in* Blondie of the Follies *(1932).*

ABOVE LEFT AND RIGHT: *Davies and Hearst gave famous costume parties, both at her Santa Monica beach house and the fabled San Simeon estate. Director Victor Fleming flanked by MGM writers Frances Marion (left) and Anita Loos; Irving Thalberg with Davies (left) and his wife, Norma Shearer.*

TOP RIGHT: *Davies on location with King Vidor and crew for* Show People *(1928), in which she gets to exercise her comic talent in the role of a movie star.*

RIGHT CENTER: *Vidor films the commissary scene, in which celebrities play themselves, including Hearst columnist Louella Parsons and Douglas Fairbanks, Sr.*

RIGHT: *In the 1933 musical* Going Hollywood, *Davies plays the fan of a crooner (Bing Crosby) and, pretending to be a maid, tries to win his heart.*

1926

- Rudolph Valentino dies.
- Garbo makes her American debut in *The Torrent*.
- Lionel Barrymore makes his first film for MGM, *The Barrier*, and stays with the studio twenty-eight years, second only to Robert Taylor's thirty-three years.
- Louis B. Mayer decides that MGM needs a western star and finds a cavalry officer, Colonel Timothy John Fitzgerald McCoy. The publicist says, "He's the real McCoy."
- Garbo's third film for MGM, *Flesh and the Devil*, makes her a star. Gossip sheets exploit the steamy love scenes between Garbo and costar John Gilbert, which does nothing to dampen interest in the film.
- MGM creates the brightest light in the history of film, 325 million candlepower, for Lillian Gish's *The Scarlet Letter*. MGM publicity claims the light's power is so great that, if concentrated, its rays would allow a person nincty miles away to read a newspaper.
- MGM becomes the industry's most profitable company, netting $6,388,200.

A veteran of vaudeville at age four, Judy Garland would join the MGM star roster nine years later and appear in numerous films with vaudeville themes.

During the silent era, when only title cards require translation, MGM distributes many foreign films, such as this German production of Goethe's Faust, *directed by F. W. Murnau.*

The film, which critics consider to be one of Lillian Gish's finest, missed its mark at the time, and she departed from MGM without completing her contract.

Following the Gish episode, Mayer realized that, in creating its own stars, MGM could exercise firmer control over their careers, even their private lives. On the surface, creating stars seemed easier said than done. As thousands of hopefuls flooded Hollywood, studios employed dozens of scouts to look for new talent. Unknown actors, willing to work for a few dollars a day as extras, thought they had arrived when they received a long-term contract, which usually started at $75 or $100 a week, three or four times the living wage at the time. Even though the studio often dropped them after six months, having a contract gave status to these lucky few.

Scouts went beyond Hollywood in their search for stars—to Broadway, where Harry Rapf claimed to have found Joan Crawford, and then to Europe, where Mayer himself took credit for signing a young actress who would come to personify the mystique and glamour of the studio.

Louis B. Mayer met Greta Garbo in 1924, on the first of his regular trips to Europe to look for talent. After his frustrating visit to the set of *Ben-Hur* in Italy, he and his family proceeded to Berlin, the center of European filmmaking in the 1920s. On the advice of Victor Seastrom, Mayer went to see a four-hour Swedish film called *Gösta Berling's Saga*, directed by Mauritz Stiller. Mayer had already screened two

of Stiller's earlier films, and now was sufficiently impressed to offer him a contract for $1,500 a week.

Garbo's early career is shrouded in myth. Did Mayer hire Garbo at Stiller's insistence, or, having seen the young actress in Stiller's film, recognize her potential from the start? The official MGM version stressed Mayer's interest in Garbo from the very beginning, though he is supposed to have criticized her figure, telling her in his often-blunt manner, "Americans don't like fat women." By the time Stiller and Garbo sailed to America in the summer of 1925, the nineteen-year-old girl had lost a considerable amount of puppy fat. Still, Loew's publicity people wondered if Mayer had made a mistake in hiring the "awkward peasant girl."

Albert Lewin, who worked for Seastrom in 1924, claimed he was among the first to see *Gösta Berling's Saga* in an MGM editing room, and he registered a very definite opinion: "There were about seven or eight of us sitting in the room. Nobody could follow the story. It was complicated, the titles were in Swedish, and nobody would have sat through the picture if it hadn't been for this girl. They just waited for her to come on. Every time she came on, all these cutters went, 'Aahhh. . . .'"

In her MGM debut, *The Torrent*, Garbo played a poor girl who becomes an opera queen, opposite Ricardo Cortez. Her acting and the enthusiastic responses of Monta Bell, the director, and William Daniels, the cameraman with whom Garbo would work on most of her future films, immediately prompted Mayer to offer her a revised contract.

Mauritz Stiller was assigned to direct her next movie, *The Temptress*, but it was not long before his arrogance and slow methods reminded the MGM brass too much of Erich von Stroheim, and Thalberg replaced him with Fred Niblo. Sadly, the man who had discovered Greta Louise Gustafsson, and changed her name to Garbo, was forced to leave MGM while his protégée would remain with the studio for all of her Hollywood films.

Garbo's screen presence began to generate electricity and anticipation at MGM. Mayer, however, waited until a steady flow of fan mail began to confirm his hunch about her potential. Garbo did not really click with the public until the end of 1926, when Thalberg cast her opposite John Gilbert in *Flesh and the Devil*, the story of a temptress who comes between best friends and then pays for the trouble she causes with her life. Gilbert's attitude toward the young beauty was cool at first. Before filming got under way, director Clarence Brown offered to introduce him to his new costar, but the leading man is supposed to have replied with a distinct lack of charm, "To hell with her—let her come meet me!"

Life, however, would soon imitate the studio's art: Gilbert and Garbo became infatuated lovers. Their passion sizzled all over the set and caused Clarence Brown some embarrassment when the two continued to kiss in front of the cameras long after he had called "Cut!" It was both the

film and the love affair that launched Greta Garbo's brilliant streak across the world's skies. With audiences clamoring for more, MGM immediately cast Garbo and Gilbert in *Love*, a version of Tolstoy's *Anna Karenina*. The studio's exuberant publicity men capitalized on the stars' infatuation with each other, by promoting the movie with the headline "Garbo and Gilbert in *Love*" (originally, the film was going to be called *Heat*, until screenwriter Frances Marion pointed out how that would look on marquees). The gossip columnist Walter Winchell coined the phrase "Garbo-Gilberting," to describe the behavior of any pair of exhibitionistic lovers. The stars would appear together in only two more films, *A Woman of Affairs*, in 1928, and *Queen Christina*, in 1934. But by 1929, their affair was over.

Even at the beginning of her career at MGM, Garbo refused to play the part of a traditional movie star. Her early experiences with photographers who shot her in revealing clothes, and with reporters who garbled her interviews, made Garbo rebel against the Hollywood publicity machine. She would surprise the world—as well as the studio—with her unconventional moods and self-willed ways, often quitting films entirely, then returning to even greater acclaim. But once MGM grasped the impact Garbo generated on the public through her refusal to talk to the press, it found a way of exploiting her reclusiveness. "GARBO TALKS!" were two

OPPOSITE:

TOP: *Garbo's inauspicious debut in* The Torrent *(1926), before MGM figures out what to do with her. She plays a Spanish singer opposite love interest Ricardo Cortez.*

BOTTOM: *Garbo, as* The Temptress *(1926), drives a succession of men (here Antonio Moreno) to their ruin.*

TOP: *Garbo with John Gilbert. Alistair Cooke once wrote of Garbo, "If your imagination has to sin, it can at least congratulate itself on its impeccable taste."*

ABOVE: *Three great Swedes— Garbo between two directors, Victor Seastrom (who plays the memorable professor in Ingmar Bergman's* Wild Strawberries *toward the end of his life), and Mauritz Stiller.*

words that said less about the advent of sound than they did about the miracle of hearing the Swedish sphinx speak in *Anna Christie*.

Behind the scenes, the studio brass was willing to put up with Garbo's demands. But prior to *Love*, she insisted on a huge increase in her salary. Mayer refused; she walked out. After waiting several months for her to return, Mayer decided what he and the studio wanted most. More than the stature of a Lillian Gish, Garbo's cool elegance and erotic appeal sold tickets. He met Garbo's terms.

The studio could well afford Garbo. By the end of 1926, MGM's profits placed it at the top of the film industry. Mayer had more than fulfilled his contractual obligations to produce a minimum of fifteen films a year. During the first full year under his management, 1925-26, MGM made some forty pictures; the following season it produced forty-five movies, and for the two seasons thereafter, the studio would surpass the much desired fifty-film mark. Some twenty-five staff directors and forty writers were supervised by Thalberg's team of five or six producers. Forty-five contract players called MGM their home. Between eight to ten of these actors would be considered stars by virtue of their salaries and special treatment, though perhaps twice as many were promoted as such to the outside world. During this time, MGM assembled an army of skilled artists, designers, carpenters,

LEFT: *Garbo is typically seductive, this time with Robert Castle in the 1929 silent movie* The Single Standard.

ABOVE: *Garbo in* Love, *the 1927 version of* Anna Karenina. *MGM provides a happy ending to Tolstoy's masterpiece: Anna's husband dies and she is reunited with Count Vronsky (John Gilbert).*

1927

◆ Warner Bros.'s *The Jazz Singer*, with Al Jolson, is the first feature film with dialogue. Sound has arrived.

◆ Even though sound is here, MGM makes two successful silent operettas, *The Student Prince in Old Heidelberg*, with Ramon Novarro and Norma Shearer, and *Rose Marie*, with Joan Crawford.

◆ Norma Shearer marries Irving Thalberg after a brief courtship. The best man is Louis B. Mayer.

◆ Lon Chaney, filling theaters with his frightening disguises, inspires a famous 1920s joke: "Don't step on it, it might be Lon Chaney."

◆ A July roster of MGM's principal contract actors shows eight "Stars" and thirty-seven "Featured Players." The stars are Lon Chaney, Jackie Coogan, Marion Davies, John Gilbert, Lillian Gish, William Haines, Ramon Novarro, and Norma Shearer. In September, Garbo moves up to star, and Gish disappears from both lists.

◆ On January 11, the idea of an "International Academy of Motion Picture Arts and Sciences" is raised at a dinner party hosted by Louis Mayer.

Greta Garbo and John Gilbert on the Love *set.*

seamstresses, lighting technicians, scene painters, and writers, many of whom would spend their entire working lives at MGM. Over the years, the studio grew from its original twenty-two acres to more than 275. With its own police force, fire department, and post office, the Culver City lot became a city unto itself.

Loew and Schenck had recognized that executive talent was even rarer than good directors or stars. In late 1925, Mayer's name was added officially to the title Metro-Goldwyn. His weekly salary jumped a thousand dollars to $2,500; Thalberg's more than tripled, from $650 to $2,000. In addition, Loew's guaranteed a minimum of $500,000 toward the profit-sharing formula split among Mayer, Thalberg, and Rubin.

Thalberg, who only three years earlier had been earning less than $25,000 a year, now began to push for an even greater share of MGM's profits. "His eighteen-hour day," wrote Jim Tully in a 1927 *Vanity Fair* sketch, "involves editing, cutting, titling, casting, advising millionaire stars, giving fatherly advice to directors, script writers and authors; passing on problems of real estate, exhibitor control, and promotional values in his productions." To the film colony at large, however, Thalberg adopted a modest appearance. During all the years he spent producing movies for MGM, he never allowed his name to appear on the screen. "Credit you give yourself," he often said, "is not worth having."

By September 1927, the top management of Loew's and

Buster Keaton, one of the great comics of the silent era, signs a contract with MGM in 1928. In The Cameraman *(1928), he competes against newsreel photographers to win the heart of Marcelline Day.*

MGM had achieved much of what it set out to do three short years earlier. That same month, Marcus Loew died of heart disease at Pembroke, his thirty-five-room baronial mansion off Long Island Sound. Twenty-five hundred people crowded the memorial service at his estate. Managers of Loew's theaters, which were closed for three days, sent an enormous floral design that read simply "THE LAST CURTAIN." Even competing theaters closed for an hour out of respect for the deceased theater magnate. Amid an outpouring of genuine affection, the usually hard-bitten show-business paper *Variety* wrote about Loew's "gentle, tender, endearing soul," and reached for the Bible to describe his business dealings: "a just Solomon, a wise Moses, a patient Job, and a kind David in judgment and in counsel."

Loew's board of directors immediately promoted Nicholas Schenck to the corporation's helm, and Arthur M. Loew, the founder's shy and retiring son, took over Schenck's job as executive vice-president. Schenck needed no time for the transition; in effect, he had been running the company's day-to-day operations since Marcus Loew's heart attack in 1923, including overseeing the details of the MGM merger the following year. He would remain at the helm of Loew's for almost thirty years, guiding it with a steady hand through its greatest triumphs and some major crises. Yet, for most of those years, he remained in the shadows, as far as the larger public was concerned, allowing Louis B. Mayer and Irving Thalberg to occupy the limelight.

TOP: *Lon Chaney in* London After Midnight *(1927). Tod Browning's thriller is one of the few "lost" MGM films: no surviving prints have been found. Starting in the late 1960s, MGM begins transferring its early nitrate pictures to more durable acetate film, in order to preserve its vast library.*

ABOVE: *Two of MGM's seasoned comediennes, Polly Moran (left) and Marie Dressler (right), ham it up at the MGM gate.*

1928

◆ Leo the Lion roars for the first time in *White Shadows in the South Seas,* which also features a synchronized score and sound effects.

◆ The Academy of Motion Picture Arts and Sciences presents its first awards. MGM wins title writing awards for three pictures—*Telling the World, The Fair Co-Ed,* and *Laugh, Clown, Laugh*—and best cinematography for *White Shadows in the South Seas.*

◆ *The Crowd,* written and directed by King Vidor, is released and becomes one of the most praised films in MGM history. It returns twice its cost and earns Vidor his first nomination for an Academy Award for best director.

◆ Marion Davies scores the biggest hit of her career with *The Patsy,* a comedy directed by King Vidor.

◆ Buster Keaton leaves United Artists to sign with MGM. Crowds cause pandemonium when he attempts to shoot location footage in New York City for *The Cameraman.*

◆ MGM builds its first sound stages.

◆ Loretta Young, fifteen, makes her first film, *Laugh, Clown, Laugh.*

White Shadows in the South Seas.

57

PART TWO

The Lion Roars

On September 23, 1926, the night the heavy-weight boxing championship between Jack Dempsey and Gene Tunney was broadcast on the air from Philadelphia, movie theaters reported a precipitous drop in attendance, in some instances by as much as half. Radio had arrived. Some people in the film industry predicted there would be little competition from a medium so different from silent pictures. When box-office returns continued to be erratic, however, Loew's decided to buy into radio's future and set up its own station. At first, WHN merely announced the programs showing at the various Loew's theaters. The same idea was later carried a step further by WMGM, which served as a publicity outlet for MGM's films and stars.

As radio became more popular, the station moved from Brooklyn to the top of the company's Manhattan headquarters. Under the management of Nils T. Granlund, well-known vaudeville artists appeared on WMGM, as part of their contract with Loew's theaters, which continued to carry live acts through most of the thirties, even though the era of big-time vaudeville had ended as a consequence of the movies, radio, and the Depression.

With the advent of radio, the thought of combining sound with pictures grew all the more tantalizing. Experiments conducted by Thomas Edison and W. K. L. Dickson in synchronizing sound to film dated back to the late 1880s, but talkies became viable only with the development of an effective loudspeaker system and the perfection

LEFT: *MGM is the last major studio to convert to sound. In* The Hollywood Revue of 1929, *the famous number "Singin' in the Rain" first appears.*

ABOVE: *Leo the Lion recording his sound debut for* White Shadows in the South Seas *(1928).*

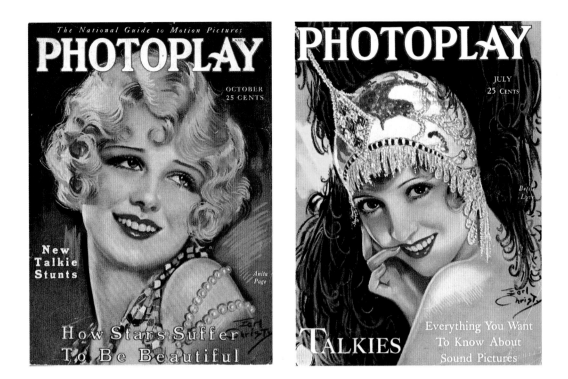

PHOTOPLAY

PHOTOPLAY

OCTOBER
25 CENTS

New
Talkie
Stunts

Anita Page

How Stars Suffer
To Be Beautiful

JULY
25 Cents

Betty Lyon

TALKIES

Everything You Want
To Know About
Sound Pictures

ABOVE: *Anita Page (left) and Bessie Love (right), two silent film stars, help MGM pass the sound barrier with flying colors in* The Broadway Melody *(1929).*

of the Vitaphone process (recording sound on discs synchronized to film).

The Jazz Singer, starring Al Jolson, opened at the Warner Theater in New York City, on October 6, 1927. At first, the movie industry remained largely skeptical. Irving Thalberg, reached for comment during his honeymoon, declared, "Novelty is always welcome, but talking pictures are just a fad." MGM did not get involved in this revolutionary breakthrough until early 1928, when agreement was reached on an industry standard based on both Vitaphone and Movietone, a process developed by the Fox studio that recorded sound directly on film. By then, pressure from Loew's exhibitors, who were losing business to theaters already equipped for sound, forced Nicholas Schenck to embark on a three-million-dollar crash program to convert the entire Loew's chain to the new technology. He also announced that MGM would begin producing up to 20 percent of its output with sound.

Eddie Mannix, the former amusement park bouncer who had been sent west by Nicholas Schenck in 1924 as an aide to Mayer, was put in charge of the complex task of overseeing the conversion of the studio's operations. Nobody at MGM knew much about the mysteries of sound, but Mannix remembered some audio experiments a young engineer, Douglas Shearer, had tried with a film trailer for one of his sister's pictures, *Slave of Fashion*. Nothing came of these, and Shearer was now working, after a stint at Warner Bros., at MGM on trick photography. Mannix entrusted him with the task of developing the studio's brand-new sound department. Some said that his sister, recently married to Irving

ABOVE: *MGM publicity has Leo hard at work promoting a sound approach to profits.*

ABOVE: Hallelujah (1929), with an all-black cast, is an unusual film for MGM, but director King Vidor wants to make the picture so badly, he reputedly offers to give up his salary.

Thalberg, helped him to get the appointment. Although she may have opened the door, it was Doug Shearer's acceptance of an enormous challenge that launched him on his career as one of the foremost sound pioneers in Hollywood.

Leo the Lion's roar was first heard in 1928, at the beginning of *White Shadows in the South Seas*. Working at a New Jersey sound studio, Shearer dubbed a music score and sound effects onto the film. The only dialogue, however, was the single word "Hello." While Mannix supervised the building of the first of two sound stages at MGM, using construction crews in three shifts around the clock, Shearer borrowed the facilities at Paramount to add musical scores, sound effects, and, eventually, dialogue to subsequent films. In *Alias Jimmy Valentine* and *The Bellamy Trial*, certain scenes of the completed films were completely reshot with dialogue, but these were makeshift efforts to buy time while MGM geared up to present its first great sound spectacle.

MGM's breakthrough from novelty to real entertainment came with the "all-talking, all-singing, all-dancing" musical, *The Broadway Melody*, based on the simple story of two sisters whose act breaks up when they fall in love with the same rakish songwriter. The film gave rise to a whole genre of backstage musicals in the thirties and also introduced the young songwriting team of lyricist Arthur Freed and composer Nacio Herb Brown to Hollywood. They were in the vanguard of an army of musical talent that came from Tin Pan Alley and Broadway.

Although *The Broadway Melody* was produced by Lawrence Weingarten, who had recently married Thalberg's sister Sylvia, Thalberg kept a close eye on its progress.

1929

◆ King Vidor makes *Hallelujah*, MGM's first all-black film. It has the first song written for the studio by Irving Berlin, "Waiting at the End of the Road." Critics love it. Parts of the South won't show it.

◆ *The Broadway Melody*, MGM's first all-sound picture, is billed at its February 1 debut as "All Talking, All Dancing, All Singing."

◆ Comedian Buster Keaton makes his last silent picture, *Spite Marriage*.

◆ Joan Crawford makes her last silent film, *Our Modern Maidens*, with Douglas Fairbanks, Jr. Their offscreen romance and marriage help make it a big hit.

◆ Lionel Barrymore directs *Madame X* and three more pictures, concluding with *The Rogue Song* (all-talking and in Technicolor), then returns to acting.

◆ Cecil B. De Mille arrives and makes *Dynamite*.

◆ Sound takes over the industry, and MGM makes record profits: $12.1 million— up $3.5 million from the year before.

Louis B. Mayer's affiliation with William Randolph Hearst often brings the studio into contact with the world's leading figures. (Left to right) Hearst, Winston Churchill, Mayer, Fred Niblo, and John Churchill.

ALL TALKING ♦ ALL DANCING
ALL SINGING

The New Wonder of the Screen

When the sights and sounds, the music and dialogue and all the wonderment of

"The Broadway Melody"

are brought to you, you will realize for the first time the true magic of the Talking Screen. Nothing like it ever before! The new thrill of a lifetime has come for you! This drama of White Nights on Broadway, of love and hate and tenderness, of stage beauties and reckless millionaires is the perfect vehicle to reveal to the world the new magic of the screen that has a voice to tell you its soul-stirring story.

Hear each throbbing minute of the screen's greatest Achievement!

—*From campaign book*

Despite being among the last to convert to sound, the success of MGM's first musical, The Broadway Melody *(1929), firmly places the studio in the vanguard of the sound revolution. It also introduces the musical team of composer Nacio Herb Brown and lyricist Arthur Freed.*

THE ADVENT OF SOUND

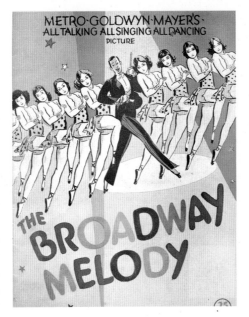

In the twenties, a number of electronics companies were devising sound-reproducing systems for use in conjunction with motion pictures. MGM hesitated to get involved in sound until it saw which of the competing technologies would prevail. In April and May 1928, about six months after the showing of *The Jazz Singer*, MGM and other studios signed agreements with Electrical Research Products (ERPI), the commercial outlet for Western Electric, to obtain licenses and recording equipment. Even so, talkies were further delayed by a shortage of sound engineers who were prepared for this new technology.

In 1928, the completed silent picture *White Shadows in the South Seas* was taken by Douglas Shearer, the head of the sound department at MGM, to a New Jersey recording studio in order to add synchronized sound effects and music in time for the New York premiere on July 31, 1928. On this occasion, the public first heard Leo the Lion (MGM's trademark) roar. Then, director Jack Conway took *Alias Jimmy Valentine* back into production and reshot the climactic sequence with dialogue at the Paramount studio (which was already equipped for sound). Shearer wrote that "audiences thoroughly enjoyed the novelty of sound coming from the screen, although they were keenly conscious of its squeaky imperfections."

Talking pictures created a whole new set of obstacles for cast and crew. The microphones could not be moved. If the actors were required to move, they had to position themselves near a hidden microphone, which might be in a bouquet of flowers, in a lamp, or under a table—just about anywhere. In addition, actors were cautioned either not to move from one hidden mike before they had finished a speech or not to start talking again until they were directly in front of another mike.

While rehearsing a scene for *The Trial of Mary Dugan* in 1929, Norma Shearer "had to remember the exact spot on the floor on which she had to sit, had to keep her head in a certain position so that the microphone would record her lines, while three cameras, each with a different lens, took long shots, close-ups, and medium shots, all from soundproof booths placed in a line before her."

Many other problems arose. Airplanes flying over movie studios often ruined scenes being shot. At MGM, a "silence" balloon was raised to warn aircraft, and red flags were tied to cords on the studio roof. An agreement for aviators to avoid these marked locations was reached among the Department of Commerce, the California Aircraft Operators Association, and the movie producers.

Some problems demanded long hours of experimentation. Discussing technical sound problems, Shearer wrote: "There was a time when we had to have special cartridges for gun shots, which would make no explosion, because light valves might be shattered." This problem was eliminated by the "electric shock absorber," which was first used in MGM's *The Big House* in 1930. On the sound track, small sounds often resembled explosions. Raindrops, for example, first sounded like dropping bullets. Technicians learned how to *damp* the sound by lining window sills with blotting paper or laying felt on the ground beyond the sight lines of the camera. The roar of rustling petticoats was subdued with nonabrasive muslin linings.

Among other original devices, the MGM sound department created a *suitcase portable* recording outfit and a *baffle board*, which helped eliminate extraneous noises from entering the microphone.

TOP LEFT: *A program for the premiere of* The Broadway Melody *(1929).*
ABOVE TOP: *Norma Shearer hopes her sound test, made at the University of Southern California, will lead to a successful sound career at MGM.*
ABOVE: *MGM's first sound stages, built in 1928, make sure the need for quiet is obeyed from all directions.*

OPPOSITE:
TOP LEFT: *Engineer Douglas Shearer shows sister Norma the latest in sound technology Here, they examine a condenser microphone.*
TOP CENTER: *Douglas explains to Norma the process of recording sound onto celluloid film (Movietone process), as opposed to recording sound onto disk (Vitaphone process).*
TOP RIGHT: *Doug positions the microphone for Norma to make a test.*

ABOVE AND RIGHT: *John Gilbert's first talkie,* His Glorious Night *(1929), is not the success the studio hoped it would be.*

LEFT: *For her first talkie,* Anna Christie *(1930), Greta Garbo speaks in both the English (above with Marie Dressler) and German (below with Salka Viertel) versions.*

ABOVE: *Greta Garbo and George Marion in* Anna Christie *(1930). Garbo's famous first line—"Gif me a vhisky, ginger ale on the side, and don't be stingy, baby!"—is spoken in a deep, husky voice that meshes perfectly with her personality and is greeted with enthusiasm by her fans and studio executives.*

RIGHT: *Silent star William Haines in* Alias Jimmy Valentine *(1929). The film is completed as a silent, then the studio comes up with the idea of adding dialogue to the finale. The cast and crew are brought back to reshoot the entire scene.*
LEFT: *A publicity still of Joan Crawford in* Untamed *(1929), her first talking film.*

Dissatisfied with one of the big numbers, "The Wedding of the Painted Doll" (shot in Technicolor in an otherwise black-and-white film), Thalberg ordered the sequence reshot. To save the time and expense of rerecording the score, Douglas Shearer suggested that the cast pretend to sing to the original soundtrack while reshooting, thus avoiding the cost of reassembling the orchestra's musicians. This technique would become an industry standard.

The Broadway Melody scored a resounding success, earning an Academy Award for best picture and recouping its cost ten times over. The golden era of MGM musicals was still a decade away, but the studio, having been the last to break into the sound era, was now leading the revolution in content, if not technology.

Not everyone at MGM relished the studio's adventure into sound. Actors, especially stars, were terrified. "It was the night of the *Titanic* all over again," one MGM actor recalled, "with women grabbing the wrong children and Louis B. singing 'Nearer My God to Thee.'" According to one Hollywood joke making the rounds, when Marion Davies was escorted to *The Jazz Singer* by an MGM publicist, she turned to him at the end and said, "M-m-mister Voight, I-I-I have a p-p-problem." William Randolph Hearst, who was not one to spare expense, hired the best speech therapist to work with Davies. It turned out she had a surprisingly good voice, which further enhanced her comic talents.

Voice experts and dialogue coaches became both a fad and a necessity in Hollywood, but for many in the industry, the limitations exposed by sound were too great to overcome. Jean Hersholt was among the relatively fortunate. Although he went from earning a silent star's salary of

$3,500 a week at Universal to $500 at MGM, he managed to sustain a long career as a featured player and even went on to have a radio series. Karl Dane, however, was not so lucky. Ironically, his big break had come only a few years earlier as the tobacco-chewing doughboy in *The Big Parade*. His comic turns with George K. Arthur were also very popular. Unfortunately, his thick Danish accent proved a major liability. His film career came to a halt in 1930, and four years later he committed suicide.

Insecurity affected actors in different ways. Many stars had no stage experience and found it difficult to handle long passages of dramatic dialogue. Others, who had been trained in the declamatory style of acting favored in nineteenth-century melodrama and had adjusted to the equally exaggerated pantomime of silent movies, found that talkies rendered such acting ludicrous or, at best, outmoded.

To reassure the public as well as themselves that the switch to sound was only a small obstacle for their stars, many studios rushed into production anthology pieces that showcased their top talent. MGM produced *The Hollywood Revue of 1929*, featuring Marion Davies, Buster Keaton, Laurel and Hardy, Conrad Nagel, William Haines, Lionel Barrymore, and Jack Benny. Norma Shearer and John Gilbert did the balcony scene from *Romeo and Juliet*, and then burlesqued it in modern English. Joan Crawford sang "Gotta Feelin' for You," and later a trio of comediennes—Marie Dressler, Bessie Love, and Polly Moran—hammed up a new song, by Arthur Freed and Nacio Herb Brown, called "Singin' in the Rain." Almost everyone made an appearance, with the conspicuous exception of Garbo, who starred that year in *The Kiss*, the last MGM silent. Her talking debut in *Anna Christie*, Eugene O'Neill's brooding drama, not only represented the final breakthrough for the most important MGM star but also marked a new chapter in Hollywood's relationship with writers.

The Hollywood Revue of 1929 *gives many of the studio's top stars an opportunity to display their voices before the public in a short skit or song.*
TOP LEFT: *The entire cast perform the film's finale,* "Singin' in the Rain" *(in Technicolor).*

ABOVE: *Marion Davies.*
RIGHT: *Lionel Barrymore directing John Gilbert and Norma Shearer in a scene from* Romeo and Juliet.
FAR RIGHT: *A dancing Joan Crawford.*

1930

◆ Greta Garbo moves to sound with the voice the world was waiting to hear in *Anna Christie*. Her English is so good, in fact, she has to add an accent in several retakes to sound more like the Swedish Anna.

◆ Lon Chaney, who swore he would never make a talking picture ("I have a thousand faces, but only one voice"), changes his mind and creates five voices for the role of the ventriloquist in a remake of *The Unholy Three*. Seven weeks after it opens, Chaney, forty-seven, dies of throat cancer.

◆ Irving Thalberg's wife Norma Shearer wins an Oscar for best actress for *The Divorcée*. She is also nominated for *Their Own Desire*.

◆ Director W. S. Van Dyke takes his cast and crew to the African jungles to shoot *Trader Horn*. Edwina Booth, the star of the film, contracts a blood desease and is reported to have died, which only adds to the legend surrounding the production of this adventure film. In fact, she dies sixty-one years later.

◆ The Roaring Twenties become the Depression Thirties, but MGM nets a record $15 million—its best year until 1946.

| Leo the Lion is the star at this MGM sales convention.

TOP: *Norma Shearer in* The Divorcée *(1930), with Chester Morris.*
ABOVE: *Anita Loos (right), one of Hollywood's most popular screenwriters, poses with cast and crew members of* Hold Your Man *(1933), a gangster film starring Clark Gable and Jean Harlow.*

OPPOSITE: *With* Our Blushing Brides *(1930), the studio begins developing a more sophisticated image of Joan Crawford, rather than continuing to promote her flapper-girl persona of the silent era.*

With the advent of sound, studios scrambled to recruit "real" writers, especially from Broadway. Playwrights Maxwell Anderson, Sidney Howard, George S. Kaufman, Moss Hart, Ben Hecht, Charles MacArthur, S. N. Behrman, Donald Ogden Stewart, wits from the Algonquin Round Table, such as Dorothy Parker, Robert Benchley, and S. J. Perelman, and the staff of *The New Yorker* all served time at MGM's writers' building. Although these writers gave clever twists to plots and added crackling sophistication to dialogue, they are not as well remembered for the films they wrote as for their barbs and anecdotes told against Hollywood.

The most famous stories, much embroidered over the years, concern the most creative talents, such as lone novelists who could not adapt their working methods or personal tastes to the assembly-line system at the studio. According to MGM's Sam Marx, William Faulkner was given the task of working on a wrestling film for Wallace Beery, but after the writer was asked to familiarize himself with Beery's *The Champ*, he emerged from the screening room, wild-eyed and white-faced, muttering, "It ain't possible!" Soon he would be asking permission to work at home; unfortunately, the studio did not realize he meant Oxford, Mississippi!

Thalberg brought F. Scott Fitzgerald, the unhappy herald of the Jazz Age, to MGM to write the scenario for *Red-Headed Woman*, based on the novel of the same name by Katharine Brush, who wrote in a style clearly influenced by Fitzgerald. Apparently, the writer could not imitate himself sufficiently well; after five weeks, he was taken off the project. He believed, however, that he might have been fired for making a drunken fool of himself at the Thalbergs' house,

JOAN
CRAWFORD
IN OUR
BLUSHING
BRIDES

WITH
ROBERT MONTGOMERY · ANITA PAGE ·
DOROTHY SEBASTIAN · RAYMOND HACKETT ·
A HARRY BEAUMONT PRODUCTION ·
A METRO·GOLDWYN·MAYER ALL TALKING
PICTURE ·

RIGHT: *The script for* The Sin of Madelon Claudet *(1932), starring Helen Hayes, undergoes numerous revisions and is finally credited to Charles MacArthur. The scene shown here, in which Hayes's character is struck by a car, is cut from the final version.*
OPPOSITE: *Clark Gable and Joan Crawford (circa 1931).*

a scene he later described in his short story *Crazy Sunday*. In the end, Fitzgerald received only one screen credit at MGM, for *Three Comrades*, and he considered that script to have been marred by changes made by producer Joseph L. Mankiewicz.

Many other great writers, such as Ernest Hemingway, John Steinbeck, and Aldous Huxley (who collaborated on a number of screenplays at MGM, including *Pride and Prejudice*), would have little to show for their efforts in Hollywood, where they came, in screenwriter Herman Mankiewicz's phrase, "in pursuit of the lump sum."

The writers who fit in most easily were those with a journalistic background, perhaps because they had been trained to turn out copy on deadline and were used to being cut and edited by others. In his memoirs, Ben Hecht, the most successful of such writers, recalled "movie writing as an amiable chore. It was a source of easy money and pleasant friendships. There was small responsibility. Your name as writer was buried in a flock of 'credits.' Your literary pride was never involved. What critics said about the movie you had written never bothered you. They were usually criticizing something you couldn't remember. . . . Of the sixty movies I wrote, more than half were written in two weeks or less."

Apart from his credited screenplays, Hecht was also the busiest script doctor in Hollywood. His discreet contributions to *Queen Christina*, *The Shop Around the Corner*, and *Gone with the Wind* went uncredited, except to his bank account. For the latter, David O. Selznick had called him in desperation, after a dozen writers had tried to please the producer, and offered him $15,000 if he could

rework the script for the most famous novel of the decade in a week. The writer, who had not read the book, listened to Selznick's lengthy recitation of Margaret Mitchell's story and then said, "That's the most involved plot I've ever heard. Can't you just throw it away and I write a new one?" Selznick was not amused.

Charles MacArthur, the brilliant and mercurial newspaperman with whom Hecht cowrote such Broadway comedies as *The Front Page* and *Twentieth Century*, became one of Thalberg's closest friends and favorite writers. His contributions to projects such as *Billy the Kid* and *The Sin of Madelon Claudet*, although not as famous as his stage efforts, resulted in excellent reviews for MGM. The latter picture, a maudlin melodrama about an unwed young girl discovering the meaning of maternal love for her child, starred his wife, Helen Hayes. When MacArthur objected that the original script was "god awful," Thalberg told him to fix it. Despite his efforts, the couple still felt acute embarrassment over the final outcome. Louis B. Mayer thought differently and wept openly at the preview. So did audiences. Helen Hayes won an Academy Award for her performance.

Like most of the Hollywood studios, MGM hired a number of famous writers without being able to use them. It was Samuel Goldwyn who first tried to elevate writers to movie stardom by gathering them under the banner of Eminent Authors (in answer to Zukor's Famous Players). Few of these writers worked out, and Goldwyn quickly turned to others who were less eminent but more reliable. Frances Marion became Goldwyn's and Hollywood's top-paid scenarist at $3,000 a week. She elected to stay on with MGM after

TOP AND LEFT: *Director Clarence Brown, cinematographer William Daniels, and crew shoot Garbo and Robert Montgomery in a scene for* Inspiration *(1931). The invention of the boom mike helps restore the camera and the actor's mobility.*

ABOVE: *For the banquet scene in* Anna Karenina *(1935), Brown and Daniels track down the entire length of the table.*
OPPOSITE: *William Daniels and director George Fitzmaurice lower the boom on Garbo and Ramon Novarro in* Mata Hari *(1931).*

the merger, partly because she admired the way Thalberg integrated writers into the whole filmmaking machinery. "No picture was ever cast unless the actors chosen met with our approval," she recalled. As evidence of her reliability, Marion amassed close to one hundred and fifty credits, and won successive Academy Awards for her work on *The Big House*, in 1930, and *The Champ*, in 1931, awards that conspicuously eluded Faulkner or Fitzgerald.

Thalberg recruited Anita Loos to supply her special brand of witty dialogue for *Red-Headed Woman*, following his disappointment with Fitzgerald. Another of the skilled scenarists of the early silent era, the diminutive Loos began writing scenarios and titles for D. W. Griffith, and published the best-selling novel *Gentlemen Prefer Blondes* in 1925. She wrote or contributed to a number of major MGM films, including *Hold Your Man*, *San Francisco*, *Saratoga*, and *The Women*. She stayed at MGM mainly because of Thalberg, and credited him with the studio's unrivaled success.

What impressed these writers about Thalberg was not just his uncanny feel for story and plot but also his team spirit and modesty. "Whenever a picture was successful, Irving said, 'We have done a good job!' " Frances Marion recalled. "Dealing with writers, he withheld any criticism that might destroy our creative forces. 'A picture is only as good as its writer. A writer only as good as his inspiration,' he said. 'I don't want to dictate what you're to write, or impose too many of my ideas on you. You're the creators, not I.' "

In fact, Thalberg often imposed himself, and sometimes assigned several writers to the same script, in succession or simultaneously. Often they would be working on the same project unbeknown to each other, a practice that was later halted by the Screen Writers Guild. Albert Lewin recalled Thalberg "in story conferences with all sorts of famous dramatists and authors, and frequently the best ideas were his. The solution of how best to design a story would often come from him."

Maintaining an assembly line of forty to fifty films a year required a large staff of writers of different talents. Schenck, Mayer, and Eddie Mannix often complained about the waste of some high-priced talent. When P.G. Wodehouse told the New York press that MGM had paid him more than $100,000, basically to do nothing for a year, Schenck raised the issue with Thalberg, who replied testily, "If you know how to make pictures without writers, let me know."

Providing both producers and directors with a constant stream of potential material, the MGM story department compiled four to five thousand reports a year on scripts or ideas, many submitted by agents. The dozen story analysts combed newspapers for reviews or mentions of novels and plays; they read most of the short stories and feature articles published by the flourishing magazine market. In addition, studio representatives in New York and many

THE EYE OF THE CAMERA

In the glow of firelight, Greta Garbo moves about the room caressing each piece of furniture and trying to "memorize" the essence of the place. Though *Queen Christina* (1934) was photographed by William Daniels, most likely, the audience paid little attention when his name flashed on screen. But when people marveled at Garbo's beauty, they were also admiring the cameraman's idealized vision of her. Daniels modestly insisted he hadn't created the "Garbo face," but had merely photographed her to fit the requirements of the scene. The star appreciated his talent, as did the studio. He photographed nineteen of Garbo's twenty-four MGM films.

The "newsreel look" of pointing a camera and shooting whatever passed in front of it was disdained by Hollywood cinematographers. They enhanced imagery through camera placement and controlled lighting. John Alton, who won an Oscar for his work on *An American in Paris* (1951), called cinematography the art of "painting with light." A still photographer can make adjustments in the darkroom, but the cinematographer doesn't get a second chance. There's no room for a misplaced shadow or an annoying reflection. A female star with "laugh lines" and bags under the eyes requires help to maintain her screen image. Soft lighting and focus and shooting through fine gauze muted Joan Crawford's freckles and blemishes, and a tiny "eye light" hovering above the lens brought Garbo's deep-set eyes out of the shadows in her close-ups.

John Arnold, another brilliant cameraman, shot King Vidor's hit *The Big Parade* (1925), and headed the MGM camera department from 1931 to 1956. Arnold cast cinematographers like the studio cast actors. Clyde De Vinna was highly regarded for his beautiful outdoor photography. Using filters and reflectors, and an unerring eye for the way the sun plays across a landscape, De Vinna captured the exteriors of such famous location films as *Trader Horn* (1931), *Eskimo* (1933), and *Treasure Island* (1934). Hal Rosson, who was noted for his subtle and imaginative lighting, shared the credit on *Treasure Island*. Jean Harlow's platinum blonde beauty was seen to its best advantage under Rosson's practiced eye, in pictures such as *Red Dust* (1932), *Red-Headed Woman* (1932), and *Bombshell* (1933). He was also noted for his work on Technicolor musicals, including *The Wizard of Oz* (1939), *and Singin' in the Rain* (1952). The high light levels required by the Technicolor process often resulted in a gaudy coloring-book look, but Rosson was able to transfer his black-and-white skills to the creation of a subtle color style.

Oliver T. Marsh shot *The Merry Widow* (both the 1925 and the 1934 versions); Joseph Ruttenberg worked on *The Great Waltz* (1938), *The Philadelphia Story*, and *Mrs. Miniver* (1942); and George Folsey was the cinematographer for *Meet Me in St. Louis* (1944), *Adam's Rib* (1949), and *Forbidden Planet* (1956). Though their names are not familiar, their great skill nevertheless comes through in the fascinating compositions of light and shadow that appear on the screen. The MGM world is brighter, darker, more romantic, and more chilling than real life because MGM cinematographers worked with the directors and the art department to enhance the mood of the scripts and increase the illusion of reality.

Robert Surtees, another great cameraman whose films include *Thirty Seconds Over Tokyo* (1944) and *Quo Vadis?* (1951), learned his craft from Ruttenberg. He, in turn, passed his knowledge on to Harry Stradling, Jr., who recalled: "The rich MGM look was governed by a long list of 'don'ts' that were drummed into my head by Robert Surtees: 'don't let the backlight hit the actor's nose' or 'never pan with a 25mm wide-angle lens.' Today we break all those rules, but a lot of the things I learned from Robert Surtees have stayed with me. One thing he used to say is that it's not terribly important how the actors are lit when they're moving so long as when they stop they look terrific.... You may have an actress sitting next to a lamp—and that's your source light—but the light isn't flattering. You have to cheat the light on her face. If she looks good, nobody will say, 'Oh, the source light is wrong.' But if she looks bad, they'll sure tell you."

TOP: *For* Letty Lynton *(1932), cinematographer Oliver T. Marsh (on crane) prepares a shot of Joan Crawford and Robert Montgomery, while director Clarence Brown stands by.*
ABOVE: *Joseph Ruttenberg lights Judy Garland for* Presenting Lily Mars *(1943).*

OPPOSITE:
TOP: *During the filming of* Hold Your Man *(1933), Clark Gable and Sam Wood observe Hal Rosson as he photographs Jean Harlow under intense lights designed to enhance her platinum blonde look.*
CENTER: *James Wong Howe (left) and W. S. Van Dyke (kneeling) work out a roulette wheel shot with Clark Gable, Nat Pendleton, and others in a scene for* Manhattan Melodrama *(1934).*

LEFT: *Director Vincente Minnelli and cameraman George Folsey photograph a scene in front of the Smith house in* Meet Me in St. Louis *(1944).*

RIGHT: *Billie Burke and Clark Gable in the mock-up interior of a car in* Forsaking All Others *(1934).*

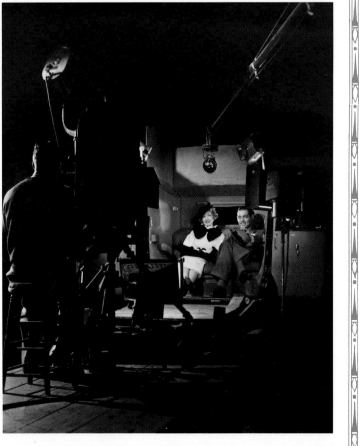

During his brief contract with MGM, Cecil B. De Mille creates Madame Satan *(1930), a bizarre musical disaster epic which culminates in a costume ball aboard a giant dirigible that is struck by lightning, forcing the entire party to bail out over New York City.*

TOP LEFT: *Kay Johnson, in the title role, wears one of Adrian's most famous costume creations.*
TOP RIGHT: *Adrian's design for Kay Johnson's dress.*
ABOVE: *A dancer portrays Electricity in the film's "Ballet Mechanique" scene.*

foreign cities kept their eyes out for anything that might remotely interest MGM, or a competitor. "A story never looks as good as when the other fellow buys it," Thalberg was fond of saying, "or as bad as when we do."

Spotting a potential story among hundreds required a certain kind of talent, but persuading a studio executive to buy it demanded more subtle skills. One of MGM's readers in this early period was Kate Corbaley, a former librarian from Stanford University. She possessed the rare ability to grasp the essence of a story and make it come alive in the retelling. Sometimes called the "Scheherazade of MGM," Mrs. Corbaley became a special favorite with Mayer, who, in common with many of the first-generation moguls, eschewed reading. Over the years, most of the supervisors came to rely increasingly on her judgment and advocacy.

The story department also served as an ideal training ground for aspiring producers. For example, Albert Lewin, a Harvard graduate, began his career as a reader at the Goldwyn studio, where Abe Lehr warned him, "You'll never get anywhere in the picture business, you've got too much education." Known as "the Professor," Lewin started at MGM as a story editor and became one of Thalberg's close associates. Samuel Marx, a struggling journalist whom Thalberg imported from the East Coast and then put in charge of the story department in 1930, became a producer some dozen years later. But nobody would make that transition faster or with a firmer sense of purpose than David O. Selznick, during his first stint at MGM in 1926-27.

Louis B. Mayer balked at hiring Selznick because of the contempt he felt for the young man's father, movie pioneer Lewis J. Selznick. A few years earlier, when MGM needed to secure certain rights involving its production of *Ben-Hur*, the elder Selznick had tried to cut himself in on the deal. During the negotiations, he told Nick Schenck that he would follow his son's advice in the matter. After David urged his

father to drop the deal, a grateful Schenck told the boy to call on him if he ever needed help.

After the bankruptcy of his father's film company, David Selznick headed for Hollywood, where he simply wanted a chance to prove himself. Hired reluctantly by Mayer, he began as a reader for producer Harry Rapf, for a trial period of two weeks, on the understanding that if he worked out, his weekly salary would be raised from $75 to a still-modest $150. He immediately came up with three usable story ideas, rewrote two scripts, and bombarded his superiors with several memos a day, suggesting a reorganization of the script department. With the methodical efficiency for which he would become known, Selznick designed a filing system for story ideas and a quota system that required each writer to increase his weekly output.

Mayer, who rarely held a good man down, offered Selznick a permanent job, with a salary that soon jumped to $300 a week. Along with his instinct for a good story and an inexhaustible energy, David O. Selznick also was extraordinarily self-confident, preferring his own ideas and way of doing things to anybody else's. In a period of just a year, he became a manager and then head of the writer's department; he quickly rose from assistant to associate story editor to assistant producer, under Harry Rapf, and finally, he became the producer of Tim McCoy westerns.

Along with director W. S. "Woody" Van Dyke, who matched his own energy and competence, Selznick hurled himself into the McCoy projects and astonished the studio brass by devising a way of shooting two of these pictures in two weeks, for a mere $80,000. Although Mayer gave a very low profile to such bread-and-butter films, they were essential both to the studio's diverse supply of product and to profitability.

Selznick's spectacular rise was suddenly cut short following an altercation he had with Thalberg over the

TOP LEFT: *A concept drawing for the ballet.*
TOP RIGHT: *From the "Ballet Mechanique."*
ABOVE: *The party is over… and it's time to crash.*

81

TWO SOLID YEARS IN PRODUCTION

THE PUBLIC HAS WONDERED: "WHAT ABOUT 'TRADER HORN'?" NOW COMES THE ANSWER AFTER TWO YEARS OF HERCULEAN LABOR, FABULOUS EXPENSE, ENGINEERED BY ARMIES OF GENIUS IN THE DEPTHS OF AFRICA, BROUGHT TO YOU NOW IN BREATHTAKING TALKIES!

TOP: *Shooting* Trader Horn *(1931) in Africa. Ironically, when the expedition returns, much of the wild animal footage isn't wild enough, and scenes have to be reshot in Culver City.*
RIGHT: *Newspaper ads further exploit the drama of making the film.*
OPPOSITE: *Cover of the campaign book provided by MGM's publicity department to exhibitors.*

production of *White Shadows in the South Seas*. Robert Flaherty, the poetic documentarist, had already spent six months filming leisurely in Tahiti, and producer Hunt Stromberg was doing little to move the project forward. With his customary zeal, Selznick proposed a complete overhaul. His plan called for Flaherty's replacement with the efficient Van Dyke, a revised story line, and, of course, himself as the producer. Resenting Selznick's interference, Stromberg went to Thalberg to have him arbitrate their conflict. Although in general agreement with Selznick's approach, Thalberg backed his senior producer. After a public confrontation with an enraged Selznick, Thalberg fired him. Not long afterward, he did replace Flaherty with Van Dyke, to finish *White Shadows* along the lines proposed by Selznick. By that time, Selznick was already busy turning things upside down at Paramount's story department.

The novelty of the talkies turned 1930 into a record year at the box office, which may have created the persistent myth that the movie industry escaped the ravages of the Depression, and even thrived. In fact, the period brought severe economic difficulties to Hollywood. As the worldwide Depression hit bottom in 1933, three of the five top film companies were operating under receivership. Loew's income had shrunk by two thirds during the previous five years; still, it remained the only major film company that continued making a profit and paying dividends to its shareholders. In large part, this prosperity was due to the fact that Loew's had to expend the least among its rivals to wire its smaller chain of theaters for sound.

Initially, the stock market crash affected individuals in Hollywood more than it did the industry itself. Thalberg was

FILMED IN AFRICA AT RISK OF LIFE

FATE AND NATURE COULD NEVER AGAIN BE SO KIND TO ANOTHER EXPEDITION SUCH AS THAT OF THE METRO-GOLDWYN-MAYER TROUPE WHICH BRAVED DEATH AGAIN AND AGAIN TO BRING THE WORLD SENSATIONS NEW TO CIVILIZATION. STRANGE TRIBES, STRANGE PLACES, THE FRONTIER OF A PRIMITIVE WORLD ARE THE BACKGROUND FOR THE DRAMA OF "TRADER HORN."

almost wiped out financially, whereas Mayer, who invested long term in real estate, was barely affected. He even compensated Thalberg for his losses, including the prospect of lower profits, by transferring to his most valued employee an additional 10 percent from his own share of the profits. He also used his influence in Washington to bail Thalberg out of a nasty tax situation. "No good deed ever goes unpunished," Noel Coward once said; Mayer's generous gestures began to nibble away at the unique partnership between the two men. In the beginning, Mayer treated him as a beloved son; later, as a prodigal who kept returning, provided he was given larger and larger portions of his patrimony.

It was during this period that relations between Mayer and Nick Schenck also deteriorated. In early 1929, Mayer was shocked when he read an announcement in a newspaper that William Fox had been talking to Loew's top management about buying out the company. Mayer's sense of betrayal at not having been consulted was heightened by his discovery that Schenck personally stood to make some eight million dollars from the deal. He swung into action, threatening to leave and using his connections with the Hearst organization and Hoover administration to block the merger. In the end, however, it was the combination of a near-fatal car crash and the stock market tumble that ended Fox's bid and saved MGM from being swallowed up a mere five years after its founding.

Afterward, Nick Schenck tried to mend fences with Mayer and his group by offering them bonuses. Both Mayer and Robert Rubin spurned the offer, but Thalberg accepted because of his financial troubles. The studio chief would never forget the treachery by his own boss. He had been accustomed to correcting people when they mispronounced the name Schenck, but now Mayer frequently would suggest that the head of Loew's be called Skunk.

During the depths of the Depression, Schenck and Mayer proposed that every staff member earning more than fifty dollars a week take a 50 percent pay cut to maintain profitability. Many in the film colony, however, brazenly continued to spend weekly salaries that often surpassed what an average family lived on for a year. Joan Crawford, more attuned to her fans than perhaps any other star, had herself photographed with extra furs and diamonds in *Photoplay* magazine, declaring that she considered it her public duty to help the economy by spending every dollar she got.

The Depression years were productive ones at MGM. Neither Mayer nor Thalberg would permit the cutbacks to be reflected in their films. The stars under contract continued to provide the fundamental basis for choosing story ideas, scripts, and literary properties. By the early thirties, each season would have its Garbo or Shearer picture, with its own somewhat predictable style. Informal production units, consisting of a specific director, cameraman, and designer, would evolve around a star, who often refused to work with anyone else. The style and look of the film became an amalgam of direction, camera work, couture, and the star.

It was this winning combination that helped Norma Shearer succeed in a remarkable variety of roles, despite the fact that, in the beginning of her career, nobody accused her of having much beauty or talent. D. W. Griffith told her she did not have the right face for the camera, and the great Ziegfeld found her lacking in glamour. Having to direct her in *Pleasure Mad* (at the Louis B. Mayer studio), Reginald Barker tried cajoling and intimidating the proper Miss Shearer into playing a spirited young sophisticate. Finally, in frustration, he complained to Mayer, who tried the same range of tricks during one of his paternal pep talks with the young actress. Listening to her long list of excuses, Mayer finally told her, "Do you know what's wrong with you? The trouble with you is you're yellow!" The young actress promised to put more life into her role.

Shearer acquitted herself better in MGM's *He Who Gets Slapped*, which gave her some reassurance about her choice of a career, though wearing a tutu as a circus bareback rider made her self-conscious about her legs. The studio, however, still had no clear idea how to develop her, and cast her in roles as disparate as a knife-thrower, a gangster's moll, a society girl, and a flapper. In just one year, 1925, she appeared in seven pictures. The exposure certainly helped. That year her name began to appear on exhibitors' polls as a box-office draw, and, in 1926, MGM publicity releases named Shearer as the studio's top female

OPPOSITE: *Advance promotion announces Greta Garbo as the star of the forthcoming* Red Dust, *with the script concentrating on the tawdry life of streetwalker Vantine. When the film is finally produced, based on a far different script, it is Jean Harlow who parlays the role of Vantine into a spectacular success.*

ABOVE: *The four reigning queens of MGM grace covers of* Photoplay, *the most popular fan magazine of the thirties.*

(Clockwise from upper left) Garbo, Norma Shearer, Joan Crawford, and Jean Harlow.

star after Marion Davies, who topped the list for political reasons. Her sudden rise to stardom happened without any apparent improvement in her acting.

Samuel Marx tells a story about a 1927 movie, *After Midnight*, assigned to guest director Viachetslav Tourjansky, who was unaware that his star was about to become Mrs. Thalberg. After the very first day of shooting, he went to see Thalberg, thinking it might not be too late to get Shearer replaced by another actress. "Why must I use this girl?" he complained tactlessly. "She is cross-eyed!" The Russian found himself relieved of his duties and banished to the boiling Mojave Desert, to shoot a Tim McCoy adventure.

After her wedding, some of the other MGM stars, notably Joan Crawford, hoped that Shearer would retire and concentrate on being a *hausfrau*, allowing them an opportunity to play the roles that were typically given to Shearer. But Mrs. Thalberg was determined to be wife, mother, and actress; she continued to depend on her husband to select important roles for her and then surround her with MGM's best talent.

Thalberg proceeded to match her with Ramon Novarro in *The Student Prince in Old Heidelberg*, a first-class production directed by Ernst Lubitsch. Although Shearer was playing a sweet Cinderella role, not unlike her own fairy-tale situation, marriage did not make her a better actress. Tired of her mannerisms, Lubitsch once shouted at her, "Mein Gott! I can get a waitress from the commissary who could do better than you!" When he asked her to do the scene again, Shearer burst into tears and sent for her husband. The cast and crew froze in anticipation, no doubt with the fate of the Russian director Tourjansky still fresh in mind; only Lubitsch remained perfectly calm. Finally, the all-powerful production chief arrived. He listened patiently to his bride's account, then kissed her and said, "Darling, I'm sure we can all learn a lot from Mr. Lubitsch."

Soon after the advent of sound, Thalberg cast her in the title role in MGM's first dramatic talkie, *The Trial of Mary Dugan*, as the amoral chorus girl who is put on trial for murdering a millionaire. This part was followed by a number of appearances alongside the studio's leading men: John Gilbert in *The Hollywood Revue of 1929*; young Robert Montgomery in *Their Own Desire*; and then, in 1930, Chester Morris in *The Divorcée*, for which Shearer won her only Oscar, as the young wife who answers her husband's infidelity with her own.

A different kind of energy emerged in *A Free Soul*, in which she portrays the high-minded daughter of a successful but self-destructive trial lawyer, based on Adela Rogers St. John's best-selling book about her father, Earl Rogers. Yet no matter what role she played, Shearer's underlying persona as an essentially pure and good woman persisted. When Clark Gable smacked her in *A Free Soul*, the impact was derived not just from the act itself—as in James Cagney's more famous act of violence perpetrated with a grapefruit that same year in Warner Bros.'s *The Public Enemy*—but from a symbolic *lese majesté* committed by an upstart actor against the first lady of MGM.

Thalberg and Shearer were so successful in maintaining her image of class, that even when she was out of her depth, as Nina in Eugene O'Neill's psychological drama *Strange Interlude*, or as Amanda in Noel Coward's highly stylized *Private Lives*, she was treated with respect by audiences and critics. But her success was due in larger measure to MGM's production values and her husband's obsessive perfectionism than to her own acting ability. For instance, Thalberg actually filmed the whole Broadway production of *Private Lives* so that Norma could study Gertrude Lawrence's every move and turn of phrase, which is not the way great actors prepare for a role. Yet Thalberg knew what he was doing. Gertrude Lawrence was,

undoubtedly, a better actress, but Norma Shearer was a star. By associating his wife with the work of famous playwrights and good actors, he achieved two goals. He produced some unusual or daring subjects he wanted to explore, while endowing Norma Shearer with a highbrow reputation. The MGM glamour factory took care of the rest.

A different star of the thirties, Jean Harlow also made the best of her limitations. Although already established as a sexpot, her career had reached a plateau by the time MGM bought out her contract from Howard Hughes in 1932. She played an extra as late as 1929, in Chaplin's *City Lights*, and wasted years under contract to Howard Hughes. Though completely miscast as a British seductress in Hughes's epic of World War I air combat, *Hell's Angels*, Harlow's natural flair for innuendo surfaced in the now-famous scene with Ben Lyon, when she utters the immortal line, "Pardon me while I slip into something more comfortable."

Then came hard-boiled roles in *The Public Enemy*, with tough guy James Cagney, and *The Beast of the City*. Her early image was further defined in *Platinum Blonde*, a title that stuck to her like one of her slinky dresses. After her first film with MGM, *The Secret Six*, producer Paul Bern, who had taken a strong personal interest in the actress, persuaded Thalberg to give Harlow a different rinse in *Red-Headed Woman*. It would be the first role to add some complexity, and even grace, to her character. But it was not until she costarred with Clark Gable in *Red Dust*

TOP: *Tired of playing lady-like roles, Shearer commissions a photographer to reveal her more alluring qualities.*

RIGHT: *Shearer insists on playing opposite exciting newcomer Clark Gable in* A Free Soul *(1931).*

"SIN MUST BE PUNISHED"

Right from the start, MGM was in trouble with *Red-Headed Woman* (1932), the Katharine Brush novel that screenwriter Anita Loos had fashioned into a leering comedy about a scheming secretary who sleeps her way to fortune. Irving Thalberg and Paul Bern had cast Jean Harlow in the lead, but before filming had even started, Thalberg received bad news from Lamar Trotti, who worked for the Motion Picture Producers and Distributors of America, Inc., which was commonly known as the Hays Office.

Led by former Postmaster General Will H. Hays, the Hays Office was formed after scandals rocked Hollywood in the early 1920s. The office was created in an attempt by the film industry to undermine city and state censorship boards and, under the threat of federal intervention, to clean up the content of movies. In 1927, Hays released a preliminary form of a new production code, a list of do's and don'ts that warned against dealing with subjects such as branding, surgical operations, and excessive or lustful kissing. The list prohibited outright "any inference of sex perversion," "miscegenation," or similar themes.

The slogans "crime does not pay" and "sin must be punished" were hallmarks of the Hays Office. So, when Thalberg submitted a script in which Harlow destroys her boss's marriage, dumps him for an elderly millionaire, escapes a murder rap, and ends up in France with another millionaire and a gigolo chauffeur, Trotti complained immediately. He termed the entire project "a very grave problem," adding that the heroine was "an out-and-out harlot... a common little tart using her body to gain her ends." Trotti objected to all the sex scenes, to

Harlow's "half-undressed" scenes, and to so many individual lines and situations "that it does not seem necessary to list them."

The Hays Office, however, was essentially toothless. It could only make recommendations, which the studios could then ignore. After shooting for *Red-Headed Woman* had started, Thalberg met with Trotti in an effort to convince him that the film would be treated as a farce. But once it was released, there were widespread complaints. A woman in Atlanta wrote that the movie was "Sex! sex! sex! The picture just reeks with it till one is positively nauseated." The Birmingham Better Films Council objected to "the part where she rubs herself against old man Gaerste in a most sensuous way." Jason S. Joy, a Hays Office official, felt obliged to apologize, saying that the movie was "one which, even though it conformed to the Code, would get us into all sorts of trouble." He noted with chagrin that "right now half of the other companies are trying to figure out ways of topping this particular picture." Even so, *Red-Headed Woman* required seventeen separate cuts before it could be screened in Massachusetts; it was banned entirely in Britain.

Sex and sensationalism in the movies increased so much that, in early 1934, the Roman Catholic church formed the Legion of Decency for the purpose of rating films. In order to counter the church, Hays introduced a new, tougher Production Code in June of that year. Considerably more explicit in its restrictions, it prohibited expressions such as "nuts" and "Oh, God" and words such as "abortion." A man and a woman—even a husband and wife—could not share a double bed.

TOP: *Jean Harlow's image is greatly influenced by the dictums of the Hays Office. By 1936, the sexy makeup and platinum blonde hair (left) give way to a more decent, natural look (right).*

ABOVE: *In* Hold Your Man *(1933), director Sam Wood is permitted to show Harlow and Clark Gable in bed together, even though the characters are unmarried (top), but by 1943, director Mervyn LeRoy cannot allow any hanky-panky between Greer Garson and Walter Pidgeon, whose characters in* Madame Curie *are married (bottom).*

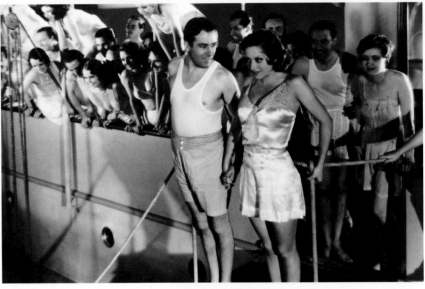

Kidnapping of children was acceptable only if "the child is returned unharmed."

By this time, the Code had some bite. Unless a movie adhered strictly to its guidelines, it wouldn't be granted the Hays Office Seal of Approval, without which the movie couldn't be exhibited in theaters. The Hays Office reviewed every screenplay before shooting, threatening to withhold the all-important seal unless offensive material was deleted. What was and wasn't permissible changed the content and tone of every Hollywood picture, from musicals and comedies to horror films.

When Joseph Breen reviewed the script to *A Night at the Opera* (1935), he cut Groucho Marx's efforts to lure Margaret Dumont into his stateroom: "You come to my room, and I'll guarantee there'll be a situation. If not, I'm not the man I used to be." (Censors in New York and Virginia went further, cutting out this exchange: DUMONT: Are you sure you have everything, Otis? GROUCHO: I haven't had any complaints yet.) Breen also scrutinized *A Day at the Races*, eliminating Groucho's quip: "I'd like a suite of rooms, two nurses, and don't call me for three months."

Although, over the years, producers and directors managed to circumvent some of the restrictions of the code, it remained in effect until 1968. It was replaced by the rating system of the Motion Picture Association of America, which is still in use today.

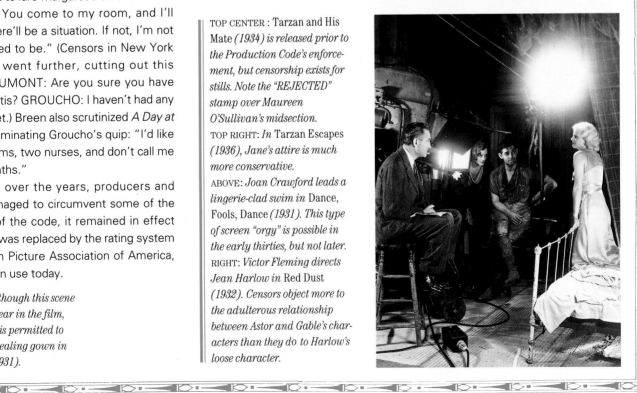

TOP LEFT: *Although this scene does not appear in the film, Greta Garbo is permitted to wear this revealing gown in* Mata Hari *(1931).*

TOP CENTER : Tarzan and His Mate *(1934) is released prior to the Production Code's enforcement, but censorship exists for stills. Note the "REJECTED" stamp over Maureen O'Sullivan's midsection.*

TOP RIGHT: *In* Tarzan Escapes *(1936), Jane's attire is much more conservative.*

ABOVE: *Joan Crawford leads a lingerie-clad swim in* Dance, Fools, Dance *(1931). This type of screen "orgy" is possible in the early thirties, but not later.*

RIGHT: *Victor Fleming directs Jean Harlow in* Red Dust *(1932). Censors object more to the adulterous relationship between Astor and Gable's characters than they do to Harlow's loose character.*

ABOVE: *At the Grauman's Chinese Theater premiere of* Dinner at Eight *(1933).*
RIGHT: *Wallace Beery and Jean Harlow in a scene from* Dinner at Eight.

that her own brand of sensitivity and her comic talents were finally revealed.

Unfortunately, Harlow's career was marked by tragedy. In 1932, she married Bern, a shy, bookish bachelor, twice her age. It was not uncommon for powerful studio executives to befriend starlets and help them in their careers. Bern's relations with several ambitious young women were well known and largely considered platonic. Less than three months after their wedding, however, Paul Bern was found dead in his Benedict Canyon home. He appeared to have committed suicide, leaving a note for his wife in which he apologized for some "frightful wrong" he had done to her. Louis B. Mayer was one of the first to arrive on the scene, and his immediate reaction was to protect Jean Harlow, a major studio asset. Mayer reportedly left Bern's house with the suicide note in his pocket but was persuaded to put it back by Howard Strickling, MGM's west coast publicity chief, who once distinguished publicity—the job of getting things into print—from public relations—the art of keeping things from the press. Together, the two men used all their influence to manage information and to quell any rumors of foul play that might adversely affect the career of their star.

In fact, the public embraced Harlow's subsequent films. Perhaps because she was so willing to satirize her own sexpot image, the astute and funny *Bombshell* won her acclaim as well as more fans. In it she mocked her role in *Red Dust*, showing the chaos behind the supposedly serene and glamorous life of a movie star. Harlow still flaunted her sexuality in skintight dresses, but her tongue-in-cheek vulgarity and raucous way with a one-liner proved that she was

an adroit comedienne. Prompted by the success of *Red-Headed Woman*, MGM had Anita Loos fashion three more wise-cracking vehicles for her. Harlow also shone in ensemble pieces such as *Dinner at Eight* and *China Seas*, more than holding her own with the other accomplished farceurs in the cast.

While Shearer specialized in high-minded, aristocratic parts, and Harlow in sexpot roles, Joan Crawford projected a distinctly contemporary and American air. In her best silent films—*Our Dancing Daughters* and *Our Modern Maidens*—she played a Jazz-Age vamp with an infectious vitality that startled the country. Her early sound films—*The Hollywood Revue of 1929* and *Our Blushing Brides*—continued in this vein, but the Depression made jazz babies an endangered species. *Dance, Fools, Dance* was a transitional film: the title indicated another jazz romp, while the actual story found Crawford forced to work as a reporter when her fortune is wiped out. Her screen chemistry with Clark Gable (still playing in a supporting role, but soon to break out as a star) so impressed Irving Thalberg that he recast and reshot *Laughing Sinners* to showcase the pair. In doing so, he set a pattern for subsequent Crawford films.

Unlike Garbo and Shearer, Crawford usually portrayed a working girl who had to rely on her wits and courage to get ahead. Typically, she was cast as a chorus girl or a secretary, a small-town woman who had to fight against snobbery and prejudice to succeed. Most of her films were original screenplays, not expensive adaptations, and they were geared to mainstream audiences who could sympathize with her

ABOVE: *A glamorous studio photograph of the platinum "Bombshell" at the height of her popularity (circa 1934).*
LEFT: *Harlow attends the premiere of* Strange Interlude *(1932) with her second husband, MGM producer Paul Bern.*
RIGHT: *A caricature of Harlow by Hollywood artist Sotéro.*

s o t é r o

spunk and her attempts at upward mobility. The formula was so successful that MGM paired Crawford and Gable three times in less than a year. By 1932, she was edging out Garbo at the box office and setting her sights on juicier roles.

Yet Crawford never reached Garbo's heights at MGM, and she remained in awe of the Swedish actress. Much to Crawford's regret, the only time they appeared in the same film—*Grand Hotel*—they shared no scenes. Several days after shooting began, they still had not met. Though the reclusive star refused to fraternize with the other members of the cast during filming, Crawford arranged to bump into her. Garbo touched Crawford's face and murmured, "Our first picture together, and we don't work with each other. I am so sorry. You have a marvelous face." (More than forty years later, recalling this incident, Crawford confided to her biographer, Jane Ellen Wayne, "If there was ever a time in my life when I might have become a lesbian, that was it.")

Garbo's career, following her talking debut in *Anna Christie*, had continued the pattern she set for behavior both on screen and in private life. While catering to her characteristic whims, MGM kept her box-office appeal strong, casting her in roles that exploited her aura of mystery and aloofness, most notably as Mata Hari, the notorious spy of World War I, later executed by the French. Following her appearance in *Grand Hotel* and *As You Desire Me*, with Erich von Stroheim, Garbo left Hollywood, manifesting her periodic restlessness and dissatisfaction with MGM's estimation of her worth. When she returned, it was with a contract that granted her more money and virtual control over her pictures. She exercised it by insisting on having John Gilbert, her former lover, as her leading man in *Queen Christina*. At first her director, Rouben Mamoulian, wanted John Barrymore to play the role, but then decided he was

too old. Next he asked Laurence Olivier, who stood in such awe of Garbo that he hardly registered on the screen test.

Garbo's eccentricities and willfulness made life difficult on the set, to which nobody was admitted except for the crew. She even told her director to leave before she would do a love scene, but Mamoulian refused. She declared that she would do only a single take of each scene, without any rehearsal, in order to keep her performance fresh. Mamoulian patiently showed her on film the improvement brought about by rehearsals and retakes. The director recalled staging the movie's famous scene—in which she memorizes the objects in the room where she had known love—as a piece of choreography: "She played it to a metronome. She had to roll over a bed and move around the room in what was a kind of sonnet in action." Mamoulian got the enigmatic and much-interpreted look on Garbo's face at the film's end by asking the actress to try to think of nothing. With *Queen Christina*, Garbo reached the zenith of her fame (it became a favorite picture of some less-idealistic rulers, including Stalin and Mussolini). Gilbert, on the other hand, hit bottom. It was to be his last picture at MGM, and he would die three years later at the age of forty-one.

While MGM's attention was focused mainly on its constellation of female stars, these ladies required impeccably groomed leading men whom they could charm, bind, or hold in thrall. The men cast opposite Garbo, Shearer, and Crawford were often limited by the perfunctory and passive nature of their roles, which required handsome looks more than acting ability. Robert Montgomery typified this type of debonair leading man. He came to Hollywood from the New York stage in 1929. At MGM, he eventually succeeded actors such as William Haines, who outgrew the juvenile roles typically assigned to him. It was not long before Montgomery was cast opposite the studio's big stars. He appeared with

THE LAUNCHING OF A STAR

In 1925, a young woman named Lucille Le Sueur left San Antonio, Texas, and arrived in Hollywood. Through the power of the MGM star machine, she was destined to become Joan Crawford. Thoroughly molded and consciously created, she was transformed into one of the greatest silver-screen legends: flapper, sex goddess, dramatic actress, star. Louis B. Mayer called her the first MGM "creation."

After her all-important screen test, she asked Harry Rapf, the producer who had spotted her in the chorus line of a Broadway review, what the test said about her. "Structure and vitality," he replied. As for structure, she modeled her looks on Gloria Swanson's, her lips on Mae Murray's. She accentuated her cheekbones, plucked her eyebrows, and suffered through dental surgery to straighten her teeth. She dieted and exercised strenuously.

Photographers used special lighting to eliminate the freckles covering her face and body. As with Garbo, the cameramen obscured her hips, concentrating instead on her long waist. The studio also decided her original name might be too difficult for fans to pronounce and sponsored a nationwide contest, inviting them to find her a new screen name. Thus, she was christened Joan Crawford. Howard Dietz, MGM's New York publicity chief, helped to forge a bond between this new star and her fans by making them a part of her creation.

Three years, twenty pounds, hundreds of

BOTTOM LEFT: *In* Untamed, *Crawford is described as "just a little jungle flower getting wilder every minute."*
BOTTOM RIGHT: *Signing autographs (circa 1933).*

magazine covers, and eighteen films later, the former chorus girl would be known as "The First Queen of the Movies." One of those early films, *Our Dancing Daughters* (1928), which was partly responsible for making her a star, also captured the frenzy and desperation of the pulsing twenties as the decade jitterbugged to a close. Then, her marriage to Hollywood's crown prince, Douglas Fairbanks, Jr., transformed her from Charleston queen into Cinderella. Louis B. Mayer took full advantage of the attendant publicity, producing the wedding and then costarring the two lovers in *Our Modern Maidens*, in 1929. Following its premiere, the couple placed their footsteps in the cement outside Sid Grauman's Chinese Theater.

Every part of MGM's apparatus conspired to separate her from the exotic Garbo and the aristocratic Shearer. Distinctly American, spunky, and down-to-earth, Crawford was put under the care of MGM's brilliant costume designer Adrian, who took over the job of creating her distinctive, glamorous look in 1929, and until 1943, he designed everything she wore on screen and most of what she wore off. Her eyes grew larger, her shoulders broader, her lips redder, and, not surprisingly, young women everywhere imitated her clothes, her walk, her talk. They dreamed that they, too, could rise from obscurity to stardom. Joan Crawford, or at least her image, represented the fantasy that anything was possible in Hollywood. The working girl could become a movie queen.

TOP: This Modern Age *(1931).*

TOP RIGHT: Grand Hotel *(1932).*

ABOVE: *Cover of* Screenland's *December 1931 issue.*

RIGHT: *Mrs. Louis Artisdale of Rochester is awarded a $500 prize for coming up with the name "Joan Crawford."*

FAR RIGHT: *An illustration of Joan, the Jazz Baby in* Our Modern Maidens *(1929).*

Norma Shearer in *Their Own Desire*, *The Divorcée*, and *Private Lives*, and with Joan Crawford in *Our Blushing Brides*. Not all were well received, and his appearance with Garbo in *Inspiration* was particularly disappointing. Occasionally, Montgomery got the challenging role he craved: he played the informer in *The Big House*, a gritty prison drama that did well at the box office, although it clearly did not fit the MGM style. Following another seven years, during which the wearisome similarity of his roles was offset only by the changing faces of his costars (Marion Davies, Madge Evans, Helen Hayes, Myrna Loy), Montgomery won his best reviews in a movie that the studio heads reluctantly allowed the unsatisfied actor to make. For his portrayal of a psychotic murderer in *Night Must Fall*, Montgomery received an Oscar nomination for best actor.

Clark Gable, too, might have become trapped in a tuxedo, had he been considered conventionally handsome. After knocking about in pictures for a while, including a small role in von Stroheim's *The Merry Widow* in 1925, Gable concentrated on a stage career, following the advice of his drama teacher, Josephine Dillon, who later became his first wife. Following his appearance in a West Coast production of *The Last Mile*, actor Lionel Barrymore, who already knew Gable, urged the young man to audition again for movies. There, he met mainly resistance. Studio chiefs, such as Darryl F. Zanuck at Warner Bros. and Thalberg himself, were of the opinion that Gable had little chance of success

ABOVE: *Robert Montgomery becomes one of MGM's leading men at the beginning of the thirties. Studio publicity reinforces his onscreen persona of social grace by stretching the truth about his wealthy background.*

RIGHT: *Montgomery (seated at table second from left) with Chester Morris and Wallace Beery (second and third from right) in* The Big House *(1930), a tense prison drama that is a big success for MGM.*

1931

◆ Clark Gable's year: Beginning as a bit player, he becomes a name after *The Secret Six* and eight movies later is the star in *Hell Divers*.

◆ Banks are still failing, unemployment rising, and theater attendance dropping, but MGM survives by pairing its biggest stars on screen. The mix of Clark Gable and Joan Crawford with sex and politics in their third film together, *Possessed*, is a smash and solidifies a costar combination that will last MGM through the thirties.

◆ MGM stars take home the top Academy Awards: Lionel Barrymore for best actor (and a lifetime MGM contract) for *A Free Soul*, and Marie Dressler for best actress for *Min and Bill*.

◆ MGM brings Alfred Lunt and Lynn Fontanne from Broadway to film *The Guardsman*.

◆ "The Star-Spangled Banner" becomes the National Anthem.

◆ The year ends on a dire financial note for the country, but MGM rings out 1931 with a $12 million profit.

Jackie Cooper, age nine, makes his first appearance on the MGM lot after signing his contract. He is entering from Washington Boulevard.

Clark Gable in the famous rain barrel scene from Red Dust *(1932). The day this scene is shot is the same day that Jean Harlow's husband, Paul Bern, is found dead.*

with his "big bat-like ears." (Zanuck also said he looked like an ape, which may have led to Gable's meticulous removal of bodily hair from his chest and underarms.)

Through the persistence of his agent, Minna Wallis, Gable landed the role of the villain in Pathé's 1931 western, *The Painted Desert*. Shortly after, MGM signed him to a contract. Following a succession of films in which, he later said, "I pulled guns on people or hit women in the face," Gable stole the show in *A Free Soul*. The studio's attitude toward Gable quickly changed. Here was a man, Thalberg declared, "every woman wanted and every man wanted to be." All the leading ladies on the lot began clamoring for Gable, and Thalberg obliged by casting him in a dozen movies in the first year of his contract. Gable gamboled with Madge Evans in *Sporting Blood*; pressed himself against Garbo in *Susan Lennox: Her Fall and Rise*; and even portrayed a clergyman who rescues Marion Davies, a fallen circus performer, in *Polly of the Circus*.

The new star's rough-hewn masculinity and magnetic appeal were most apparent when he costarred with the studio's most alluring females, such as Joan Crawford and Jean Harlow. In the first of three films he made, in 1931, with Crawford—*Dance, Fools, Dance*—Gable played a racketeer and she, a rich girl who has fallen on hard times. By their second picture together, aptly named *Laughing Sinners*, the two stars were having a secret affair. In the third, *Possessed*, the whole set was aflame with their passion, the

kind not seen at MGM since Garbo and Gilbert were lovers. Crawford and Gable were both already married, and the gossip began to worry Louis Mayer. He called in the two actors separately and read them the riot act: they would have to choose between each other or a career. The actors promised to behave, though Crawford would claim that the affair continued on and off until Gable's death thirty years later.

Mayer may not have approved of adultery, but he was perfectly happy to see Gable's magnetism paired with Jean Harlow's feral sexuality on the screen. They first appeared together in *The Secret Six*, in 1931. The following year, it was their saucy love scenes in *Red Dust* that finally established Gable as the number one male star at MGM. But he felt that he still had to prove himself as an actor. Gable so disliked his role as a dance director in the Joan Crawford vehicle *Dancing Lady* that he adopted a course of passive protest, calling in sick and having his tonsils, then appendix, removed. Mayer was furious. When he received a call from Columbia Pictures, asking to borrow Robert Montgomery for the male lead in an insignificant comedy, the studio boss hatched one of his acts of revenge. Since Montgomery was not interested in the role, Mayer told Columbia's boss Harry Cohn, "We've got a bad boy down here I'd like to punish."

For an actor to be loaned out from MGM to a second-rate studio such Columbia, in 1934, was the equivalent of being banished from the court of St. Petersburg to Siberia. (The practice of loaning out contract players when they

TOP: *In a lobby card for* Red Dust, *Clark Gable, without a mustache, with Jean Harlow and costars Donald Crisp and Tully Marshall.*
ABOVE: *A mustached Gable plays piano for the chorus girls during the filming of* Dancing Lady *(1933).*
RIGHT: *Gable by Sotéro.*
OVERLEAF: *Director Victor Fleming filming the jungle storm sequence in* Red Dust.

TRIED AND TRUE

Though MGM would stake its future in large part on its ability to produce vehicles for its major stars—the Garbos and Gables—the studio turned repeatedly to its invaluable roster of feature players to provide not only strong support but, in many cases, dynamic leading performances. MGM depended on these professionals for their solid and efficient work. Indeed, they were often the best aspects of the films in which they appeared. There were many at MGM: Marjorie Main, Spring Byington, Jean Hersholt, and Keenan Wynn among them. But perhaps the greatest of these actors were Lionel Barrymore, Marie Dressler, and Wallace Beery.

Barrymore, a member of the famous acting dynasty that included his younger brother John and his sister Ethel, had been performing in films for fifteen years when he signed a contract with MGM in 1926. Lionel developed into a dependable character actor, one whose booming voice and authoritative presence would become a mainstay of MGM films. A team player, he also tried his hand at directing, composing, and painting during his decades at the studio. His virtuoso turn as a drunken lawyer in *A Free Soul* (1931) won him both an Oscar and a lifetime contract from Mayer, who good-naturedly accepted the nickname "Lionel B. Mayer" for his own histrionics off the set.

Barrymore appeared in most of the prestige movies made by the studio, and also raised the level of B-movies, adding gravity and conviction to flimsy plots of films such as *The Devil Doll* (1936). As arthritis restricted him more and more to a wheelchair, he became identified with patriarchs and curmudgeons, with grandfathers, bankers, politicians, and doctors —notably Dr. Gillespie in the long-running *Dr. Kildare* series.

On the only occasion when the three Barrymores appeared together on screen—in *Rasputin and the Empress* (1933)—it was Lionel who took the title role of the mad monk. He also appeared with his brother in hits such as *Grand Hotel* (1932) and *Dinner at Eight* (1933).

Marie Dressler's long career in entertainment began in musical comedy and vaudeville. She made her film debut in 1914, costarring with Charlie Chaplin in Mack Sennett's *Tillie's Punctured Romance*. By 1927, the show-business career of the large-boned, homely actress had run dry, and, at fifty-eight, she seemed to have no prospects of any kind, let alone in films. At that point, screenwriter Frances Marion persuaded Irving Thalberg to cast Dressler as one of the gin-guzzling slum dwellers in *The Callahans and the Murphys* (1927). However, MGM withdrew the film following vehement opposition from Irish Americans who objected to the unflattering portrayal of the Irish.

Despite this disaster, during the next three years Thalberg assigned Dressler other comic character roles, including the bibulous mistress of Garbo's father in *Anna Christie* (1930). Of Dressler's scene-stealing performance, *The New York Times* wrote that "her speech, expressions and her general gesticulations make this far and away her outstanding film characterization." Garbo, who was dissatisfied

TOP LEFT: The Champ *(1931)* *wins featured actor Wallace* *Beery an Academy Award.*
TOP CENTER: *Frank Morgan* *as the Guardian of the Gates* *in* The Wizard of Oz *(1939), in* *which he also plays Professor* *Marvel and the Wizard.*
RIGHT TOP: *Billie Burke, the* *second wife of stage impresario* *Florenz Ziegfeld, plays Glinda* *the Good Witch in* The Wizard *of Oz. Here, Burke is shown* *alongside Clark Gable in* Forsaking All Others *(1934).*
RIGHT BOTTOM: *Lionel* *Barrymore plays the Mad* *Monk in* Rasputin and the Empress *(1932), which co-* *stars Frank Morgan, John* *and Ethel Barrymore, and* *Tad Hamilton.*
ABOVE: *Beery with Marie* *Dressler in* Min and Bill *(1930).*

with her own performance, was so impressed with Dressler's that, after seeing the finished film, she drove to the home of the older actress to pay personal tribute with a large arrangement of chrysanthemums.

That same year, Dressler appeared in nearly a dozen movies, including *Min and Bill* (1930), for which she received the Oscar for best actress. She was now billed as the world's greatest actress by the studio that was home to such queens as Garbo and Crawford. By the time Dressler died of cancer three years later, she had become one of the most beloved stars in America and on the MGM lot. She occupied the top spot on the coveted exhibitors poll of box-office attractions three years in a row, more than fulfilling Thalberg's gamble of bringing her out of poverty and obscurity.

Wallace Beery had been a star for well over a decade before he earned an MGM contract in *The Big House* (1930). A former circus roustabout, he started out in slapstick shorts, playing in drag in the short-lived *Sweedie* series. In the twenties, Beery alternated between appearing in a series of military comedies and in villainous roles in westerns and swashbucklers. With his gravelly voice and burly physique, he injected a welcome sense of toughness into such MGM adventures as *The Secret Six* (1931) and *Hell Divers* (1932), brawling in both with Clark Gable. Beery's brawny appeal worked equally well in comedies and in soap operas, particularly when he was teamed with Dressler in *Min and Bill* and *Tugboat Annie* (1933). Beery won an Oscar for *The Champ* (1931), a maudlin boxing story that dwelt on his devotion to his son (Jackie Cooper), and then had prominent roles in the all-star *Grand Hotel* and *Dinner at Eight*. After a robust turn as Long John Silver in *Treasure Island* (1934) and an endearing performance as a shy tippler in *Ah, Wilderness* (1935), Beery embarked on a series of B-movies. Once again, he concentrated on service comedies and westerns, many of them with Marjorie Main. Beery's unique mixture of menace and charm proved irresistible at the box office, even when he approached his material casually. He provided MGM with an almost unbroken string of profitable movies.

Another well-loved MGM character actor was the fumblingly imperious Frank Morgan, a studio fixture who played everything from Jean Harlow's philandering uncle in *Bombshell* (1933) to a ghost in *The Cockeyed Miracle* (1946). He will always be best remembered for his multiple roles in *The Wizard of Oz* (1939). No matter how small her roles, Marjorie Main's rustic mannerisms and gravelly voice made an indelible impression in more than twenty-five MGM films, including *The Women* (1939) and *Meet Me in St. Louis* (1944). With her quavering voice and giddy manner, Billie Burke was almost an exact opposite to Main. Burke's flightiness was a welcome addition to many high-society comedies, in particular, *Dinner at Eight*. And, from the early 1940s on, Keenan Wynn, the son of comic actor Ed Wynn, added fast-talking support to numerous films as varied as *The Clock* (1945) and *Kiss Me Kate* (1953).

1932

◆ Irving Thalberg attracts Depression audiences by putting an all-star cast in *Grand Hotel*. It wins the Oscar for best picture, grosses twice its cost, and sets the industry standard for star-ensemble films.

◆ Olympic swimming champion Johnny Weissmuller makes *Tarzan, the Ape Man*, with the reluctant permission of the BVD underwear company, where he has an exclusive contract. MGM gets Weissmuller released by having all its players photographed in BVDs.

◆ Helen Hayes wins a best actress award for her first MGM film, *The Sin of Madelon Claudet*. Already a Broadway star, she has come to Hollywood mainly to be with her husband, writer Charles MacArthur, but now all the studios want her.

◆ Jean Harlow's platinum hair is made red for *Red-Headed Woman*. The story scandalizes the Hays Office because it violates its primary rule that the sinner must pay.

◆ In *Grand Hotel*, Greta Garbo says, "I want to be alone."

◆ MGM makes an $8 million profit, the only studio that doesn't lose money in 1932.

Johnny Weissmuller is welcomed to MGM by Madge Evans. He begins his fifteen year swing to immortality as filmdom's most famous Tarzan.

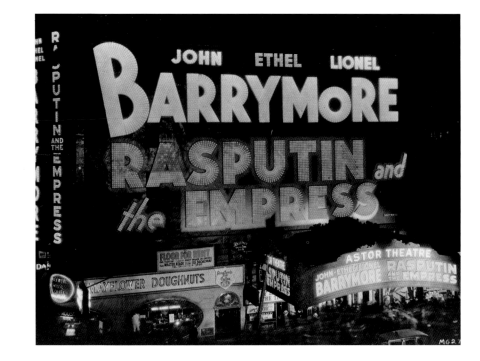

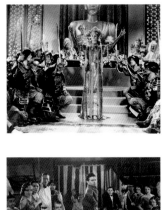

TOP: Rasputin and the Empress *(1932) is the only film to bring together the three Barrymore siblings. The magic of the famous last name obviously means more than the title itself.* CENTER: The Mask of Fu Manchu *(1932). Prior to becoming a great MGM star, Myrna Loy appears in such roles as the evil daughter of Fu Manchu (Boris Karloff).* BOTTOM: Freaks *(1932), director Tod Browning's study of deformity, is one of the most unusual films the studio ever produces.*

were not being used formed the basis of complex bargains and trade-offs in the studio era; sometimes the currency was goodwill, more often hard cash, since the money from the loan-out, usually much higher than the actor's salary, went straight into the studio's pockets.) Director Frank Capra had almost given up any hope of making *It Happened One Night*, until one day he was summoned by Harry Cohn. "We've got to make the picture now," he informed the director, "Louis Mayer wants to punish Clark Gable." The picture not only swept the Academy Awards for 1934 but, unexpectedly, devastated the men's undershirt industry, once audiences saw that Gable wore his shirt next to his skin.

MGM's growing success was based, in large part, on its ability to produce films for Shearer, Harlow, Crawford, Gable, and Garbo; and in later years, for actors such as Spencer Tracy, William Powell, and Myrna Loy. Star power and the studio's ability to show off and blend its array of creative and technical talent had, by the early thirties, developed into a recognizable MGM style. Its first great demonstration came with the production of *Grand Hotel*. In 1930, Robert Rubin had astutely snapped up the film rights to Vicki Baum's best seller by investing a few thousand dollars in the Broadway adaptation. MGM would make money from the play and a fortune from the film.

The story, consisting of the comings and goings of guests in a large European hotel, offered little in the way of a central plot but created great interest in the various characters and the atmosphere. It provided the studio with an excellent opportunity to display an ensemble company of stars. In addition to Greta Garbo, top billing went to the brothers John and Lionel Barrymore, Joan Crawford, and

Wallace Beery, with supporting roles filled by well-known feature actors Lewis Stone and Jean Hersholt. Through carefully conceived and interwoven subplots, the screenplay succeeded in blending the action and desires of the various characters: Garbo's Grusinskaya, a ballet prima donna weary of life, is resurrected through love by John Barrymore's baron, another hopeless character who has fallen on hard times and has resorted to stealing people's jewels and money to survive. Crawford's Flaemmchen is a young, adventure-hungry stenographer, whose material desires are softened by the sad aspect of Lionel Barrymore's Kringelein, a man doomed by illness but determined to enjoy his last days. Wallace Beery's character, Preysing, becomes the pivot around which the first couple is cast apart and the second is brought together: he catches the baron trying to steal his money (so that he can join Grusinskaya the next morning on the train for Vienna) and bludgeons him to death with a telephone.

Thalberg worked for several weeks on the story line with assistant Paul Bern and director Edmund Goulding. Once casting and script had been agreed upon, production proceeded like clockwork. The studio's top exponent of style—Cedric Gibbons—created an art deco environment that extended from the hotel's sleek, modernistic lobby to the lamps, wall sconces, and abstract art seen in the rooms' interiors. Production wrapped in February, some scenes were reshot after previews in March, and the film opened in April to a huge box office. Almost a year later, it received an Oscar for best picture, the only category for which *Grand Hotel* was nominated. It was an appropriate comment, since the film transcended its individual contributors. Even such

TOP LEFT: *"What magic power in these names—here is the million dollar cast." This catch phrase is used to promote* Grand Hotel *(1932), as are the blazing lights of the Astor Theater during the film's premiere run in New York City.*

TOP RIGHT: *Kringelein (Lionel Barrymore) and Flaemmchen (Joan Crawford) confront Preysing (Wallace Beery) in a scene from the movie.*

CENTER: *The melancholy dancer Grusinskaya (Garbo) with her maid (Rafaela Ottiano).*
ABOVE: *Here, Edmund Goulding directs Crawford and Lionel Barrymore, while Lewis Stone and John Barrymore (on couch) wait in place for a continuation of the sequence.*

famous hams as Wally Beery and Lionel Barrymore harmonized perfectly with the rest of the ensemble. In a sense, the picture itself became the star.

Paul Bern's death, in 1932, made a strong impact on Irving Thalberg. The producer's health, which had never been robust and was further undermined by his incredibly active schedule, buckled under the weight of his grief. He had lost a close friend and colleague, whose opinions and general culture he trusted. While Mayer and Strickling were busy trying to avoid a scandal, Thalberg, who wept through the entire funeral service, went into a long depression. He lost his customary appetite for work and told Mayer that he wanted to be released from his contract, which only recently had been renewed until 1937. If the studio boss would not agree, then at the very least, Thalberg wanted a year's sabbatical.

ABOVE: *Artwork from the promotion book of* Grand Hotel *(1932) illustrates "above-the-title billing." In spite of this, the stars' personalities take a back seat to characterization and ensemble acting.*

RIGHT: *Goulding shoots an "exterior" scene with Lionel and John Barrymore and Joan Crawford. This* Grand Hotel *entrance is actually a "front" built on the sound stage, with wooden walls, insulation, and catwalks showing.*

TOP: *The realized lobby set.*
ABOVE: *Gibbon's conception of the lobby set.*
RIGHT: *Lewis Stone (right) repeats the same line in the opening and closing scenes of the film: "Grand Hotel—always the same. People come, people go, nothing ever happens."*
OPPOSITE: *An overhead shot of Cedric Gibbons's art deco-inspired lobby set.*

Tarzan The Ape Man

By the time MGM brought *Tarzan, the Ape Man* before the cameras in 1932, the white lord of the jungle, who had been created in 1914 by novelist Edgar Rice Burroughs, had previously appeared in a number of films, the first of them in 1918. Jungle thrillers had long been a staple at every Hollywood studio and were hardly considered risky business. MGM had already produced *Trader Horn* in 1931, and the year before an independent *Tarzan* serial starring Frank Merrill was released. MGM finished *Kongo* in 1932, and RKO was readying *King Kong*.

Louis B. Mayer made sure, however, that the MGM *Tarzan* would never be confused with other jungle movies. Right from the start, it was planned as a big-budget spectacular. It would have more animals, more stunts, more perilous traps, more natives. It would have breathless plotting by Cyril Hume and Ivor Novello. (Who cared if they paid little attention to the original novel?) It would feature five-time Olympic swimming champion Johnny Weissmuller as Tarzan and Maureen O'Sullivan as Jane. The distinguished C. Aubrey Smith and Neil Hamilton added weight to the cast.

And *Tarzan* was crisply directed by W. S. Van Dyke, whom Irving Thalberg had previously sent into the African jungle for *Trader Horn*. For that film, which was based on a best-selling book about the great white hunter, the cast and crew had suffered through seven months of dysentery and other tropical disorders. Edwina Booth, its female star, contracted a blood disease which ended her career. The expedition returned with more than 200,000 feet of film but, unfortunately, not much of a story. In reworking the script with new scenes and dialogue, the studio writers needed names for two of the warring African tribes. They ended up dubbing one of them the Gibboneys,

after MGM art director Cedric Gibbons, and the other the Joconeys, in honor of Joe Cohn, the head of production. The two tribes went on to enjoy a long history in the numerous *Tarzan* sequels, which used up the masses of jungle footage shot by Van Dyke.

Perhaps most importantly, *Tarzan, the Ape Man* would have sex. The scenes between Weissmuller and a scantily clad O'Sullivan were considered racy, even by precensorship standards. The result was wildly popular. Another studio would have immediately capitalized on its success (the sequel to *King Kong* appeared within nine months of the original), but MGM exploited *Tarzan* in its own manner, waiting two years to release the equally profitable *Tarzan and His Mate*. This sequel gave art director Cedric Gibbons his only directing credit (Jack Conway assisted him).

The success of the sequel proved Mayer's contention that the series should be handled as a prestige item. When a preview for *Tarzan Escapes* (1936) proved disappointing, Mayer ordered extensive reshoots in order to maintain the quality of the series. Three years would elapse before *Tarzan Finds a Son* was released. Rather than suggest that his relationship with Jane was anything but platonic, the script called for Tarzan literally to "find" the conveniently orphaned Boy (Johnny Sheffield).

By the 1940s, the series was growing threadbare. Weissmuller, who had yet to appear in any other role, was allowed to don clothes in *Tarzan's New York Adventure* (1942), a potboiler in which Jane and Tarzan come to the Big Apple to rescue their kidnapped Boy. It would be the last of the series at MGM. O'Sullivan retired from movies to raise a family that included Mia Farrow. Weissmuller moved to RKO for six more *Tarzan* movies, and then starred in the *Jungle Jim* series.

TOP: *A portrait of Weissmuller by Cecil Beaton for* Tarzan, the Ape Man *(1932), the first in a series of highly successful films based on the novel by Edgar Rice Burroughs.*

ABOVE: *Champion swimmer Johnny Weissmuller diving into his private pool, keeping fit between* Tarzan *films.*
BELOW: *A Sotéro rendering of Weissmuller.*

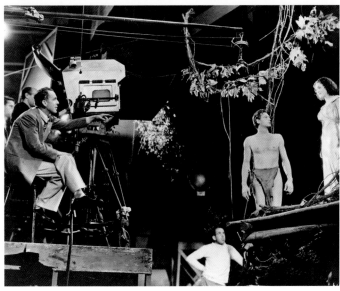

ABOVE: *MGM art director Cedric Gibbons is credited with directing* Tarzan and His Mate *(1934), but he receives assistance from veteran Jack Conway. Here, Conway guides the actors through the romantic tree nest scene. Rear projection and matte paintings will fill in the details.*

TOP: *A tender moment with Maureen O'Sullivan, as Jane, in the post-Production Code* Tarzan Escapes *(1936).*

RIGHT: Tarzan and His Mate *is the second film in the popular MGM series.*

Mayer was aware that his production chief received offers regularly to run rival studios, and he grew alarmed enough to summon Nick Schenck and Robert Rubin from the East Coast. After several days of stormy meetings, Schenck asked his brother Joseph (the chief executive of United Artists) and Eddie Mannix to act as mediators. Thalberg finally agreed to carry on at MGM after he was given the option to buy up to 100,000 shares of Loew's stock at considerably less than their market value, 20 percent more than Mayer would be able to purchase, and double the options awarded to Rubin. In effect, the deal acknowledged Thalberg's supremacy at MGM but at the cost of alienating not only Mayer, with whom relations had already been deteriorating, but also Schenck, who resented being forced to reward MGM executives with profits derived from the enterprise built up by both Marcus Loew and himself.

Thalberg resumed the burden of his duties, instead of following his impulse to take time off. A few months later, following the 1932 Christmas party for the MGM family, he went home and suffered what was believed to be a heart attack. It was clear that he would be out of commission for weeks, possibly months, and this setback led to his decision to take an extended leave of absence. Mayer, once again, sent for Schenck, but this time he had a different motive. Thalberg's recalcitrance and illness had demonstrated the fragility of depending on a single production chief. Perhaps it was time to think the unthinkable: a future without Thalberg, or at least one in which his monolithic power might be divided among other producers.

The inner circle of supervisors that Thalberg had gathered around him included Harry Rapf, Hunt Stromberg, Bernie Hyman, Lawrence Weingarten, John Considine, and Albert Lewin. They were able producers who had benefitted from Thalberg's guidance and could be counted on to handle

the majority of MGM's schedule of forty to fifty films a year. With Schenck's approval, however, Mayer immediately recruited a couple of outside producers to manage the more ambitious projects. One of these men was Walter Wanger, who had worked at Paramount and Columbia, and the other was David O. Selznick, the man whom Thalberg had fired from MGM several years before and who was now RKO's production chief.

Thalberg was understandably upset. He could not deny the studio's need and right to replace him during his illness, but he argued against dividing the kingdom into potentially feuding fiefdoms. Just before departing, he received an unusual letter from Mayer apologizing for their quarrel, but justifying his and Schenck's actions as their duty to the company. However, he continued, "Anyone who has said that I have a feeling of wrong towards you will eventually have cause to regret their treachery, because that is exactly what it would be, and what it would be on my part if I had any feeling other than what I have expressed in this letter towards you. I assure you I will go on loving you to the end."

In late February, the Thalbergs embarked on a sea voyage to Germany and France, traveling in great style with their friends Charles MacArthur and Helen Hayes. In April, Thalberg received a cable from Mayer informing him of the total reorganization of the studio. The post of production chief had been abolished. All unit producers, Thalberg among them, would report directly to Mayer. He ended the message, "AM DOING THIS FOR YOU."

In courting David O. Selznick, Mayer was not only looking for an executive with Thalberg's kind of vision, taste, and energy, he was also interested in establishing a unit production system (as opposed to a central producer) similar to the one that Selznick had successfully implemented at RKO,

ABOVE: *Irene Mayer weds producer David O. Selznick. (Left to right) Margaret Mayer, Louis B. Mayer, Irene, David, Edith Mayer, and her husband, R. William Goetz.*

OPPOSITE:

LEFT: *A conceptual poster for* Tarzan, the Ape Man *(1932).*
TOP: *Top talent is used for* Strange Interlude *(1932), adapted from Eugene O'Neill's experimental play. (Left to right) Norma Shearer, Clark Gable, a sound technician, director Robert Z. Leonard, cinematographer William Daniels, and a crew member. In the film, the action freezes while the characters' prerecorded thoughts are played. Here, the technician plays recorded asides as Gable and Shearer hold their poses.*

1933

◆ MGM releases its second all-star movie, *Dinner at Eight*, with Marie Dressler, John Barrymore, Wallace Beery, Jean Harlow, Lionel Barrymore, Lee Tracy, Edmund Lowe, and Billie Burke. It is one of the biggest moneymakers of the Depression.

◆ In *Dinner at Eight*, John Barrymore, as the dissolute matinee idol, always favors his left side, "The Great Profile," and is never photographed from the right.

◆ John Gilbert replaces the unknown twenty-six-year-old Laurence Olivier at the last moment as Garbo's costar in *Queen Christina*. Gilbert's career is declining, and he makes one more film before his death three years later at age forty-one.

◆ *Queen Christina*'s closing shot of Garbo standing at a ship's figurehead staring pensively ahead becomes one of the most famous shots in movie history. Generations will wonder, What was she thinking? The director told her to think of nothing.

◆ Twenty-five hundred theaters close as the Depression deepens. Unions threaten a general studio strike when temporary wage cuts are imposed.

Irving Thalberg and Norma Shearer visit Lyon while on vacation.

THE LAUNCHING OF A FILM

The film *Queen Christina* was launched in February 1934. With it came the extraordinary promotional efforts of the MGM publicity department. As for all of their big-budget productions, a lavish campaign book was created that inspired exhibitors across the country with endless ways to showcase the picture, bring in bigger crowds, and take advantage of the attention already showered on the film by newspapers, department stores, and merchandisers. It highlighted the rave opening night reviews and pointed out the fashion trends that quickly followed. "New sleeves were born to intrigue femininity, new silhouettes were widely advertised, new collars and necklines saw the light of day…" And included were pre-written articles, poster art of a daz-zling variety, and promotional items ranging from clothing, toys, and perfume to books and car accessories.

Queen Christina was Greta Garbo's first picture in two years. Following *Grand Hotel*, she had "retired" and gone back to Europe, returning only after MGM met her terms. The film had its world premiere at New York's Astor Theater, "always an extraordinary Broadway event," and costarred her former lover John Gilbert. But as the campaign book stressed, "It"s GARBO—GARBO!—no matter where you look on these pages and once that magnetic name is properly exploited far and wide in every conceivable fashion the crowds begin to turn towards your theater. The supreme actress of this generation is still the magnetic ideal of millions of moviegoers."

TOP LEFT: *On the Astor Theater marquee, the name Garbo is all important, while the title appears in very small type.*
TOP RIGHT, ABOVE, OPPOSITE: *Pages from the campaign book.*
BOTTOM LEFT TO RIGHT: *The lobby of the Astor Theater.*

An All-Star Rebound to Normal
Between Camera Shots of "Dinner at Eight"

Metro-Goldwyn-Mayer's brilliant all-star production. Left to right: Standing—EDMUND LOWE (Dr. Talbot)...GEORGE CUKOR, Director...LIONEL BARRYMORE (Oliver Jordan) JEAN HARLOW (Kitty Packard)...PHILLIPS HOLMES (Ernest). Sitting—MADGE EVANS (Paula Jordan)...LOUISE CLOSSER HALE (Hattie Loomis)...BILLIE BURKE (Millicent Jordan)...MARIE DRESSLER (Carlotta Vance)...KAREN MORLEY (Lucy Talbot)...GRANT MITCHELL (Ed Loomis)...A DAVID O. SELZNICK PRODUCTION.

In Hollywood, you see it every day in the making of pictures — **the pause that refreshes** with ice-cold Coca-Cola. It breaks the stress and strain of shooting scenes over and over. It is cooling relief from the hot kleig lights. It banishes drowsy yawns and hot, thirsty faces. It's the way to snap back to normal and be alert ... Because, an ice-cold Coca-Cola is more than just a drink. It combines those pleasant, wholesome substances which foremost scientists say do most to restore you to your normal self. Really delicious, it invites a pause, a pause that will refresh you.

Coca-Cola

TOP: *The cast of* Dinner at Eight *(minus John Barrymore but with director George Cukor) taking a break during the filming to enjoy a a cool, refreshing Coca-Cola. This type of promotional advertising is very popular with the MGM publicity department.*

ABOVE: *The stars of* Dinner at Eight *(1933) grace the cover of some sheet music for the film. (Top to bottom) Marie Dressler, John Barrymore, Wallace Beery, Jean Harlow, Lionel Barrymore, Lee Tracy, Edmund Lowe, and Billie Burke.*

after taking the job there in October 1931. Heading into the worst year of the Depression, Selznick managed to streamline production at the studio, releasing more than forty pictures while reducing their total cost by as much as one third. But, in doing so, he argued that he had no desire to supervise personally such a large production slate. Instead, he organized individual producers, including himself, into units with their own budgets and staff, and then granted them autonomy to decide what films to make. He coined the phrase, "executive producer," to describe his overall function.

Selznick, who had married Louis Mayer's younger daughter, Irene, over her father's objections, hesitated to accept Mayer's offer. He was one of the rare breed of Hollywood insiders who was determined to make his mark not because of his family connections but in spite of them. He was also reluctant to tamper with the MGM setup. He admitted to being inhibited by the giant shadow cast by Thalberg, whom he had come to admire greatly. "I regard him as the greatest producer the industry has yet developed," he wrote in response to Mayer's first offer. "I intend to try goddam hard to equal his achievements, and I hope one day to surpass them. I cannot do this at MGM for two reasons: first, if I did succeed, it would be with the assets and facilities that he has been so largely responsible for developing . . . . His record is too excellent for me not to regard him as the master of that particular situation; and I should think very little indeed of his organization if they did not regard him as their master."

Mayer moved to allay this last concern by offering each one of Thalberg's top supervisors the freedom to form his

ABOVE: *Jean Harlow against the leaning board created so that actors can rest without wrinkling their costumes. Photographing Harlow for* Dinner at Eight, *William Daniels stated, "Her beautiful hair has a silky texture that can be brought to the screen only by the most careful lighting. When she was filmed in contrast to any other player, we had to juggle our lights to give them a break beside her dazzling whiteness. We photographed her in white clothes and white settings as much as possible."*

A Metro-Goldwyn-Mayer PICTURE   A Cosmopolitan Production   Produced by DAVID O. SELZNICK
Directed by W. S. VAN DYKE

own production unit within MGM. Each one would also be given screen credits for the films he produced. This practice was contrary to Thalberg's well-established policy, but in line with Mayer's practical knowledge of human nature. In the same canny way, Mayer waited for the right moment to press Selznick into taking the job at MGM. It happened when the producer felt vulnerable following a corporate shuffle at RKO. Mayer redesigned his offer into an extremely tempting package: $4,000 a week for two years, the title of vice-president on a level with Thalberg and Mannix, supervision of MGM's top projects, and first choice of stories and stars. Although Selznick's ultimate goal was to establish a company of his own, it was difficult to pass up the opportunity of producing pictures backed up by the greatest studio in the industry. Not surprisingly, after he accepted, *Variety* heralded his return to MGM with the headliner, "The Son-in-Law Also Rises!"

Selznick's first project, a film version of George S. Kaufman and Edna Ferber's Broadway play *Dinner at Eight*, invited direct comparison with Thalberg's ensemble piece, *Grand Hotel*. He even used many of the same actors—Wallace Beery, the Barrymore brothers, and Jean Hersholt—while the rest of the cast displayed MGM's deep reserves of talent: Jean Harlow, Marie Dressler, Billie Burke, Lee Tracy, Edmund Lowe, and Madge Evans. For his choice of director, on the other hand, Selznick overlooked the studio regulars and brought in George Cukor, who had worked for him at RKO. He also imported Herman Mankiewicz and Donald Ogden Stewart, two of the top-paid wits in Hollywood, to polish the screenplay by Frances Marion.

Following its success, Selznick went on to produce

TOP: Manhattan Melodrama *(1934) contains the first onscreen meeting of beloved team William Powell and Myrna Loy.*
ABOVE: *"A girl, a gambler, and a district attorney!" is the exclamation for the film in which Myrna Loy shares romance with both William Powell and Clark Gable. Here director W. S. Van Dyke and cinematographer James Wong Howe execute a tricky mirror shot with Gable and Loy.*

1934

◆ *The Thin Man* reunites William Powell and Myrna Loy in the second of their thirteen films together. Louis B. Mayer is against the casting of two serious actors in a comedy and gives it a B-movie budget. It's shot in sixteen days, almost every scene in one take. It's a smash, making Powell and Loy, as Nick and Nora Charles, one of the favorite husband-and-wife teams in the movies.

◆ The appearance of Asta (real name Skippy) in *The Thin Man* starts a national craze for wire-haired terriers, but on the set Skippy bites Loy. He appears in all the *Thin Man* movies anyway, as well as *The Awful Truth* and *Bringing Up Baby*.

◆ Clark Gable, now a star, demands more money. MGM refuses and decides to "punish" him by loaning him out to Columbia Pictures—which Gable calls "Siberia"—for a film he doesn't want to make. *It Happened One Night* wins Oscars for best actor, best actress, best picture, best director, and best writing (Adaptation).

William Powell (seated far right) and Myrna Loy (to his right) on the set of The Thin Man, *based on the novel by Dashiell Hammett.*

SHORT SUBJECTS

6 LAUREL - HARDY

8 OUR GANG

12 FLIP THE FROG

8 CHARLEY CHASE

4 NOVELTIES
(2 reels each)

THE NEWS REEL THEATRE
HEARST METROTONE NEWS

104 ISSUES OF
HEARST-METROTONE NEWS

12 Around the world with
BURTON HOLMES

THE
BOY
FRIENDS

8 M-G-M COLORTONE REVUES

8 THE BOY FRIENDS

6 M-G-M DOGVILLE COMEDIES

EVERY SUNDAY
EXPLOITATION

A TABLOID
MUSICAL

WITH JUDY GARLAND
DEANNA DURBIN
DIRECTED BY FELIX E. FEIST

TOP: *MGM produces Laurel and Hardy comedies, Metrotone newsreels, and others.*
ABOVE: *The* Our Gang *kids promote world unity at the start of World War II.*

LEFT: *Stars, such as Judy Garland and Deanna Durbin, sometimes get their start in shorts.*

The first shorts were the first films ever made, but as those early efforts paved the way for the development of feature-length movies, the term "shorts" came to refer to the one- and two-reel films, usually not more than thirty minutes in length, that were shown, as a bonus, together with the feature presentation.

At MGM, shorts came in a variety of styles—newsreels, travelogues, comedies, musicals, thrillers, and cartoons. Most were given the same high production values that the features received. Before the advent of news on television, newsreels were extremely popular. MGM's newreels, under the banner of Metrotone News, were produced biweekly by William Randolph Hearst.

MGM shorts, while several cuts above a screen test, sometimes gave actors a chance to prove themselves worthy of feature film roles. Deanna Durbin, for example, debuted in the musical two-reeler *Every Sunday* (1936) and went on to become a star. Other performers achieved fame directly in shorts, notably Laurel and Hardy, the most successful comedy team in film history. The two joined forces in 1926 at the Hal Roach studios. Roach's shorts, including the Charlie Chase comedies and a series with Thelma Todd and ZaSu Pitts, were distributed by MGM through a deal Roach made with Nicholas Schenck. Roach also produced the *Our Gang* comedies and, in 1938, sold the rights to MGM.

With the rise of television in the fifties resulting in a decline in movie receipts, studios were forced to cut costs. Shorts were among the first to go, and even though they continue to be made, they have not yet reclaimed their former status in mainstream entertainment.

The stars of Anna Karenina *(1935): Fredric March as Vronsky (left), Garbo as Anna (middle), and Basil Rathbone as Karenina (right). The film marks Garbo's tenth year in American films and includes some of William Daniels's most famous close-ups of her. Daniels said, "She does things not so much by gestures or postures, but by little things in her eyes. That is why she is superior in close-ups."*

Night Flight, from the book by Saint-Exupéry, starring Clark Gable, Helen Hayes, and the Barrymore brothers. Then he teamed Gable with Joan Crawford in *Dancing Lady*, a semimusical that revived her career, following the failures of *Rain* (for United Artists) and *Today We Live*. For the gangster drama, *Manhattan Melodrama*, Selznick brought in another actor whose popularity had been ebbing. Not only did William Powell become one of MGM's favorite leading men, but the movie brought him together for the first time with Myrna Loy. The picture gained an extra measure of notoriety as the last thing outlaw John Dillinger saw before he, or someone thought to be him, was gunned down by the FBI in front of Chicago's Biograph Theater.

Perhaps Selznick's most successful MGM production was *David Copperfield*. Period pieces, which inevitably entailed great expense, were out of favor during the Depression. It took months of bombardment with the famous "DOS" memos before Schenck and Mayer agreed to finance the project. A confirmed Anglophile who at one time dreamed of studying at Oxford, Selznick had had a childhood passion for the novels of Charles Dickens. Throughout the production, he carried his own tattered copy of the classic tale his father had given him as a boy.

In his zeal to remain faithful to the original and to ensure a warm reception by a European audience, Selznick rebuffed MGM's efforts to cast Jackie Cooper, the studio's favorite child star at the time, in the role of young David. Instead, the film introduced a charming English boy, named Freddie Bartholomew, to the world. The youngster stayed on in Hollywood and became a popular child actor of the thirties. The adaptation was by Hugh Walpole, a fashionable English writer between the wars, who also appeared in the film as the pompous Vicar of Blunderstone. *David Copperfield* became a global success, ringing up two million dollars in profits and leading to a new attitude toward period pictures and the filming of classic literature at MGM.

In early 1935, Selznick announced his plans to leave MGM that summer to form his own company, but he remained long enough to finish adaptations of Dickens's *A Tale of Two Cities* and Tolstoy's *Anna Karenina*, a more faithful remake of the silent version that starred Garbo and Gilbert eight years earlier. Although it was his only collaboration with Garbo, the actress pressed him to remain and produce all her pictures.

Among the Thalberg men, Hunt Stromberg proved to be the most independent and productive. At the same time that Selznick was adapting great works of literature to film, Stromberg's unit was making hits that resulted in the establishment of extremely successful series, such as the delightful *Thin Man* movies. Stromberg was also the first to team Jeanette MacDonald and Nelson Eddy, in *Naughty Marietta*. The film's success led to the popular duo's appearance in seven more pictures. When MacDonald, who aspired to be a diva, voiced misgivings about appearing in the first of these schmaltzy pieces, Mayer (in one of the typical moments that earned him the nickname "Lionel B." after Lionel Barrymore, another great ham) went down before the actress on his knees and sang "Eli, Eli," the traditional Jewish lament. Mayer's secretary, Ida Koverman, happened to come into the office at that moment, holding Jeanette's contract, and observing the star, with tears in her eyes, quickly got her to sign on the dotted line. The musical operetta clicked so well with the public that Mayer quickly cast MacDonald and Eddy in *Rose Marie*, which would provide a global publicity bonanza for the Royal Canadian Mounted Police.

In films such as *Treasure Island* and *The Great Ziegfeld*, Stromberg employed to great success the production philosophy laid down by Mayer and Thalberg: surround a good story with the best possible cast, crew, and sets. Familiar to generations of readers and previously adapted into a silent movie, *Treasure Island* was essentially

121

OPPOSITE: *One of the largest sets ever constructed for the spectacular "A Pretty Girl Is Like a Melody" number, originally written by Irving Berlin for the 1919* Follies.

LEFT: *The premiere book of* The Great Ziegfeld *(1936) emphasizes the film's musical numbers and cast, including William Powell, Myrna Loy, and Luise Rainer.*

BELOW: *(Clockwise from upper left) Heather Dane is a "Gown of Bells," Diane Cook a "Paradise Shower," Mary Jane Halsey a "Silver Mirage," and Lorna Lowe a "Sequin Fountain."*

"presold" and became a tremendously entertaining hit. MGM assigned their top feature players—Lionel Barrymore, Lewis Stone, and Wallace Beery—along with thirteen-year-old Jackie Cooper in the leading roles. Director Victor Fleming kept the pacing swift and the adventure crackling. Three cameramen provided a pungent atmosphere of smoke-filled pubs and plotting pirates, as well as the epic sweep of schooners and deserted islands.

The studio spared no expense for *The Great Ziegfeld*, a biography of the famous Broadway impresario (and the first of three MGM film titles to use his name). Produced by Stromberg, it was a colossal musical that only MGM could afford. With William Powell as Ziegfeld, Luise Rainer as his first wife, Anna Held, and Myrna Loy as his second wife, Billie Burke, the plot had enough drama and heartbreak to win Rainer an Oscar. The songs included specialty numbers by such Broadway veterans as Fanny Brice (who sang her signature tune "My Man") and Ray Bolger, such chestnuts as "Shine On Harvest Moon" and Irving Berlin's "A Pretty Girl Is Like a Melody," showcased in a mammoth production number with hundreds of dancers, an enormous revolving set, and Dennis Morgan lip-synching the lyrics to Allan Jones's voice. It would become only the second musical to win an Oscar for best picture.

Irving Thalberg returned to Los Angeles in August 1933, fifteen pounds heavier and well rested. The studio's

RIGHT: *Maurice Chevalier kisses* The Merry Widow *(1934), played by Jeanette MacDonald.*

OPPOSITE: *The back cover of the campaign book for* The Painted Veil *(1934) offers a choice of posters to exhibitors for promotion in their lobbies.*

top brass formed a welcoming committee, and Louis B. Mayer made sure the press captured all the smiles and handshakes as he greeted his prodigal son. But the homecoming offered a different prospect for Thalberg. He, who had once commanded and energized thousands, now moved into a bungalow on the MGM lot to launch his production unit with only one of his former lieutenants. Al Lewin, who alone had resisted Mayer's blandishments, elected to continue working directly under Thalberg. Many of the other producers, not surprisingly, would also continue to rely on Thalberg's advice.

The new unit system fostered a spirit of competition inside MGM, with Thalberg and Selznick locked in friendly combat on center court. Thalberg had been unexpectedly gracious toward Selznick and praised *Dinner at Eight*, which cost less than half the amount expended on his own *Grand Hotel* and brought in a million dollars' profit. Thalberg began his comeback with a remake of the operetta *The Merry Widow*. For this new version, featuring Jeanette MacDonald and Maurice Chevalier, he hired director Ernst Lubitsch, who had previously directed the stars in two Paramount musical comedies. Lubitsch managed to capture the sophistication of the original operetta while steering its sexual comedy far from the shoals of censorship. As Jeanette MacDonald observed of Lubitsch, "He could suggest more with a closed door than all the hay-rolling you see openly on the screen nowadays, and yet he never offended."

Thalberg then began to prepare two new vehicles for Norma Shearer, *Marie Antoinette* and *The Barretts of Wimpole Street*, which brought him into unexpected conflict with William Randolph Hearst: the press lord wanted both these parts for Marion Davies. Although his blonde, comic mistress would have been completely miscast in the role of the dark, tragic Elizabeth Barrett, Hearst waged an ugly campaign, forbidding his newspapers to mention the

name of Norma Shearer. Thalberg won Mayer's backing, but only because Hearst had lost much of his fiscal clout during the Depression, and had annoyed Mayer by switching his support to Roosevelt against the studio boss's friend, Herbert Hoover, in the 1932 election. With such political and artistic disagreements mounting, Hearst's Cosmopolitan Pictures finally left MGM, in 1934, and moved to Warner Bros.

That same year, the Marx Brothers came to Culver City, after their previous films, made at Paramount studios, had done poorly at the box office. Intuitively, Thalberg understood that the improvisational clowning of the brothers (now without straight man Zeppo) withered under the rigors of shooting scenes in bits and pieces, often out of sequence and with many retakes. He suggested that they rehearse their material and then test it in front of live audiences, as a kind of preview, to see where they could adjust the jokes and comic routines. *A Night at the Opera*, which resulted from this process, is considered one of their greatest films. The Marx Brothers, whose popularity had waned considerably, were suddenly in vogue again. Many considered this reversal in their fortunes a result of Thalberg's genius.

Around this time, Thalberg turned his attention to *Mutiny on the Bounty*, a completely new kind of movie for him to undertake. He attributed his choice of filming the popular novel by Charles Nordhoff and James Norman Hall to David Selznick's previously successful experience with historical material. Thalberg encountered many problems during its production, beginning with Clark Gable's resistance to playing the role of Fletcher Christian. "The public," he told the producer, "will never believe me as a first mate in the British navy."

Worried not only about his accent but also about having to shave his trademark mustache, Gable feared he would

TOP: *Island natives greet the arrival of the* Bounty.

ABOVE: *Clark Gable shares a romantic moment with Movita in* Mutiny on the Bounty (1935)

LEFT: *Captain Bligh (played by Charles Laughton) and his officers are cast adrift by the gang of mutineers.*

RIGHT: *Gable as first mate Fletcher Christian, with mutiny growing in his heart.*

◆ *Mutiny on the Bounty* wins the Oscar for the best picture, the last winner in history to capture no other award.

◆ Clark Gable has to be threatened and bribed to appear in *Mutiny*, which turns out to be his best MGM film so far. What he hates is having to shave off his mustache.

◆ MGM releases *A Tale of Two Cities* with Ronald Colman, Basil Rathbone, and Elizabeth Allen. Colman's role becomes his all-time favorite, and for it he shaves off *his* moustache.

◆ The Marx Brothers make their sixth film, *A Night at the Opera*, their first without Zeppo. Allan Jones plays the straight man romantic lead who sings Irving Berlin's "Alone," the only hit song from any Marx Brothers movie.

◆ Peter Lorre makes his American screen debut as a demented surgeon in *Mad Love*.

◆ Spencer Tracy's twenty-year tenure at MGM begins with *The Murder Man,* which also features James Stewart in his movie debut.

look ridiculous wearing knee britches and a pigtail. Kate Corbaley told him it was not a question of britches or wigs but of "maleness and independence." Eddie Mannix drew him aside and said, "You've got the personality for Fletcher Christian. Besides, you're the only guy in the picture who has anything to do with a dame."

The story presented another problem for Gable. He could not understand why Fletcher Christian would tolerate the treatment Captain Bligh inflicted on his men. "Two days on that ship and I'd be knocking that stinking captain flat on his back!" he complained to Frank Lloyd. The director went to his bungalow and fetched a little book containing the Articles of War, issued for that period by the British Admiralty. Gable read the rules on punishment, which meted out "hanging from the yardarm until dead" for even the most minor infractions.

Meanwhile, the production experienced other problems. Charles Laughton, the terrible Captain Bligh, suffered from seasickness. Apart from a few background shots in Tahiti, Lloyd filmed most of the outdoor scenes off Catalina Island and Santa Barbara. Several exact replicas of the *Bounty* were made, including an eighteen-foot version that was designed to increase the scale of the waves, but it got lost in rough weather. Then, after a camera barge was overturned, taking down a crew member along with the camera equipment, the storms scenes were moved to Lot Three in Culver City. Nicholas Schenck, concerned about the $1.7 million cost of the picture, feared that it would become "the biggest flop in the studio's history," and arranged for a quiet opening. But *Mutiny on the Bounty* was quickly recognized as one of the finest films ever produced by the studio. It would win the Academy Award for best picture in 1935.

TOP: *Jeanette MacDonald in Naughty Marietta (1935). This Hunt Stromberg production begins a successful cycle of operetta films that team the actress-singer with Nelson Eddy.*

ABOVE: *The famous stateroom scene from the Marx Brothers' A Night at the Opera (1935): the pileup begins!*

Nelson Eddy has his locks trimmed by the studio barber following the completion of Naughty Marietta.

MAGIC COUPLES

TOP LEFT: *Spencer Tracy and Katharine Hepburn hold up traffic in* Adam's Rib *(1949).*
TOP RIGHT: *On location for* Rose Marie *(1936), Nelson Eddy assists Jeanette MacDonald with her makeup.*
ABOVE: *Garbo and Gilbert in* Flesh and the Devil *(1926). Garbo's title card reads: "When I blow out the match, that is an invitation to kiss me."*

Movies have always reflected the hopes and dreams of the public, especially in terms of romance. Since almost every movie genre—from mysteries to swashbucklers, from war to love stories—features a leading man and woman, it is not surprising that thousands of different screen couples exist on film. Only a relatively few couples created real magic, and of these, a surprising number worked for MGM.

At the studio with "more stars than there are in heaven," Louis B. Mayer and Irving Thalberg acted as divine matchmakers. If a couple proved successful in a film, it was likely they would be recast as a team, especially if they were both under contract to MGM. Thalberg, for example, noticed a chemistry between Joan Crawford and Clark Gable when they costarred for the first time in *Dance, Fools, Dance* (1931). He set the story department to finding scripts that would suit the two actors. Subsequently, Crawford and Gable made eight films together, in most of which she played the working girl who rose to fame and glamour, and he was the rugged he-man who loved her. Judy Garland and Mickey Rooney, the perennial happy-go-lucky teenagers, costarred in nine MGM movies. And Myrna Loy and William Powell, the quintessential happily married couple of the forties, made thirteen films together in as many years.

What made a great screen couple? The answer is as difficult to determine as it is to explain what makes a relationship work in real life. Like all great lovers, screen couples exude mystery and wonder. "We're inevitable," John Gilbert tells Greta Garbo in *Queen Christina* (1934), "don't you feel it?" She does and so do

we. Great lovers always seem inevitable, part kismet and part coincidence.

Casting two actors together creates a third entity, a single ideal. And no movie studio in the world paired couples together with as much frequency as MGM. In some cases, screen couples served to perpetuate a series, such as Johnny Weissmuller and Maureen O'Sullivan in the *Tarzan* films, or Lew Ayres and Laraine Day in a succession of *Dr. Kildare* episodes. But the great MGM screen couples came to symbolize a singular aspect of romance: Greta Garbo and John Gilbert (Temptation); Clark Gable and Jean Harlow (Lust); Joan Crawford and Clark Gable (Glamour); Myrna Loy and William Powell (Sophistication); Jeanette MacDonald and Nelson Eddy (Sentimental Love); Judy Garland and Mickey Rooney (Good, Clean Fun); Greer Garson and Walter Pidgeon (Enduring Love); Spencer Tracy and Katharine Hepburn (Mutual Admiration).

Perhaps the popularity of these couples can be attributed to moviegoers' longing for the romantic ideals these costars projected on screen. Certainly, their popularity also was a reflection of the times. Jeanette MacDonald and Nelson Eddy sang sentimental arias to each other, lavishly adorned in period costumes, while the world suffered through the Great Depression. Their love was always chaste and their relationship was as idealized as someone like Louis B. Mayer could imagine. In *Mrs. Miniver* (1942), Greer Garson and Walter Pidgeon stoically endured the hardships of World War II. (Winston Churchill said that the movie did more for the war effort than a fleet of destroyers.) But the common bond and

the lasting appeal of the majority of screen couples from this era also had to do with equality of the sexes.

We may think of the liberated woman as a phenomena of the seventies, but just look at the female characters of the thirties and forties. They were women who stood up to their men. Women who could wisecrack, work, even fight, if necessary, for the things they wanted and for the men they loved. They were equal partners in solving a crime, running a business, singing duets, or dancing on Broadway. These women held their own with men in the bedroom, the boardroom, and even the barroom, when necessary. In a classic scene from *The Thin Man* (1934), Myrna Loy discovers that William Powell has consumed six martinis, and tells the waiter, ". . . bring me five more martinis, Leo, and line them right up here."

These women matched their men, drink for drink, or any other way, and the men loved them for it.

The influence of MGM's screen couples continues today on late-night television and in video rental stores, where these movies of yesteryear are still popular, reinforcing the fantasies created by Hollywood's most powerful dream machine. Obviously, we still want to believe that, in real life, Loy and Powell or Garson and Pidgeon stay happily married for decades. "Ah! Sweet mystery of life," as Jeanette MacDonald and Nelson Eddy would croon. And the mystery was this: Why can't real life work like the movies?

TOP LEFT: *Joan Crawford and Clark Gable made a total of eight films together between 1931 and 1940.*

ABOVE: *William Powell and Myrna Loy play Nick and Nora Charles in the* Thin Man *series.* LEFT: *Promotional art for* After the Thin Man *(1936), the third film in the popular series.*

ABOVE: Romeo and Juliet (1936): Portraits of Leslie Howard as Romeo (top) and Norma Shearer as Juliet by Dan Dayre Groesback.

RIGHT: *Shearer and Ralph Forbes, as Paris, are front and center at the Capulet ball. The choreography is by Agnes De Mille.*

CAPULET'S GARDEN

Thalberg's other production-in-progress was inspired by the great stage actress Katharine Cornell, who had appeared in a revival of *Romeo and Juliet*, his favorite Shakespearean play. She was both a family friend and the godmother of the Thalbergs' second child, but the producer had his wife, not Cornell, in mind for the screen version. Norma Shearer was petrified by the idea of performing Shakespeare and, at age thirty-three, felt too old to play the role of fourteen-year-old Juliet. Her fears were partially alleviated by the casting of forty-two-year-old Leslie Howard as Romeo and fifty-three-year-old John Barrymore as Mercutio. At one point, Thalberg was prepared to replace Barrymore, who often lost his voice and suffered memory lapses because of his drinking. But his next choice, William Powell, refused to take away his friend's role.

Thalberg spent two years preparing Shakespeare's classic for the screen. On Cukor's suggestion, and over Cedric Gibbons's objection, he brought Oliver Messel from England to design the lavish sets and costumes. He engaged

LEFT: *Leslie Howard on the realized set of Juliet's garden. Set design is shared by Cedric Gibbons and Oliver Messel. Shot on the world's largest sound stage, the castle and Juliet's garden and balcony cover 52,000 square feet of floor space.*

ABOVE TOP: *Artist's rendering of Romeo's approach to Juliet's balcony.*
ABOVE: *A miniature model that helps guide the set builders and is used for planning camera placement.*

133

1936

◆ *The Great Ziegfeld* wins best picture. Luise Rainer wins best actress, playing the first Mrs. Ziegfeld. Myrna Loy portrays Ziegfeld's second wife, Billie Burke, who also happens to be an MGM contract player.

◆ The real fury in *Fury* is with the autocratic director, Fritz Lang, who is so hated on the set that there's a rumor electricians are rigging an accident for him. The rumor gets out. Suspense. Lang lives. The publicity is huge. *Fury* is huge. Spencer Tracy becomes a major star.

◆ Tracy and Gable appear in the first of their three films together, *San Francisco*, even though neither one wanted to make it. Tracy is uneasy playing a priest because he has disappointed his father by not becoming one in real life. Gable doesn't like being sung "at" by Jeanette MacDonald.

◆ Leo, the MGM lion, is full-screen in *No Place Like Rome*, where he's among the lions that some actors are tossed to.

◆ Jimmy Stewart and Eleanor Powell costar in *Born to Dance*. Stewart is forced to sing "Easy to Love," and their stand-ins elope from the set.

Spencer Tracy in Fury, *an unusual study of mob violence directed by Fritz Lang*

ABOVE: *Jeanette MacDonald in* San Francisco *(1936), MGM's biggest moneymaker of the year. The star is pleased to have a change of pace in an action melodrama. Although it is her only teaming with Clark Gable, publicity exclaims: "They were born to fall in love!"*

Cornell professor William Strunk, an expert on Elizabethan language, and the English actress Constance Collier to help Norma in verse diction. Although *Romeo and Juliet* was received with respect by critics, it failed to generate much enthusiasm and lost almost a million dollars, confirming Schenck's belief that Shakespeare was basically box-office poison.

Thalberg's final production seemed uncharacteristic of the kind of film produced at MGM: the adaptation of Pearl S. Buck's *The Good Earth*. "The public won't buy pictures about American farmers," Mayer reminded him, "and you want to give them Chinese farmers?" But Thalberg wanted, in his own words, "to catch the soul of China," through the simple story of a peasant couple who are destroyed by greed.

After fighting Mayer, he finally got Schenck's approval of the project and budget. Then the obsessive producer dispatched an expedition of researchers, led by art director Alexis Touloubov, to China; from there, they shipped back eighteen tons of furniture, artifacts, material objects, and farm implements, to authenticate every aspect of the film's visual details. With similar intentions, director George Hill went along with a film crew and brought back almost two million feet of film.

In seeming contradiction, Thalberg cast two Caucasian actors in the central roles of the Chinese couple: Paul Muni, who began his career playing old men in the Yiddish theater,

and the Viennese actress Luise Rainer. "I'm about as Chinese as Herbert Hoover," Muni told Thalberg, as he worried about his makeup, his voice, and the youthfulness of the character he was to portray. But Thalberg was so determined to cast him in the role that he made a deal with Warner Bros. to exchange Clark Gable for Muni and Leslie Howard (whom he used in *Romeo and Juliet*). Muni, famous in the theater for his makeup artistry, plucked out half his eyebrows and used a so-called Mongolian fold above his eyelids. With his hair partly shaved, his cheeks somewhat sunken through dieting, Muni further enhanced his character by interviewing and observing dozens of Chinese men, determined to avoid the stereotyped Oriental of the movies.

Thalberg hired a succession of writers to adapt the book, finally ending up with a stack of different versions taller than himself. He also had problems keeping a director on the project. First, George Hill committed suicide in 1934; then Victor Fleming, who took over the project, asked for a completely new screenplay. But Fleming eventually would leave because he needed an operation. In the end, Sidney Franklin became the director of record, filming yet another version of the script.

An eleven-month shooting schedule began in February 1936, on a five-hundred-acre farm in the San Fernando Valley community of Chatsworth, about fifteen miles from the studio. Here, a walled city was created, surrounded by a reshaped countryside, with terraced fields planted with

TOP: *The earthquake shatters the nightclub following Jeanette MacDonald's third rousing rendition of the film's theme song "San Francisco."*

ABOVE: *Victims of the earthquake seek shelter while San Francisco burns in the background.*

TOP: *Margaret O'Brien and Busby Berkeley during the filming of* Babes on Broadway *(1942).*

ABOVE: *Mickey and Freddie Bartholomew play paddle ball on a studio backstreet (1937).*
LEFT: *Roddy McDowall and Mickey Rooney play with Lassie (1943).*

KIDS ON THE LOT

At Metro-Goldwyn-Mayer, Irving Thalberg and Louis B. Mayer created a child-star machine that was to last for decades. From Jackie Coogan's appearance in *The Rag Man* (1925), which marked the debut of the studio in child-star movies, to Dean Stockwell's part in *Anchors Aweigh* (1945), MGM boasted more top juvenile actors—Jackie Cooper, Mickey Rooney, Judy Garland, Freddie Bartholomew, Margaret O'Brien, Elizabeth Taylor, Roddy McDowall—than any other studio in Hollywood.

In those days, child labor laws were less stringent than they are now, but they were still enforced throughout the movie industry. In order to comply with these laws and to ensure that the stars' time was used in the most effective way, MGM provided such essentials as education and medical care. Actors were taught by on-site tutors, and there were even formal classrooms, but it was, at best, a haphazard system given the hectic schedule of production. With the constant pressure of budgets and deadlines, MGM was far more interested in finishing its movies.

On-site hospital care was a necessity for young performers. Though they carried the adult burden of full-time employment in addition to their schooling, these actors were still susceptible to childhood disease and illness. More than once, production on the famous *Our Gang* series had to be shut down because of an outbreak of measles, mumps, or chicken pox.

Life for child actors at MGM was filled with contradictions. Though they portrayed all-American kids on screen, they actually grew up isolated from childhood experiences—and they grew up fast. Accustomed to handling adult responsibilities, such as auditions, rehearsals, memorization, practice, and stunts, they were stars and wage earners first, children second. Their only peers were each other, and, like Rooney and Garland, they often formed life-long friendships.

Child actors had little control over their fortunes or fates within the studio. Decisions were made *for* them, not *by* them, and their futures were decidedly uncertain. Few of them were able to make the difficult transition into adult stars. Notable exceptions were blockbuster talents such as Elizabeth Taylor, Mickey Rooney, and Judy Garland, but success did not guarantee their happiness, as they faced an adult world without having experienced a real childhood.

Ultimately, the life of a child actor was both complicated and difficult, despite efforts by the studio to create an atmosphere of comfort and support. Many youthful careers were launched in front of the MGM cameras, but the stars often paid an exorbitant price along the way.

TOP: *Jackie Cooper attends the Los Angeles premiere of* Mata Hari *(1931).*
ABOVE TOP: *A make-shift class-room on the set of* Ben-Hur *(1925).*
ABOVE: *Elizabeth Taylor and friends leave the new MGM school (1943).*
BELOW: *Mickey Rooney, Deanna Durbin, Judy Garland, and Jackie Cooper have lunch together (1936).*

Chinese vegetables, grown the Chinese way. An artificial river was built to bring in water for their cultivation, and then it was allowed to run dry for the catastrophic scenes of famine.

For the climactic sequence depicting a plague of locusts, African newsreels were first used. But neither Thalberg nor Franklin was satisfied with these long shots. What they needed were close-ups of the actors trying to fight off the menacing swarms. They asked Buddy Gillespie in the special-effects department to help them; he devised numerous tricks needed for the different shots: for the close-ups, he photographed coffee grounds and also pieces of burned cork being shot from a pressure gun against a vast white sheet. For medium-length shots, Gillespie rounded up all the pickled grasshoppers in town, which were placed on a taut canvas and intermixed with woodchips. When the canvas was jiggled, the dead locusts appeared to be swarming. Luckily, there also happened to be a genuine infestation of grasshoppers in Utah at the time. He sent a crew to film them and then had barrelfuls of the live pests brought back to use in the close-up shots. Careful editing of these various elements created a powerful, if expensive finale to the film.

Thalberg paid the same thoughtful attention to the aural effects of the film. One evening he happened to hear a radio performance of an early tonal composition by Arnold Schönberg. The next day he asked Salka Viertel, a favorite writer of Garbo's, whose salon served as a meeting point for many of the European exiles, to invite the composer to the studio. At the meeting with Schönberg, the producer explained the epic scope of the picture: the countryside of China, plagues of locusts, famine, floods, the clash of human passions, and in the middle of a climactic thunderstorm, a woman giving birth to a baby—what a splendid challenge to

any composer! Schönberg responded with a general analysis of how badly music and sound were handled in films. He mentioned that if he ever worked on a picture, he would want complete control over the sound, including the spoken words. Thalberg respectfully pointed out that the director may want to handle the actors. In the end, Thalberg used a score generated by MGM's music department, inspired by Chinese folk songs.

Sadly, Thalberg did not live to see the completion of *The Good Earth*. By the summer of 1936, the burden of his work and the battles for his projects had worn him out. He did not go to the New York opening of *Romeo and Juliet* in late August. Over the Labor Day weekend, the Thalbergs revisited Monterey, the scene of their honeymoon. By the time they returned, Thalberg had caught a cold and was developing pneumonia. On September 13, the producer wired his regrets that he would miss MGM's annual family picnic. Only a few within the inner circle at MGM knew just how grave his situation was, but none was prepared for the news the next morning that Irving Grant Thalberg had died in his sleep. According to one legend, his last words to Norma were, "Don't let the children forget me." According to another, he warned Norma not to marry—at least not an actor.

Hollywood was shocked by his sudden death. All production was halted as every studio paused for silence at the time of his funeral on September 17. MGM closed for the day, the only time in its history. Tributes poured in from President Roosevelt, from the heads of rival studios, stars, directors, fellow workers. For a man who had lived only thirty-seven years, and never took a screen credit at MGM, Thalberg was very widely known and, on the whole, deeply loved. Everybody, including people such as Erich von

ABOVE: *The dapper William Powell walks to the set of* Libeled Lady.

LEFT: *Sheet music cover for Cole Porter's "I've Got You Under My Skin" from* Born to Dance *(1936), starring Eleanor Powell.*

BELOW: *In* Libeled Lady *(1936), Harlow, Powell, Loy, and Tracy are "four stars in love, laughter, and legal complications."*

OPPOSITE: *One of the sets of Hunt Stromberg's opulent production of* Rose Marie *(1936), Jeanette MacDonald and Nelson Eddy's second operetta together.*

139

Stroheim and F. Scott Fitzgerald, who sometimes thought of him as an adversary, acknowledged his talent, likable nature, and dynamic contribution to the whole industry.

Over fifteen hundred people—the cream of the film colony—jammed into the Synagogue B'nai B'rith to hear Rabbi Edgar Magnin compare the relationship of Irving and Norma Thalberg to that of *Romeo and Juliet*, "the greatest motion picture I have ever seen." Singer Grace Moore sobbed through the Twenty-third Psalm. Thousands crowded outside, waiting for the opportunity to catch a glimpse of the numerous celebrities, though the stars themselves had come to bid farewell to the only producer they would consider a star.

While many at MGM mourned and missed Thalberg, stories circulated suggesting that Louis B. Mayer was not among them. One had it that the studio chief danced the rumba on the day of Thalberg's death; another, that after the funeral services at Forest Lawn, Mayer turned to Eddie Mannix and said, "Isn't God good to me?" Funeral jokes are a Hollywood pastime, and these reflect, if not the facts, at least the way people in the movie community thought of Louis B. Mayer. There is a lesser-known, but perhaps more plausible, death scene, in which a sentimental Mayer patched things up with the dying Thalberg, expressing regret for the previous few years of estrangement during what was certainly a unique and remarkable partnership in the history of moviemaking.

ABOVE: *Thalberg's final production before his untimely death is* The Good Earth *(1937), an adaptation of Pearl S. Buck's novel. The film's final title card reads: "To the memory of Irving Grant Thalberg, we dedicate this picture—his last great achievement."*

RIGHT: *The good earth: a five-hundred-acre farm in Chatsworth, California, was transformed into Chinese farmland.*

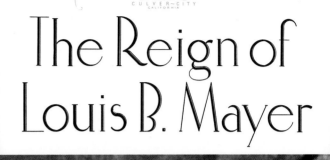

PART THREE

The Reign of Louis B. Mayer

While the stories told about the end of Louis B. Mayer's famous partnership with Irving Thalberg may have been ambivalent, the tributes that he either arranged or permitted to immortalize his former crown prince were concrete and visible. The most prominent new edifice at the entrance to the MGM lot, housing all the central administrators' and producers' offices, including Mayer's own, became the Thalberg Building. Completed in 1937, the heavily air-conditioned structure was more commonly referred to by its nickname, the Iron Lung. At Mayer's instigation, the Academy of Motion Picture Arts and Sciences established the Irving G. Thalberg Memorial Award to acknowledge the work of exceptional producers. It is still considered one of the most prestigious awards in the Hollywood community.

The creative personnel at MGM, particularly the producers, would miss Thalberg's guidance, but Albert Lewin was the only one among them to resign. He had been Thalberg's closest assistant, and so it was not surprising that he received numerous offers from rival studios. In 1937, he left to become a producer at Paramount. Mayer assigned Bernie Hyman to take over the Thalberg Unit and put the finishing touches on *The Good Earth*, which was nearing completion when Thalberg fell ill. It was released in early 1937, with a simple title card at the beginning, which read, "To the memory of Irving Grant Thalberg, we dedicate this picture—his last great achievement." So for the first and

LEFT: *Eleanor Powell dances on a giant drum in the title number from* Rosalie *(1937), one of the largest musical sequences ever filmed.*

ABOVE: *Louis B. Mayer at his desk in the air-conditioned Thalberg Building.*

145

1937

◆ MGM releases *The Good Earth*, starring Paul Muni and Luise Rainer. Thalberg has wanted to make this film since 1931 when the Pulitzer Prize-winning novel was published. He dies during production. Two million feet of background film are shot in China. It costs a record $2,816,000. Rainer wins the award for best actress for the second time in a row.

◆ Eighteen scripts later, MGM releases *A Day at the Races* to the great relief of Groucho Marx, who performed endless retakes for director Sam Wood, who kept using the first or second take anyway.

◆ Spencer Tracy wins the award for best actor for *Captains Courageous*.

◆ Twenty-six-year-old Jean Harlow dies while filming *Saratoga*, starring Clark Gable. A double finishes the film. Her fiancé, MGM star William Powell, is heartbroken.

◆ Fifteen-year-old Judy Garland's star ascends in *Broadway Melody of 1938*, in which she sings "Dear Mr. Gable" (based on "You Made Me Love You") to a photograph of the "King."

Luise Rainer in The Good Earth, *a role that wins her a second consecutive Oscar for best actress.*

ABOVE: *In 1938, Jeanette MacDonald and Nelson Eddy are at their zenith.* The Girl of the Golden West *(1938), a musical melodrama, based on a play by David Belasco, stars the singing duo as a saloon owner and a bandit.*

OPPOSITE: *A Jacques Kapralik caricature of the Marx Brothers in* A Day at the Races *(1937). From the late thirties on, the artist makes collages from assorted materials for most of MGM's films, images of which appear in posters and in-house publications.*

only time the producer's name was credited to one of his films released by MGM.

Another Thalberg project with the Marx Brothers, *A Day at the Races*, was taken over by his brother-in-law, Lawrence Weingarten, while Hunt Stromberg, who had previously worked with Jeanette MacDonald and Nelson Eddy in their first two films together, inherited the filming of Sigmund Romberg's operetta *Maytime*. Stromberg found himself finishing a project that was quite different from what Thalberg had envisioned. Louis B. Mayer had already stepped in to take a more active role, not only in the larger matters of assignment and casting but also in concept and execution. With *Maytime*, Thalberg had been planning to reprise the sophisticated sexual antics of Ernst Lubitsch's *The Merry Widow*, and to make it the studio's first 3-color feature production. Mayer, who saw *Maytime* as another opportunity to exploit the popularity of MacDonald and Eddy, ordered the script rewritten, insisting that Jeanette MacDonald's image be kept lily-white, and scrapped the costly idea of shooting it in color.

Similarly, Mayer asked Stromberg to complete *Marie Antoinette*, on which Thalberg had spent three years and $400,000 of the studio's money. In addition, half a dozen writers had already worked on revisions of the script. Mayer was in favor of continuing with this big-budget costume drama because it promised the kind of prestige that he needed to maintain MGM's reputation, which had been built up so carefully over the years.

Ever since Marion Davies had given up her claim to it, the role of Marie Antoinette had belonged to Norma Shearer. There had, however, been rumors before Thalberg's death

CLICK

THE NATIONAL PICTURE MONTHLY • 10¢ • JULY, 1938

MARIE ANTOINETTE

NORMA SHEARER

See Page 10

OPPOSITE: *The July 1988 cover of* Click *magazine juxtaposes Norma Shearer's face with the real face of the woman she portrays,* Marie Antoinette *(1938).*

RIGHT: *During a filming break, magnificently attired dancers find ways to relax on the floor of the Versailles set.*

that this movie would be Shearer's last, that she would retire to look after her ailing husband and two small children. Now, bitter wrangling broke out between Thalberg's estate, which laid claim to a continuing portion of the company's sizable profits, and Loew's management. After six months, the lawyers for each side agreed that the original profit-sharing agreement should run until the end of Thalberg's contract in 1938. Then the estate would receive a certain percentage of the profits earned from exploiting the pictures MGM made in the fourteen years since its founding. And, as part of the overall settlement, Norma Shearer agreed to star in six MGM pictures over the following three years, including *Marie Antoinette.*

Director Sidney Franklin had been at Thalberg's side during all the years of preparation for the historical film. They had planned to shoot it in color, which would enhance propmaster Edwin Willis's extraordinary collection of the most expensive period furniture ever assembled. Willis, with the encouragement of Cedric Gibbons and Adrian, spared no effort or money to put Versailles to shame. The custom-tailored outfits worn by Shearer were another example of the excessive spending on the project. Often cited is the fox trim on a cape worn by her that Adrian had sent to New York to be dyed the same color as her eyes.

When work finally resumed on *Marie Antoinette,* the studio decided to shoot the picture in black and white rather than in Technicolor, which was still in an experimental phase. No doubt this saved money at the time, but it also meant that all the expensive sets and costumes would show up in shades of gray. When Franklin protested against the decision to reduce the ninety-day shooting schedule to two months, Mayer and Stromberg replaced the director with the ubiquitous Woody Van Dyke just a few days before the start of principal photography. Norma Shearer had been consulted and agreed to the change, but it was a decision she later regretted. The film was only a modest success, which the pro-Thalberg camp attributed to the compromises forced on the picture by Mayer. Others blamed Van Dyke's hurried direction and Norma Shearer's mannered acting, operatic even within the absurdly grand setting.

Following settlement of claims by the Thalberg estate, MGM was legally absorbed into the parent company, which meant that the studio's top management now shared, with the New York executives, in Loew's profits. And these continued to grow, rising from $7.5 million in 1935 to $10 million the following year, and to a record $14.3 million in 1937. Mayer could well be pleased when his annual salary and bonus exceeded $1.3 million, making him, for the first of several years, the highest-paid executive in the United States. When reporters found it curious that the man who wrote Mayer's checks was paid less than Mayer, the reclusive Nicholas Schenck laughed it off by saying, "Louie likes that kind of thing."

Indeed, this was the period of the imperial Mayer, of fact and legend. Ensconced on the third floor of the Thalberg Building—in a white-on-white office so large that Sam Goldwyn once complained, "You need an automobile just to reach your desk"—Mayer sat on a specially elevated chair behind a round desk, manipulating telephones, bells, and knobs that controlled the window slats and adapted the

TOP, ABOVE, AND RIGHT:
*Versailles sets, created by
Cedric Gibbons and his
associate William Horning for*
Marie Antoinette: *the entrance
hall, the exterior garden, and
the music room, each one built
on a sound stage.*

LEFT: *Gibbons and Horning
survey one of the ninety-eight
set models—this one of the Paris
Opera—that are constructed
for* Marie Antoinette.

THE ANATOMY OF A FILM

In the early 1930s, MGM began a monumental effort to film the story of the French
queen Marie Antoinette. The lavish sets,
decorations, costumes, and makeup were
unequaled for the time, and the film remains
one of the most epic productions that ever
came out of Hollywood. Critics have remarked
that the actual court of Versailles in the late
1700s couldn't have been more sumptuous
than its Hollywood counterpart in the 1930s.

Norma Shearer had been slated to play the
leading role in 1933, when Irving Thalberg
began developing on the idea. After Thalberg's
untimely death in 1936, Shearer stopped
working. She returned to play Marie, heading
up a large and talented cast, which included
Tyrone Power as the handsome Swedish
count Axel von Fersen, Robert Morley (who
had been discovered on the London stage by
Hunt Stromberg) as King Louis XVI, and
Joseph Schildkraut as the crafty duke
d'Orleans.

Casting the film was perhaps the easiest
task. By far the more complicated problem
was authentically recreating life at the French
royal court of the eighteenth century. The
summer before filming began, Stromberg had
compiled 8,000 photographs from Paris and
collected first editions of eighteenth-century

French history books. Nathalie Bucknall, head
of research at MGM, reviewed this material
with all the department heads, and research
technicians Carter Spetner and Dave Barkell
made prints from pictures in the rare books.

Cedric Gibbons, the highly cultured MGM
art director, and William Horning supervised
the building of ninety-eight palace sets
representing the palace at Versailles. None of
these were exact duplications. This decision
was deliberate, since the original entry to the
palace is at the end of a long wall, there is no
grand staircase inside, and the famous 300-
foot-long Hall of Mirrors could not be used in
shooting any significant scenes. Apparently,
though, the sets proved authentic enough: the
French government honored Gibbons with a
formal decoration.

Edwin B. Willis, head of the prop
department, spent three months in France
purchasing a stunning assortment of
antiques—furnishings, paintings, statues,
scrolls, art objects, and even original letters—
in all, the largest single consignment of
antiques ever received at L.A. harbor customs.

He then employed expert woodcarvers to
make reproductions and frames for the palace
interiors. Charles Holland, the studio's chief
draper, supervised the making of elaborate

ABOVE: *Over two thousand wigs
are hand made by the Max
Factor company, including
eighteen specially designed for
Norma Shearer by Sydney
Guilaroff.*

TOP LEFT: *Several years before the cameras roll, extensive research begins in order to ensure historical accuracy.*
TOP RIGHT: *Furniture storage inherits ornate antiques purchased by Edwin Willis on a buying expedition in France.*
CENTER: *Artists paint murals on a wall of the Versailles set.*
BOTTOM: *A handmade chandelier from the glass department is hung for the ball.*

festoons from brocades, fringes, galloons (trimmings), and gimps (ornamental braids) purchased in France by Willis.

Max Factor & Company made 903 ornate white wigs for the principals and 1,200 less fancy wigs for the extras. Shearer herself wore eighteen designed by chief hair stylist Sydney Guilaroff. In the wig-making department at MGM, workers laboriously sewed hair into lace nets. More than 750 million human hairs were required for some 5,000 wigs. In order to keep the wigs in shape and tightly curled, a modern wig-baking oven was purchased.

The process of creating makeup for famous historical characters began with the sketching and molding of masks and busts. For example, using well-known portraits of Louis XVI as a guide, Jack Dawn, the head of the makeup department, sculpted a head of the king.

Adrian's costumes for Norma Shearer generally followed the styles in the period books Stromberg had collected and in surviving portraits of Marie Antoinette, including one by Élisabeth Vigée-Lebrun. Some 2,500 costumes were made with the help of a corps of seamstresses, fifty of whom were brought to Los Angeles from Guadalajara, Mexico, to sew on thousands of sequins and do elaborate embroidery. The team also assembled intricate costumes for 151 character actors and a large group of extras.

Many fabrics were specially woven in Lyons, France. One of Shearer's gowns was made of cream organza over metallic silver lamé, trimmed with silver, passementerie (a fancy ornamental braid), sequins, beading, and paste stones. Over 500 yards of white satin were used for the queen's wedding gown. Shearer's grand ballroom dress is adorned with cleverly arranged bias-cut swags of silver tissue. The bias cut was an element of fashion contemporary in the 1930s, but the overall beauty of the garment surpassed criticism.

The authentic understructure for Marie Antoinette's enormous gowns had to be engineered in the machine shop, and a special dressing room was placed right on the sound stage, since the heavy, awkward costumes were difficult to maneuver. Though Adrian's costumes could be deemed "flights of fancy," they accomplished their purpose in being luxurious to the camera's eye.

Marie Antoinette has been criticized for fictionalizing the last days of the French court before the Revolution, but it survives as one of MGM's most expensive, prestigious movies of the thirties. In the end, the real stars are the amazing production values.

153

harsh California sunlight to whatever mood he wanted to create. The office contained a private room and its own elevator so that Mayer could entertain visitors incognito, without having to expose them to a battery of secretaries.

Despite the grand image he liked to project, Mayer remained remarkably accessible to his employees, in contrast to Thalberg. The producer's antechamber had been famous for always being crowded with people, some of whom had to wait days, sometimes weeks, to speak to him. Mayer's intimidating manner was offset considerably by Ida Koverman, his executive secretary for many years, who acted as a sort of den mother to the frequent suppliants. The studio boss was proud of the fact that she had worked at one time for his friend—and President of the United States—Herbert Hoover.

From his suite, Mayer negotiated the business of making films and staged his real and feigned tantrums, fainting fits, and other histrionics, which were designed to keep his stars in line. Robert Taylor, who made fifty-nine films for MGM between 1934 and 1967, countered the public view of Mayer as a tyrannical and abusive male prima donna who outacted his actors. "As I knew him," Taylor said, "Mr. Mayer was kind, fatherly, understanding, and protective." There is an oft-repeated story that perfectly illustrates the different sides of Mayer's personality. After he became a star, Taylor was urged by his agent to make a private appointment to see Mayer about renegotiating his contract. While Taylor went into the huge office to make the request, his agent waited outside. Mayer launched into a glowing description of his

pride in his two daughters. "If God had given me a son," he told the handsome actor, "if He had blessed me with such a great and wonderful joy, I can think of nobody I would rather have wanted than a son exactly like you." After a lengthy monologue in much the same vein, Taylor left Mayer's presence in a daze.

"Well," asked the agent, "did you get the raise?"

"No," the actor replied, "but I got a father."

Whenever he was asked for a raise, the MGM boss would tailor his response to the individual star. For instance, he was delighted to learn that Walter Pidgeon had grown up in Saint John, New Brunswick, where he, too, had spent his childhood. When Pidgeon first came to see him about a raise, Mayer hoped this hometown connection would lead to a common understanding. "Mr. Mayer," the suave actor replied, "I still think I deserve a raise and I'm sure you'll do right by a Saint John's boy. I'll leave it to you." The mogul felt obliged to double Pidgeon's salary.

Mayer exhibited the friendly side of his personality whenever he visited the studio commissary for lunch. Although he had a private suite, appropriately called the Lion's Den, where he broke bread with top executives and cronies, he also made a point of working the tables in the general dining room, talking to as many of his employees as possible, sometimes spending half an hour going from one table to the next. The MGM commissary was renowned throughout Hollywood for its subsidized lunches. (Executive Al Lichtman once said, "MGM is the only place in the world where you can make $5,000 a week and free meals.") The specialty of the house was its legendary chicken soup, made kosher style with large chunks of chicken and matzoh balls. Served every day, it was a meal in itself and cost only thirty-five cents. The practice came, Mayer was fond of retelling, from a promise he had made to his sainted mother as a young man. He had told her that if he

OPPOSITE: *Robert Taylor at the time of* The Gorgeous Hussy *(1936).*

ABOVE: *In the commissary: (left) Gable, without a mustache, eats a solitary lunch (1931); Johnny Weissmuller (right) tackles a huge steak with spinach to keep up his strength (1934).*

TOP LEFT: *A window card for the first teaming of Mickey and Judy in* Thoroughbreds Don't Cry *(1937).*

TOP RIGHT: *A job in the publicity art department usually meant long hours for artists such as those in this 1939 photograph.*

ABOVE: *A theater ad for* Dramatic School *(1938), Mervyn LeRoy's first production for MGM.*

ever was successful, he would always share just such a chicken soup with his employees. Any chef hired at the commissary, therefore, was required to come to the Mayer residence to learn how to prepare the soup.

Despite his social and casual gregariousness, Mayer ran his kingdom from above, rarely visiting sets or getting involved in production details, other than approving budgets or voicing criticism at internal previews. He was kept minutely informed of the progress and problems on films by his executives and unit producers, who shared the third floor with him. Besides producers Harry Rapf, Hunt Stromberg, Bernie Hyman, and Larry Weingarten, the ruling elite after Thalberg's death included Benjamin Thau, nominally in charge of all contract negotiations, but who, in fact, served as Mayer's executive assistant, and, of course, Eddie Mannix, general troubleshooter for management and staff, who ran an effective spy system of informers to keep Mayer *au courant* on subjects ranging from liaisons to union troubles. Referring to Mannix's early days as Schenck's bouncer, the writer Elliot Paul remarked that he policed MGM by creating "a class of psychos called Mannix-depressives."

J. J. Cohn, general manager from the Goldwyn days, had been replaced by Mannix and put in charge of the first of MGM's B-picture units, which made up an increasing share of the studio's output. A few years earlier, two old hands with backgrounds in distribution, Al Lichtman and Sam Katz, had been sent to the West Coast by Nick Schenck. Initially, Mayer resented their presence, just as he had the arrival of Eddie Mannix, but they were included in the executive committee that served to carry out Mayer's commands. Lichtman, whom Mayer knew from Metro Pictures twenty years before, refined the method of charging distributors a higher percentage for the studio's prestige pictures. Loew's income increased dramatically in 1937, the first year of the new system. Katz had been a former partner in the Balaban-

Katz theater chain that went bankrupt in 1932 and was known as an industry tyrant. Katz's early responsibilities at MGM were vaguely defined to embrace several areas, including the organization of musical production.

Howard Strickling, in charge of MGM's formidable publicity machine on the West Coast, also belonged to Mayer's inner circle. Indeed, publicity was the pump propelling the studio's flow of products and stars into national and global consciousness. Some one hundred and fifty people worked on both coasts, in various divisions, handling the advertising and promotion of new pictures. The New York office took care of coverage in national magazines and on radio networks located on the East Coast, while Culver City dealt with prerelease publicity. Each production carried a photographer and publicist who fielded interviews with stars and directors, and provided the stories that filled newspaper columns.

MGM also took out small ads in magazines, featuring Leo the Lion telling millions of readers what film was being shot where in an effort to generate interest months or years in advance of the actual release. National tours by the stars were arranged through more than thirty regional offices, whose chief task was to handle each film released in that territory and deal with local advertising. Finally, there were separate departments to handle promotional tie-ins, fan magazines, and fan mail for the stars.

The task of publicizing MGM's films in the late thirties was made considerably easier by the constant recognition showered on the studio's achievements by the industry. In 1936, MGM films received five out of the ten nominations for best picture, and won with *The Great Ziegfeld*. Luise Rainer, practically an unknown actress, captured the Oscar for her performance in the same film. The award had been expected to go, in a sympathy vote, to Norma Shearer for *Romeo and Juliet*. Douglas Shearer went home with

TOP LEFT: *A theater ad for* The Great Waltz *(1938), a film inspired by Mayer's enthusiasm for Johann Strauss's waltzes and for which cameraman Joseph Ruttenberg wins an Oscar for best cinematography.*

ABOVE: *A window card for* Captains Courageous *(1937), a film based on Rudyard Kipling's novel, featuring Freddie Bartholomew, Lionel Barrymore, Mickey Rooney, and Spencer Tracy in his first Oscar-winning role.*

RIGHT: *A window card for* The Ice Follies of 1939, *in which Crawford plays a Hollywood star who helps her old skating friends back east put on a show.*

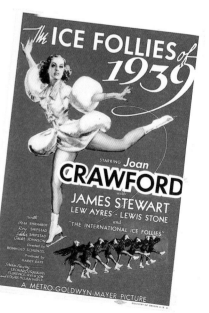

another of his many statuettes for sound recording, this time for his work in *San Francisco*. Awards were also bestowed on MGM for dance direction, shorts, and technical achievements.

Following Thalberg's death, the studio's acclaim continued. In 1937, the twenty-five-year-old Rainer stunned Hollywood by winning the Oscar again, for her role in *The Good Earth*. This time she beat out Greta Garbo, who had given one of her finest performances in *Camille*. Although the Swedish sphinx had dominated the screen for a dozen years, she would never win an Oscar for one of her performances. (Actually, it was rumored that Mayer originally had hired the Viennese-born Rainer, who had built her acting reputation with Max Reinhardt's theater company in Berlin, "to scare Garbo out of her arrogance." Studio bosses were known to resort to such stratagems to handle difficult stars. Jack Warner once paid a young Errol Flynn look-alike to do nothing but sit in the studio commissary while the star had his lunch.)

MGM's glory was slightly offset by the fading brilliance of some of its stars. The 1937 Brand Index, published by Harry Brand, president of the Independent Theater Owners of America, had labeled Garbo and Crawford "box-office poison." Increasingly, Garbo's films were considered a highbrow draw, which prompted one acidulous Irish critic to remark, "If Miss Garbo really wants to be alone, she should come to a performance of one of her films in Dublin." Rouben Mamoulian had attempted to humanize Garbo's somewhat unrelenting, tragic persona by having her laugh in *Queen Christina*, but he encountered enormous resistance from the actress. Indeed, a few years passed before Garbo realized that it was time for her to change. For her first comedy, *Ninotchka*, the publicity department sought to bring in audiences with its latest incarnation, "GARBO LAUGHS."

OPPOSITE:

LEFT: *In* Broadway Melody of 1940, *Eleanor Powell rehearses with Fred Astaire.*

CENTER AND RIGHT: *The mirrored dance floor is prepared for Fred and Eleanor, who perform on it in the film's big number, a tap version of Cole Porter's "Begin the Beguine."*

ABOVE: *Eleanor Powell, a Broadway dancer, in* Broadway Melody of 1936 *(1935). In a number from the film, she bridges two pianos, the left one played by Roger Edens.*

TOP RIGHT: *Powell atop a drum in the title number of* Rosalie *(1937).*

159

Joan Crawford, who had always been jealous of Norma Shearer's special status as Thalberg's wife, was hoping that after the producer's death she would have a better chance of getting the parts normally reserved for Shearer. But when she was cast as Peggy O'Neal Eaton, an innkeeper's daughter in a nineteenth-century costume drama, *The Gorgeous Hussy*, she received disappointing reviews. Neither the critics nor her fans were willing to accept Crawford in a role so far removed from her glamour-queen image. "Century-old costumes," one New York paper opined, "do not go well with the pronounced modernity of her personality." Crawford continued to work hard, making three pictures a year, and was rewarded with a renewed contract at $300,000 a year. Mayer always maintained that the best investment he made was in stars. "We are the only company," he would often remind his people, "whose assets all walk out the door at night."

One of those assets, Jean Harlow, died tragically of uremic poisoning in June 1937, while filming *Saratoga*. She was only twenty-six. Even before she passed away, however, the kind of steamy pictures the platinum-blonde sex goddess had made with Gable were falling out of fashion at MGM, partly because of constant pressure from the censors and partly because of Mayer's own preference for a more virginal and sweet ideal of womanhood, as typified by Jeanette MacDonald and, later, Greer Garson.

Mayer did not abandon the studio's *grandes dames*, but he was acutely aware that public taste changed con-

ABOVE: *Jean Harlow with Clark Gable in her last film,* Saratoga *(1937). Her death before the end of production necessitates finishing her scenes with a double.*
LEFT: *Jean Harlow in* Wife Vs. Secretary *(1936).*

◆ Spencer Tracy wins his second consecutive Oscar as best actor for *Boys Town*.

◆ *Young Dr. Kildare*, the first in MGM's popular hospital series, premieres.

◆ Clark Gable and Myrna Loy are voted the king and queen of Hollywood in a national poll. They star together in *Too Hot to Handle*.

◆ MGM releases *Three Comrades*, Erich Maria Remarque's novel that is banned in Hitler's Germany. Because of the German export market, any innuendo or inference that could be construed as anti-Nazi is deleted from the final production.

◆ More screen tests were made for *Marie Antoinette* than ever before in movie history. A record-breaking number of 151 players are cast. The final cut includes Norma Shearer, Tyrone Power, John Barrymore, Robert Morley, and Anita Louise.

◆ *Marie Antoinette* marks Norma Shearer's return to the screen after the death of her husband, Irving Thalberg, in 1936. Their love and devotion and success are still adored in Hollywood.

◆ MGM buys the rights to Marjorie Rawlings's best-selling novel, *The Yearling*.

The Irving Thalberg Memorial Building.

stantly, and that he must keep looking to the future. Although MGM's films of the twenties and early thirties were notable for the sophisticated, adult themes chosen for their powerful female stars, by the middle of the latter decade, with Thalberg's passing, there was a noticeable change in emphasis. Male leads, family themes, and child stars were growing in favor. This shift was reflected in the exhibitors' poll for 1938, which featured five MGM stars in its ranking of the top-ten box-office attractions. Myrna Loy, then at the height of her popularity, was the studio's only female star on the list, along with Clark Gable, Robert Taylor, Spencer Tracy, and Mickey Rooney.

Spencer Tracy won the first of his consecutive Oscars in 1937, for his role as the curly-haired Manuel in Rudyard Kipling's *Captains Courageous*, which also provided thirteen-year-old Freddie Bartholomew with his best role since *David Copperfield*. Tracy received his second Oscar the following year for his portrayal of Father Flanagan in *Boys Town*. Significantly, Tracy's supporting actor in both these films was not a woman but a boy; in the latter, it was a youngster named Mickey Rooney, who, by 1939, would oust Shirley Temple as Hollywood's number-one box-office attraction.

Born Joe Yule, Jr., in 1920, Mickey Rooney first appeared on the stage in his parents' vaudeville act when he was just fifteen months old. His film debut came at age six; the following years saw him playing bit parts at several Hollywood studios, including MGM. David Selznick brought

TOP: *Spencer Tracy, Mickey Rooney, and other cast members in a scene from* Boys Town *(1938). Director Norman Taurog begins a long tenure at MGM with this fictional treatment of an actual school for delinquent boys.*

ABOVE: *Spencer Tracy, Freddie Bartholomew, and Lionel Barrymore in* Captains Courageous *(1937).*

161

THE STILL IMAGE

The mandate of the MGM still portrait department was to create images worthy of public worship. Howard Strickling, the head of publicity, told his stable of photographers: "I want lots of glamour."

Clarence Sinclair Bull, who headed the portrait department for four decades, was also the studio's top still photographer. He shot more portraits of Greta Garbo than all other photographers in Hollywood combined, and he found her easy to work with, remarking, "I never said 'hold it.' All I did was light her face and wait and watch, and when I saw the reflected mood, I clicked the shutter. That face was the most inspirational I ever photographed."

Laszlo Willinger, an MGM still photographer in the 1930s, worked under contract for five years with almost every star on the lot. He recalled: "The first sitting I did was with Margaret Sullavan, and it was a hell of a good sitting. The assistant to the head of publicity took the proofs, weighed them in his hand, and said: 'It wasn't a big sitting, was it?' He never even looked at the stuff." As for glamour, Willinger insisted: "You couldn't have happy sex in a studio portrait. Sex and earnestness … together they spelled glamour."

In 1925, George Hurrell came to Hollywood from Chicago after studying with the renowned photographer Edward Steichen. Matinee idol Ramon Novarro and actress Norma Shearer were Hurrell's first subjects, and when Howard Strickling saw their portraits, he arranged for Hurrell to shoot Garbo, Joan Crawford, John Gilbert, and Wallace Beery.

Hurrell became famous for a smashing series of photographs of the ladylike Shearer. He said that, "the idea was to get her looking real wicked and sirenlike. However, she wasn't that type in real life. She had such a big forehead that it made her look too intellectual for the kind of roles she wanted to play. We fixed

ABOVE: *A George Hurrell portrait of Luise Rainer. The star of films such as* The Great Ziegfeld *(1936) and* The Good Earth *(1937), Rainer was a European stage actress before coming to Hollywood.*
BELOW: *Photographer Clarence Sinclair Bull, head of the portrait department, takes Robert Taylor's picture on the set of* Camille *(1937).*
OPPOSITE: *Myrna Loy, MGM's witty first lady of screwball comedy and queen of Hollywood, in an elegant collage from a Laszlo Willinger portrait (circa 1938).*

that by pulling her hair over to one side, getting her head down, and putting some 'mood feeling' into her."

Hurrell's portraits of Hollywood stars were first showcased in *Esquire* magazine, where the name of the game was sex appeal, with all the heavy eye-shadow and the voluptuousness of white satin. He occasionally used props and, in one case, a snarling beast at Jean Harlow's side to supercharge the presentation. Hurrell remembered that "Harlow's face was much more difficult to light. Her eyes were deep-set, and you had to get the light under them, or else her eyes would look too dark or be lost." But "Joan Crawford's face was the closest to perfection. Perfect proportion, except for a heavy jaw, and her eyes were very large. A portrait session in the studio could take anything from three hours to a whole day, but Crawford was a great one for it. She loved all that posing. She'd do anything as long as it wasn't in a bathing suit."

The thirties were a decade of exaggeration, and Hurrell's glorification of the world's most beautiful women made him one of the most highly paid professionals in the business. Many of his portraits are avidly collected today.

Other, lesser-known still cameramen at MGM during the thirties and forties included Virgil Apger, who created stills of Ray Bolger and worked on such films as *Sweethearts* (1938) and *Mrs. Parkington* (1944); Eric Carpenter, who was known for his studies of Judy Garland, Joan Crawford, Greer Garson, and Esther Williams; and Eugene Robert Richee, who did portraiture and publicity stills for *Kismet* (1955); as well as Ted Allen and Ruth Harriet Louise. And this is just a sampling of the talent and artistry in the portrait department at MGM during the studio's golden years.

TOP LEFT: *A miniature window card for* Life Begins for Andy Hardy *(1941), in which Andy (Mickey Rooney) goes to New York to find a job and learns the realities of life. It is Judy Garland's last* Hardy *picture.*

TOP RIGHT: *A Jacques Kapralik caricature of Mickey and Judy for* Andy Hardy Meets A Debutante *(1940).*

ABOVE: *Guests at Lewis Stone's November 1938 birthday party include (left to right) Fay Holden, Stone, Ann Rutherford, Cecelia Parker, Mickey Rooney, and Louis B. Mayer.*

him back to the studio in 1934 to play Clark Gable as a child in *Manhattan Melodrama*. In 1935, on loan to Warner Bros., Rooney received rave notices for his role as Puck in Max Reinhardt's *A Midsummer Night's Dream*. It would be as Andy Hardy, however, that Rooney would enter the hearts of American audiences.

In 1937, Lucien Hubbard, whose unit specialized in low-budget movies, produced a routine B-picture that brought back together a cast that Hunt Stromberg had used effectively in *Ah, Wilderness* two years before. In *A Family Affair*, Lionel Barrymore played a small-town judge, named Hardy, whose uncompromising sense of justice brought him into conflict with his fellow citizens. His own family frequently opposed him, with the exception of his teenage son, Andy, who was originally intended to play a secondary role. Had Mayer not insisted on placing greater emphasis on the character of Andy, it might have been just another part given to the seventeen-year-old Mickey Rooney in his thirty-third picture.

The response to *A Family Affair* and to Rooney was so positive that Mayer asked Hubbard to produce another *Hardy* picture—this time concentrating on the relationship between the judge and his son—with the intention of making it a series. When Hubbard left the studio, Mayer placed the production in the hands of J. J. Cohn and director George B. Seitz. Lionel Barrymore, already busy with another role, was replaced by Lewis Stone, and Fay Holden became Andy's Ma. Andy, of course, could not be played by anyone but Mickey Rooney.

Mayer's growing enthusiasm for the subsequent *Hardy* films almost became a personal crusade for him. He would sit through previews next to Carey Wilson, the veteran producer-writer, in order to transmit his criticisms directly. After a scene in which Andy Hardy refused to

eat—to indicate how lovesick he was—Mayer went into a rage: "Don't you know a boy of sixteen is hungry all the time?" he screamed. "You tell me you were brought up in a good American home—in the kitchen! You lied to me! You've let Andy insult his mother! No boy would tell his mother he wasn't hungry!" Then Mayer told Wilson exactly how to rewrite the scene.

When Mrs. Hardy became seriously ill in *Judge Hardy and Son*, Wilson composed a lengthy, tearful prayer for Andy to recite. Mayer accused the writer of turning the simple, good-hearted lad into a Hollywood character. And then the head of MGM went down on his knees and recited an appropriately simple prayer, which was faithfully transcribed by Wilson and recited by Rooney in the film.

With the public clamoring for more *Hardy* pictures, Mayer kept the pressure on his producers to make at least three to four new movies a year. In all, MGM churned out sixteen *Hardy* pictures, often at the rate of one every three months, and, in the process, grossed more than $25 million. Production values and scripts were mediocre by MGM standards, but at one point Mayer even asked his staff not to make them better—he was concerned that too much slickness would destroy the unsophisticated innocence of middle America, upon which the series was founded. Mayer considered the *Hardy* family series among the finest pictures that MGM produced under his leadership, and one of his proudest moments came when the series was given a special award by the Academy in 1942 for "furthering the American way of life."

The MGM factory had always turned out, with clockwork efficiency, a large number of low-budget films, but in the Thalberg era, creative attention was focused primarily on those special pictures that would endure beyond a couple of weeks, repaying the years of careful preparation

TOP LEFT: *Lewis Stone, as Judge Hardy, and Fay Holden, as Mrs. Hardy, one of the screen's most enduring and endearing couples, in a scene from* Life Begins for Andy Hardy *(1941).*
TOP: *In* Love Finds Andy Hardy *(1938), Mickey Rooney is pursued by Judy Garland (in her first* Hardy *role), series regular Ann Rutherford, and Lana Turner, who begins a lengthy career at MGM with this film.*

ABOVE: *Esther Williams begins her long career at MGM with* Andy Hardy's Double Life *(1943), and is seen here kissing Mickey Rooney in an underwater scene from the film.*

165

BEHIND THE SCENES

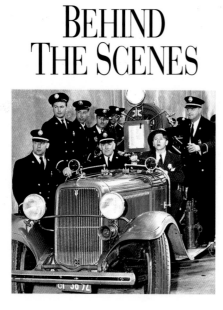

When all is said and done, it is the motion pictures of Metro-Goldwyn-Mayer that audiences will remember, along with the faces and voices of the stars and the names of the directors, producers, designers, and cinematographers. But behind each film there were countless individuals whose contributions audiences never saw on the screen. And behind MGM there were thousands of employees, many of whom spent their entire working lives in Culver City, a world unto itself.

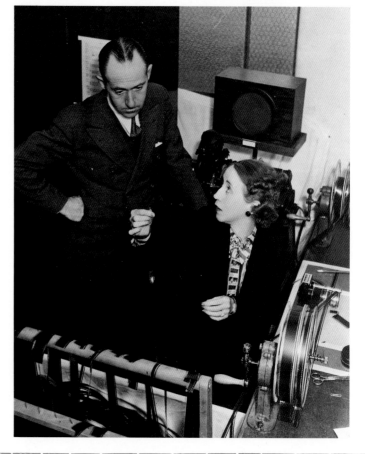

OPPOSITE:

TOP LEFT: *Mickey Rooney with MGM firemen.*

LEFT CENTER: *Relaxing in the employee lounge.*

LEFT BOTTOM: *Eating lunch in the commissary.*

BOTTOM RIGHT: *Editor Margaret Booth (seated) with cutting manager Danny Gray.*

ABOVE: *MGM employees pour out of Sound Stage 15 after a meeting.*

FROM TOP RIGHT: *Maintaining the wardrobe department inventory; extras kill time by playing cards between takes; answering fan mail; keeping order on the set (where* The Girl of the Golden West *is being filmed); cashing a paycheck (in this case, a young Angela Lansbury); and removing finished still photographs from the dryer.*

TOP LEFT AND RIGHT: *Storyboard art for the chase sequence at the Witch's castle in* The Wizard of Oz *(1939). The art helps the film-makers visualize the scene and plan its execution.*

ABOVE: *Judy Garland in* Broadway Melody of 1938 *(1937). Her partner in the finale, Buddy Ebsen, is initially cast as Oz's Scarecrow and actually begins filming in the role of the Tin Man. But his makeup makes him ill, and he is replaced by Jack Haley. Although Ebsen's songs are rere-corded by Haley, the group versions of "Off to See the Wizard" are not, and his voice remains on the soundtrack.*

required to make them. When a formula or genre clicked, as in the *Tarzan* and *Thin Man* pictures, the films were care-fully spaced a year or two apart, to keep the public interested. Mayer, on the other hand, began to pay more attention to what were known in the trade as B-pictures, though he did not encourage the use of the term. For him, the *Hardy* pictures presented an opportunity to satisfy American audiences with simpler fare, one based on family dinners, not on elegant parties.

While generating millions of dollars for MGM, the series also succeeded in generating millions of fans for the studio's growing stable of young talent. The fourth *Hardy* film, *Love Finds Andy Hardy*, in addition to starring Ann Rutherford, who played Rooney's regular girlfriend, fea-tured two young teenagers who competed for Andy's attention. One was Lana Turner, considered by many as too glamorous for a family picture ("I spent most of my time fending off Mickey Rooney," she recalled), and the other was a young girl who did not have Lana's looks but certainly could sing.

Judy Garland had been under contract to MGM since age thirteen, but her lucky break did not come until lyricist Arthur Freed and arranger Roger Edens recruited her to sing "Dear Mr. Gable," based on the song "You Made Me Love You," to the actor at his thirty-sixth birthday party on February 1, 1937. Garland's impact on the assembled elite was so electrifying that she was cast in *Broadway Melody of 1938* and sang the same song to a photograph of the star while writing a letter to him.

That film marked the breakup of the songwriting team of Arthur Freed and Nacio Herb Brown. The latter departed for New York, though the two men would still occasionally

ABOVE: *L. Frank Baum's widow, Maude, on a visit to the studio, reads through a first edi-tion of her husband's book with Judy Garland.*

write songs together. Hired by Thalberg as a songwriter at the beginning of the sound boom in 1929, Freed had written lyrics for MGM's musicals, including its first two, *The Broadway Melody* and *The Hollywood Revue of 1929*. Then, in late 1937, he was given the chance to be a producer when he told Mayer—who loved music of all kinds—that he had an idea for a film: a musical version of L. Frank Baum's children's classic, *The Wizard of Oz*.

After the publication of *The Wizard of Oz* in 1900, Baum wrote fourteen more books about the land of Oz. Over the years, several silent *Oz* films had been made, including one by Baum's own production company. Samuel Goldwyn, who had acquired the film rights to *The Wizard* in 1933, sold them to MGM for $75,000. Still, Mayer had reservations, despite the huge success of Disney's recent fantasy production, *Snow White and the Seven Dwarfs*. While it was relatively easy to bring a fairy tale to life through animation, MGM's plans called for the creation of a fantasy world using actors and real sets, an effect that had rarely been tried. The proposed budget of approximately $2.5 million made it an even bigger gamble. Accordingly, Mayer assigned Mervyn LeRoy to oversee the project, with Freed acting as associate producer.

In the first of his several attempts to find someone to fill Thalberg's shoes, Mayer had lured Mervyn LeRoy away from Warner Bros. in 1937. A top-flight director with a reputation for being able to handle any genre—from gangster movies and social dramas to musicals and comedies—LeRoy had previously directed two pictures for MGM in the early thirties, including *Tugboat Annie*, which became the studio's most profitable picture of 1933. Now at MGM, LeRoy was paid an incredible salary of $6,000 a week (twice the

TOP: *An early script of* The Wizard of Oz *includes a sequence in which Dorothy slides to safety on a rainbow. The sequence is never developed beyond this artist's conceptual rendering.*

ABOVE: *Garland performs "Over the Rainbow," the number that will become her lifelong signature song.*

BELOW: *A "Daily Music Report," dated 10/7/38, shows that Judy Garland made eight prerecordings of various lengths for "Over the Rainbow," six of which were printed.*

◆ *Gone with the Wind* wins eight Academy Awards out of the twelve categories for which it is nominated, and receives two special awards.

◆ For MGM, 1939 is the golden year. In addition to *Gone with the Wind*, MGM releases *The Wizard of Oz*, *Babes in Arms*, *The Marx Brothers at the Circus*, and *The Women*, starring Joan Crawford, Norma Shearer, Rosalind Russell, Mary Boland, Joan Fontaine, and Paulette Goddard.

◆ Garbo sings, Garbo dances, and Garbo laughs in *Ninotchka*, her twenty-third film for MGM.

◆ It takes three weeks for studio technicians to create the snow for *Goodbye, Mr. Chips*, which is filmed in England. As the snow scenes go into the can, one of the worst blizzards in years comes down outside the sound stages.

◆ Clark Gable signs a new seven-year contract. In the previous seven years, he's made twenty-five films for MGM.

◆ Hedy Lamarr makes her MGM debut in *Lady of the Tropics*.

The reigning queen of MGM, Norma Shearer, presents the reigning prince, Mickey Rooney, with the gift of her portable dressing room. Inside, Rooney gazes at her photograph.

amount Mayer earned, not counting stock options and bonuses). In return, MGM expected LeRoy to guide the selection of story material and to take control of the most important productions.

In the role of Dorothy, Freed and Roger Edens envisioned their new protégée, Judy Garland. The head office in New York, already concerned about the budget, preferred an established star. Mayer tried to get 20th Century-Fox to loan out their top box-office draw of recent years, Shirley Temple. When that failed, an attempt was supposedly made to bring back Deanna Durbin from Universal. As so often happened in Hollywood, Judy Garland got the role of her life by default.

Freed's first choices for the cast included W. C. Fields as the Wizard; Edna May Oliver as the Wicked Witch; Fanny Brice as her counterpart, the Good Witch of the North; Ray Bolger as the Tin Man; and Buddy Ebsen as the Scarecrow. In fact, only the last two actors were cast, but they appeared in reversed roles.

Originally, a trained animal was considered for the part of the Cowardly Lion, with an actor providing the off-camera voice, but lyricist Yip Harburg enthusiastically recommended Bert Lahr, having worked with Lahr on Broadway. One hundred and twenty-four Munchkins were promised by Baron Leo Singer, an Austro-Hungarian vaudeville impresario who specialized in booking midget acts, a major vaudeville attraction in Loew's theaters and other circuits in the twenties. Even Singer, though, did not have enough small people to make up the army of Munchkins, so Major Doyle, another agent, rounded up the rest.

Freed had talked to his close friend Jerome Kern about writing the score but then decided to hire Harburg and composer Harold Arlen, whose Broadway musical comedy *Hooray For What!* had impressed Freed. (He also made note of the play's director, Vincente Minnelli). More than a dozen writers worked on the *Oz* screenplay, including the whimsical Ogden Nash. The final version credited

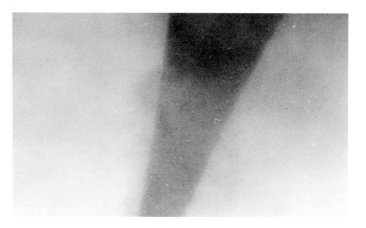

OPPOSITE:

TOP LEFT: *A miniature model of the Kansas farm set is used for long shots. Here, the tornado is seen approaching just to the right of the house.*

BOTTOM: *A canvas cone becomes a tornado.*

ABOVE: *Bert Lahr, Jack Haley, Charley Grapewin, Ray Bolger, and Clara Blandick head for the cellar as the tornado approaches.*

RIGHT: *A page from the "Cyclone" conductor's score, arranged by Herbert Stothart, George Bassman, and George Stoll.*

171

THE CREATION OF A FANTASY

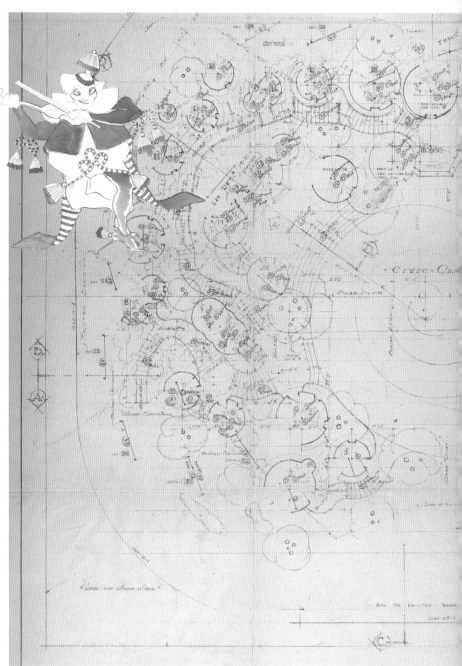

I n early 1938, producer Mervyn LeRoy and Arthur Freed set about adapting a story by children's book author L. Frank Baum as a vehicle for MGM's rising young star Judy Garland. The challenge was to create a total illusion using live actors and real sets. Art director Cedric Gibbons, along with William Horning, Jack Martin Smith, and their team of designers, sketch artists, draftsmen, carpenters, and special-effects artists, brought to life Baum's fantasy world, first, through conceptual renderings, storyboards, and blueprints; then, actual sets and matte paintings; and, finally, an array of special effects.

Artisans worked around the clock. Some sixty sets were designed and redesigned, built and rebuilt, utilizing half a dozen stages for over six months. The art department was responsible for creating such unique props and set decorations as a witch's gargoyled hourglass and moving, talking trees. Yards of painted muslin became backdrops for Munchkinland, a haunted forest, and various Emerald City locales. Costumes and sets were lit with banks of brutally hot lights and filmed in relatively early three-strip Technicolor. A. Arnold Gillespie set about creating a tornado, flying monkeys, a good witch's traveling bubble, and a melting wicked witch. Matte paintings were combined with live shots in a process created by Warren Newcombe, creating illusions such as a distant Oz, the borders of Munchkinland, and a Kansas prairie.

Between the Depression and the impending war, Hollywood enjoyed a brief but truly golden time, which was highlighted by Garland singing "Over the Rainbow." Since its premiere in August 1939, *The Wizard of Oz* has become one of the world's greatest classics.

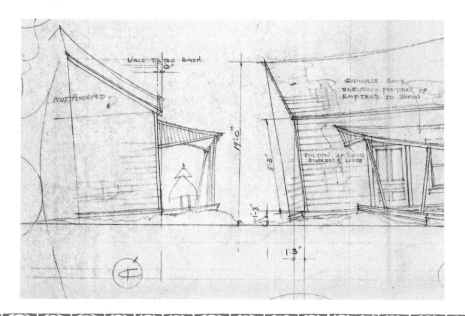

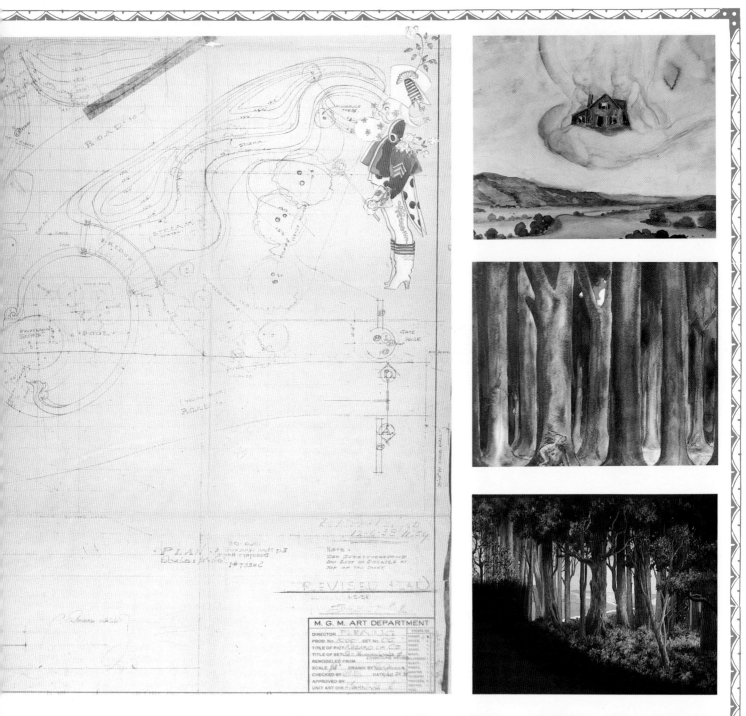

OPPOSITE:
TOP LEFT: *A rare test frame of Munchkinland.*
BOTTOM: *A blueprint detail of the house after crashing.*

ABOVE: *The blueprint for Munchkinland. Although built to quarter scale, it is the largest set in the film. In the top corners are Adrian's watercolor designs for two Munchkins.*

FROM TOP RIGHT: *Two conceptual renderings and a matte painting.*
RIGHT: *The finished set for the edge of Munchkinland.*

M. G. M. ART DEPARTMENT

173

255 FLEMING - EXT. POPPY FIELD
STAND-6 ET
HOLE — 30

TOP LEFT AND CENTER: *A matte painting for the Emerald City, executed with pastel crayon on black board, has tiny holes in the columns which allow light to pass through and create the twinkling effect seen in the film.*

FAR LEFT: *The steps leading to the Wizard's chamber.*

LEFT: *The stars' stand-ins wait in the carriage as the set is prepared for the ride through Oz.*

ABOVE: *A concept not used for the exterior of the Emerald City. The rounded column motif is incorporated into the final design.*

RIGHT: *Another section of the extravagant set.*

FAR RIGHT: *The beauty parlor where the Cowardly Lion has his mane permed.*

ABOVE: *In the climactic show-down of* The Women *(1939), Mary Haines (Norma Shearer), her claws sharpened with "Jungle Red" polish, is ready to get back her man from tigress Crystal Allen (Joan Crawford). (Left to right) Phyllis Povah, Paulette Goddard, Crawford, Rosalind Russell, Shearer, Mary Boland, and Florence Nash.*

LEFT: *(Bottom left to right) Norma Shearer, Rosalind Russell, director George Cukor, producer Hunt Stromberg, and Paulette Goddard; (top left to right) Joan Crawford, Joan Fontaine, Mary Boland, Phyllis Povah, and Florence Nash.*
OPPOSITE: *A theater brochure for* The Women.

three screenwriters: Noel Langley, Florence Ryerson, and Edgar Allan Woolf.

Following almost a year of preproduction, after which Freed turned his attention to *Babes in Arms*, filming of *Oz* began in October 1938. So did the problems. One director followed another. Norman Taurog, the first, never actually filmed any footage, except the Technicolor tests. Then Richard Thorpe was removed after LeRoy decided he lacked the appropriate touch for the fantasy. During his one week of service, George Cukor managed to refine Garland's appearance as Dorothy as well as that of Bolger's Scarecrow, Then, Victor Fleming came aboard and scrapped everything that had already been shot.

Buddy Ebsen, whose lungs gave out temporarily in reaction to the aluminum powder used in his Tin Man makeup, had to be replaced. LeRoy brought in Jack Haley, which meant that all the solos sung by Ebsen had to be rerecorded. Then Judy Garland caught a cold, and her absence, alone, added one hundred fifty thousand dollars to the budget. Some of the flying monkeys crash-landed when their wires snapped. Margaret Hamilton, the actress who played the Wicked Witch, suffered severe burns when a fire effect was set off prematurely. Betty Danko, her stand-in, was also injured when the broom used in the skywriting sequence exploded. Even the cairn terrier playing Toto was out of action for several days after someone stepped on her.

In February 1939, Fleming left the production to replace George Cukor, once again, this time as director of *Gone with the Wind*, which was being produced independently by David O. Selznick. Although Fleming got the final credit for directing *Oz*, it was veteran King Vidor who stepped in and shot many of the sepia-tinted sequences in Kansas, including "Over the Rainbow." The movie's signature song almost did not make the final print. Sam Katz, executive producer of the musical division, declared that the score was "above the heads of children," while others worried that nobody would hum the tune or buy the sheet music, or else that its inclusion would make the picture too long. Freed insisted on keeping the song, which became a classic. It won an Oscar for best song; in fact, the highlight of the 1940 award ceremonies was Garland's rendition of it, which she sang after accepting her own special Oscar for outstanding performance as a screen juvenile.

The Wizard of Oz opened in the middle of August 1939, by which time the whole country, bombarded by an unprecedented publicity campaign, had been "Ozified." At Loew's Capitol Theater on Broadway, Judy Garland, along with Mickey Rooney, appeared between showings of the film and did a twenty-six-minute song-and-dance routine, with encores that sometimes stretched to forty minutes. A wide variety of toys, dolls, and dresses tied in to the movie flooded the marketplace. Despite an excellent reception at the box office, *Oz* failed to score a profit until its first rerelease almost ten years later. It then became a national icon after its licensing to CBS in 1956. Each television broadcast of the film added millions of new fans and made *Oz* the most watched movie in history.

While *Oz*'s huge production costs limited its profitability, MGM's lower-budget fare brought in tons of cash. Within two months of its opening, receipts from *Oz* were eclipsed

THE WIZARDS OF STYLE

"The MGM Look" meant splendor in all things—cinematography, costumes, and sets. And the man who dressed most of MGM's most glamorous stars—Garbo, Crawford, Shearer, and MacDonald—was the brilliant designer Gilbert Adrian.

In 1930, his first films for MGM—*Madame Satan* and *Our Blushing Brides*—demonstrated his theatrical imagination. A cubist with a passion for straight lines and big, startling details, Adrian often contrasted black against white, which carried the maximum impact on monochromatic film. His most extreme ideas were reserved for Joan Crawford. To downplay her hips, Adrian broadened her shoulders by designing a dress with enormous ruffled sleeves for her role in *Letty Lynton* (1932). It created a sensation among retail manufacturers. The following year, in the film *Today We Live,* he dramatically squared Crawford's shoulders. Although the look had already appeared in Paris collections, it was Adrian's creations for the star that sold the idea to the world.

When designing Garbo's wardrobe for *Mata Hari* (1931) and *Queen Christina* (1934), Adrian capitalized on her androgynous looks and square waistline. He then transformed her angular qualities, by using softer shades and shapes, into a more romantic look that suited the heroines of *Anna Karenina* (1935) and *Camille* (1937). He de-emphasized her broad shoulders with detailing on the fabric around her wrists and throat.

Adrian made news by dressing Norma

TOP LEFT: *Gilbert Adrian.*
TOP: *In* Letty Linton *(1932), Adrian creates the large-shoulder look for Joan Crawford.*
LEFT AND ABOVE: *Greta Garbo as* Mata Hari *(1931) and Adrian's sketch for the dress she wears.*
OPPOSITE TOP: *Garbo and Ramon Novarro in* Mata Hari.

Shearer in a light suit with a dark blouse in *The Divorcée* (1930). The lavish budgets accorded to Shearer's *Romeo and Juliet* (1936) and *Marie Antoinette* (1938) gave him fabulous opportunities to display his flights of fantasy. Perhaps the best examples of his imaginative genius can be found in the costumes for *The Wizard of Oz* (1939). His two other Technicolor works of the same period (*Sweethearts*, 1938, and the fashion show in *The Women*, 1939), plus the couture work he did after leaving MGM, showed his more sophisticated side.

The designer, who was friendly with most of the MGM stars, was also known for his sense of humor. Learning that Crawford was soon to divorce her second husband, he cracked, "Well, she'll be footloose and Franchot-free!" While he worked quickly and was amazingly prolific, he did not design everything worn at MGM in the thirties. Gile Steel did most of the period men's wardrobe, and Dolly Tree worked on the less important films. Myrna Loy, who liked subtle clothes, requested Tree after being outfitted in several films by Adrian, and Tree sometimes designed for Jean Harlow.

The new decade of the forties brought many changes to MGM. Garbo, Shearer, Crawford, and MacDonald had all left by 1942. The studio halted production of lavish historical films, and as producers and directors became more involved in costume design, Adrian lost much of his autonomy. His wife, Janet Gaynor, had given up her acting career after they married, and when Adrian's contract expired in 1941, he also retired.

For most of the 1940s, the elegant couturier Irene contributed smart fashions to such films as *Weekend at the Waldorf* (1945), *B. F.'s Daughter* (1948), and *Easter Parade* (1948). Her friend and colleague Walter Plunkett specialized in period pictures, most notably *Green Dolphin Street* (1947) and *The Three Musketeers* (1948). Against Irene's wishes, Louis B. Mayer hired Helen Rose away from 20th Century-Fox specifically to design for the musicals. After Irene's departure, however, Rose did most of the modern-dress pictures, too.

Both Plunkett and Rose loved working with Vincente Minnelli, who had once designed costumes. Said Plunkett, "Minnelli is the most demanding perfectionist, but I get along with him very well. If there's something exquisite around the hem of the skirt, tell him and he'll have her sit some way so that it shows." Rose's designs for Minnelli's *The Bad and the Beautiful* won the Academy Award for Black and White Costumes in 1952. Arthur Freed occasionally asked the celebrated theatrical designer Irene Sharaff to work on specific projects, including *Meet Me in St. Louis* (1944), the ballet in *An American in Paris* (1951), and *Brigadoon* (1954).

Rose made big news in retail fashion with the V-necked white chiffon gown she designed for Elizabeth Taylor in *Cat on a Hot Tin Roof* in 1958, but declining studio production meant that there was not much demand for her work in the next five years. Plunkett left the studio in 1963, saddened that he had been asked to pinch pennies on the epic *How the West Was Won*. Finally, in 1969, MGM held an auction and the splendid gowns were all sold.

ABOVE: *An Adrian design for Marion Davies.*

179

NELLY - CHANGE #14
1940 - 17 yrs.
INT. POLICE BALL

ABOVE AND TOP RIGHT: *A white party dress for the police ball of* Little Nellie Kelly *(1940), as worn by Judy Garland and designed by Dolly Tree.*
RIGHT CENTER: *Dolly Tree's white negligee design for Jean Harlow in* Libeled Lady *(1936).*
RIGHT: *A hat designed by Adrian for Rosalind Russell in* The Women *(1939).*
FAR RIGHT: *Lana Turner discusses designs with Irene for* Slightly Dangerous *(1943).*

OPPOSITE: *Joan Crawford is the* Dancing Lady *(1933) in Adrian's chiffon and sequin gown.*

by those of films such as *Babes in Arms* and *Andy Hardy Gets Spring Fever*, both featuring Mickey Rooney. By the end of the thirties, it seemed clear to Mayer that MGM was gaining as much, if not more, from creating and distributing its formula pictures or series as from its superspecials or big-budget musicals, which in the previous two seasons had included the huge but not so profitable *Marie Antoinette* and *The Great Waltz*. The change in production attitude was so profound that the most prestigious picture of the time, *Gone with the Wind*, might not have had anything to do with MGM if David O. Selznick had not needed Clark Gable so badly to play Rhett Butler.

Several studios, including MGM, had turned down the screen rights to Margaret Mitchell's novel, both before and after it became a phenomenal best seller. There are at least two versions of why MGM rejected it: "Forget it, Louis," Thalberg is supposed to have told Mayer, "no Civil War picture ever made a nickel." Albert Lewin recalled bringing his chief a lengthy synopsis of the novel in the summer of 1936, at which point Selznick was trying to close a deal for the rights and thought MGM might be interested. Thalberg responded that he was too tired to burn Atlanta; within weeks the producer was dead. Selznick had also felt apprehensive about the scope of the thousand-page saga, but he bought the rights to the book after Jock Whitney, the main investor in Selznick International Pictures, pressured him to do so.

LEFT: *Vivien Leigh, as Scarlett O'Hara, attends the Wilkes plantation barbecue in David O. Selznick's* Gone with the Wind *(1939).*

ABOVE: *Scarlett realizes the wastefulness of war as she makes her way through a sea of wounded soldiers to the train depot to locate Dr. Meade.*

183

While the overwhelming tide of opinion, registered inside the film colony and through a write-in campaign from the fans, pointed to Clark Gable as the only possible actor to play Rhett Butler, it seemed far from inevitable at first. Ronald Colman showed enough interest to begin studying a southern accent. Errol Flynn and Gary Cooper were being mentioned as other possibilities. Gable himself remained cool, voicing his characteristic reservations. "People didn't just read that novel," he recalled to a reporter in the fifties, "they lived it. They formed passionate convictions about its characters. . . . They had a preconceived idea of the kind of Rhett Butler they were going to see. . . . Suppose I don't come up with what they already have me doing. Then I'm in trouble."

As an independent producer, Selznick had few actors under contract, which was both an advantage and a weakness. He could go after whomever he wanted, but there would be strings attached. Warner Bros., for example, had offered him an attractive package that included Errol Flynn, Bette Davis, and Olivia de Havilland, but the studio wanted distribution rights in return. Selznick, however, was under exclusive contract to distribute through United Artists. *And* he still wanted Gable.

Louis Mayer, whose offer to buy the production outright in May 1938 Selznick had turned down, now pressed his advantage. He exacted a deal a few months later to distribute the picture, following the expiration of Selznick's contract with United Artists, in exchange for $1,250,000 and the services of Clark Gable. MGM would keep half the profits, after deducting fifteen cents from every dollar of income to cover distribution costs. Selznick would benefit not only because of Gable's appearance in the film but also because of the relationship with MGM, which would allow him to use many of the studio's best production people, including directors and cameramen. After all, *Gone with the Wind* was the kind of film that in a different day could have been produced only by MGM.

Gone with the Wind quickly became the most successful film in history, grossing some $13.5 million in its first year. (By comparison, the top seven studios made combined profits of just over $19 million in 1939, with the lion's share—50 percent—reaped by MGM.) In a creative approach to distribution, the studio instituted a new fee schedule, charging exhibitors an unprecedented 70 percent of their box-office take, while guaranteeing them a minimum 10 percent profit. Five years later, Mayer bought out Selznick's share. MGM continued to make money from *Gone with the Wind* until the sale of the studio's film library many decades later.

Gone with the Wind virtually swept the Academy Awards for 1939, winning eight out of the twelve categories in which it had been nominated. MGM, which had produced four of the ten pictures nominated for best picture, also picked up two Oscars for *The Wizard of Oz* as well as

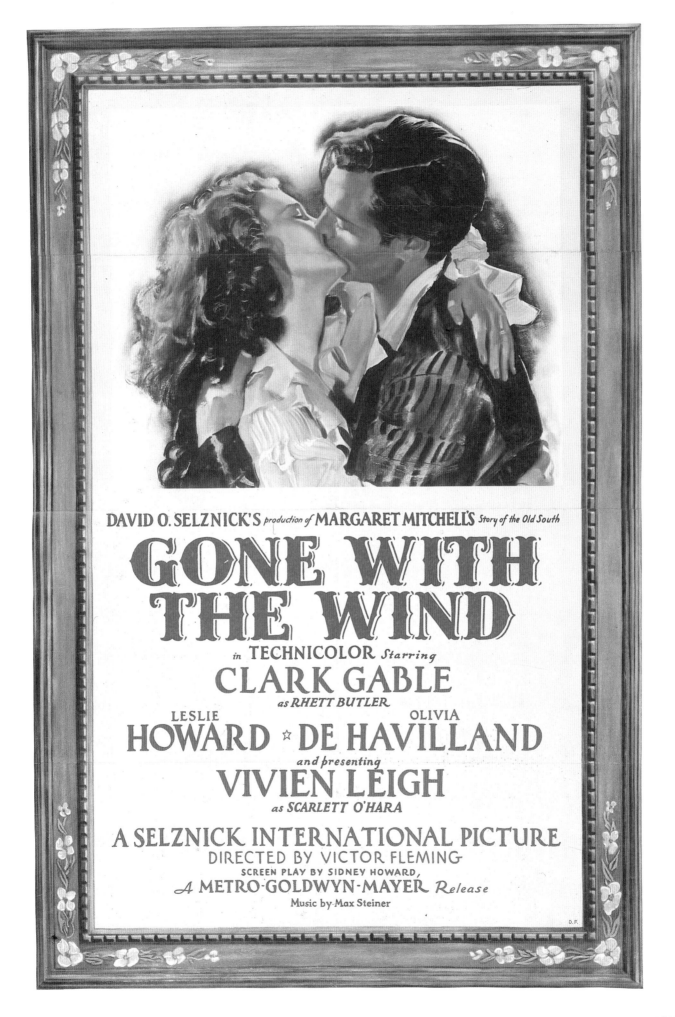

THE ART OF ART DIRECTION

ABOVE: *A miniature model of the* Romeo and Juliet *(1936) Verona Square set.*
RIGHT: *Property head Edwin Willis, Cedric Gibbons, and Gibbons's assistant Fred Hope survey the blueprint to the set.*

OPPOSITE: *Under the direction of Cedric Gibbons, the MGM art department executed exquisite sets in a variety of styles. (Clockwise from top) A weekend fishing cottage for heiress Myrna Loy to entertain reporter William Powell in* Libeled Lady *(1936); the stairs in* Ninotchka *(1939) that Garbo and Melvyn Douglas climb while rear projected images give the impression they are on the Eiffel Tower; the art deco bar for* Grand Hotel *(1932); the country home of socialite Norma Shearer in* The Women *(1939); and the elevator lobby to Clark Gable's office in* Wife Vs. Secretary *(1936).*

The first thirty years in the history of MGM saw the rise and demise of many stars, directors, and producers. Only one man was untouched by the winds of change: supervising art director Cedric Gibbons.

When MGM was formed in 1924, Gibbons already had a decade in art direction behind him. It is impossible to determine the extent of what Gibbons personally designed, but his influence was pervasive. He nurtured the talents of many of the finest designers in Hollywood, and coordinated the thousands of details woven into the imagery of each film. He was a brilliant executive, an attribute that inspired the confidence of studio heads as well as of the hundreds of people he supervised: set decorators, scenic artists, prop-persons, draftspersons, carpenters, plasterers, miniature and effects specialists, researchers, and historical consultants. The unit art directors Gibbons trained—including Merrill Pye, Paul Groesse, William Horning, Preston Ames, Randall Duell, and Jack Martin Smith—were loyal to their mentor, who, in turn, defended them in conferences with producers and directors. The accomplishments of the entire department proved that quality need not be sacrificed in the mass production of movies.

Despite Gibbons's belief in Louis B. Mayer's philosophy of making beautiful movies about beautiful people, it would be unfair to ignore the versatility of his department. After all, MGM had both Andy Hardy *and* Norma Shearer; treehouses for Tarzan as well as penthouses for Garbo; and thrillers and gangster yarns, which exposed the tawdry glitter of urban life. When Joan Crawford rose from poverty in films such as *Possessed* (1931) and *Mannequin* (1938); the dinginess of her origins was not minimized. Of course, it was the luxury of Crawford's new surroundings that the customers paid to see—and that Gibbons and company embellished into sublime fantasy. At MGM, rich meant *very*

rich. *Our Dancing Daughters* (1928), which was designed by Richard Day under Gibbons's guidance, typified the unabashed opulence that became the hallmark of the studio. This film also showed the influence of Gibbons's visit in 1925 to the Paris Exposition des Arts Décoratifs, the event that launched art deco. From the late twenties through most of the thirties, Gibbons gave glamorous MGM stars sleek, modern habitats, spacious and white. The blondeness of satin-clad Jean Harlow in *Dinner at Eight* (1933) is glorified by the dizzying whiteness of her bedroom, one of the most famous sets in Hollywood history.

Gibbons assembled a magnificent research library for elaborate historical reconstructions, such as those in *David Copperfield* (1935) and *Green Dolphin Street* (1947), but authenticity was less important than visual liveliness. Details were never allowed to overwhelm the characters; on the contrary, the scale was exaggerated to give characters greater freedom of movement. The real-life Versailles seems cramped when compared to the version in *Marie Antoinette* (1938). Gibbons and his associates excelled even when there was no documentation or reality upon which to draw. Generations have perceived a genuine emotional reality in the alternative worlds of *The Wizard of Oz* (1939) and *Forbidden Planet* (1956). Likewise, the fantastic environments for such musical numbers as the "Broadway Ballet" in *Singin' in the Rain* (1952) are etched on the consciousness of millions.

Like Walt Disney, Gibbons did not have to lift a pen in order to be a creative force. If it was up on the screen, it was because Gibbons approved it. His name appeared on virtually every American-made MGM film produced before his retirement in 1956. The man who designed the Academy Award statuette won eleven of his own in the course of his career.

The third film made at MGM's Denham studio in England is Goodbye, Mr. Chips *(1939), based on James Hilton's story about a schoolmaster who discovers love in middle age. It marks Greer Garson's debut and wins Robert Donat an Oscar for best actor.*

TOP LEFT: *The young Chips (Donat) arrives to take his teaching post.*

TOP RIGHT: *A middle-aged Chips with his pupils.*

ABOVE: *Donat and Garson in a publicity still.*

one for best actor, which went to Englishman Robert Donat for his title role in *Goodbye, Mr. Chips*, made at MGM's Denham studio in Great Britain and the last of the overseas productions that MGM mounted before the outbreak of World War II.

Loew's Incorporated had set up a presence in England mainly to battle the quota imposed on the exhibition of foreign films. It seemed a natural and attractive choice to supply England, and the rest of the English-speaking world, from a London-based studio with authentic films that combined MGM's production expertise with England's fine acting traditions. Michael Balcon, an English producer, was hired to oversee production at Denham, but Mayer intended to retain overall control by choosing properties and supplying MGM directors and many of his top stars.

Accordingly, *A Yank at Oxford*, the first MGM picture to emerge from Denham, showcased fewer British actors than could be found sitting around a single table at the MGM commissary in Culver City. Mayer shipped over director Jack Conway, along with Lionel Barrymore, Maureen O'Sullivan, and Robert Taylor, who played the principal role of an American like a bullock in ye olde china shoppe. Yanks also played many of the subsidiary parts. But when Balcon hired an up-and-coming English actress, whom Mayer had not heard of, to play the second female lead, he was severely reprimanded. Vivien Leigh's next role would be that of Scarlett O'Hara.

A film that reflected stronger Anglo-American cooperation was *The Citadel*, based on the best-selling novel by A. J. Cronin. It starred Robert Donat and MGM contract player Rosalind Russell. Victor Saville, who replaced Balcon as pro-

ABOVE: *Robert Donat and Rosalind Russell in* The Citadel *(1938), based on A. J. Cronin's story of an unscrupulous doctor.*

duction chief, also hired a number of fine English actors to round out the cast, among them Ralph Richardson, Rex Harrison, Emlyn Williams, and Cecil Parker. Donat's next major role was that of the beloved schoolmaster in the movie version of James Hilton's sentimental novel *Goodbye, Mr. Chips*.

As the Nazis moved into Austria, the Low Countries, France, and finally the rest of Europe, Loew's lost control over its European theaters and distribution channels. Surprisingly, the company managed to maintain a presence in Germany until the summer of 1940, but it came at a cost. Jewish-sounding names were frequently removed from the credits of films. Back in 1938, Mayer's concern over the potential loss of the German market had led him to invite a representative of the Third Reich from the Los Angeles consulate to a screening of *Three Comrades*, a film that was based on Erich Maria Remarque's novel about the tensions of Weimar politics leading to Hitler's rise to power. The official wanted to change the story's anti-Nazi bias, but producer Joseph Mankiewicz refused and was backed up by Mayer.

The fall of France, in June 1940, provided the strongest indication to Americans that Hitler would become more than a regional bully. This defeat led immediately to the establishment of the Motion Picture Committee Cooperating for National Defense, the first of several efforts by the industry to provide factual films, mainly shorts, to inform, inspire, and exhort within the boundaries of America's professed neutrality. MGM quickly produced a number of pictures with timely themes—*Flight Command*, *They Met in Bombay*, and Robert E. Sherwood's play

TOP: *Margaret Sullavan and Robert Young in* The Mortal Storm *(1940), MGM's first feature film to openly criticize Nazism. Frank Borzage directs a script based on Phyllis Bottome's novel about individuals separated by ideologies.*
ABOVE CENTER: *Vivien Leigh and Robert Taylor in* Waterloo Bridge *(1940), based on Robert Sherwood's tragic-romantic play set in World War I England.*
ABOVE: *In* The Shop Around the Corner *(1940), Margaret Sullavan and James Stewart play two feuding employees who discover they are each other's secret penpals. Ernst Lubitsch directs.*

1940

◆ MGM releases *The Philadelphia Story*, bringing Katharine Hepburn sweet revenge. Two years before, she'd been called "box-office poison" and chased from Hollywood. She found success again on Broadway in *The Philadelphia Story*, bought the screen rights, got MGM to gamble, and everybody won. MGM had a huge hit. Jimmy Stewart won his only Oscar. Hepburn won a long-term contract with star terms and privileges. Cary Grant insisted on and got top billing and top pay, then donated his entire fee of $125,000 to the British War Relief Fund.

◆ Original screenplay category is added to the Academy Awards.

◆ MGM starts a nationwide search for Jody in *The Yearling*.

◆ Hepburn asks for *Woman of the Year* as her next film; and as her costar, an actor she greatly admires but hasn't met: Spencer Tracy.

◆ William Powell elopes with actress Diana Lewis after a three-week romance.

◆ Lana Turner elopes with bandleader Artie Shaw.

◆ The war in Europe closes eleven countries to English-language films. Movie profits dive, and MGM loses $1 million but is still at the top of the industry.

Strange Cargo *opens at the Capitol Theater in New York. It is the last of eight films to team Clark Gable and Joan Crawford.*

189

1941

- Pearl Harbor is attacked on December 7. The United States enters World War II.

- Hepburn and Tracy meet on the set of *Woman of the Year* and become lovers until his death parts them in 1967.

- Tracy waltzes and Bergman sings in *Dr. Jekyll and Mr. Hyde*. Both firsts.

- Greta Garbo appears in a bathing suit in her final movie, *A Two-Faced Woman*. It fails. She's thirty-six when she retires, having made twenty-four movies for MGM, her only Hollywood studio.

- In *Love Crazy*, Powell switches from Thin Man to crazy man, playing a husband who pretends insanity to keep his wife (Myrna Loy) from divorcing him. A smash.

- *Life Begins for Andy Hardy* is the eleventh in the series and the biggest one yet. It's the third and last for Judy Garland. She and Mickey will be together again in *Babes on Broadway* and *Girl Crazy*.

- Mickey Rooney leads box-office receipts for the third year in a row.

- MGM makes $11 million in profits, more than any other studio.

Judy Garland plays with Chou Chou, her pet poodle, in her dressing room for Life Begins for Andy Hardy.

ABOVE AND RIGHT: Modern Screen *and* Photoplay *cover the many film stars who volunteer to fight in World War II, including MGM's Clark Gable, Robert Montgomery, and James Stewart, among others.*

OPPOSITE: *With the world at war, MGM keeps spirits up with lavish musicals such as* Ziegfeld Girl *(1941). The Follies girls and stars shown in this magazine spread are (left to right) Georgia Carroll, Alaine Brandeis, Nina Bissell, Lana Turner, Judy Garland, Hedy Lamarr, Irma Wilson, and Virginia Cruzon.*

Waterloo Bridge—but these were principally vehicles for stars Robert Taylor, Clark Gable, Rosalind Russell, and Vivien Leigh. Films such as *The Mortal Storm* and *Escape*, however, made strong comments on the more tragic effects of Nazism. The release of *The Mortal Storm*, the story of a German family cruelly torn apart by Hitler's fascist ideology, was the principal reason behind Joseph Goebbels's decision to shut down Loew's Berlin branch in 1940.

In contrast to the somber dramas and spy thrillers dealing with the war overseas, *The Bugle Sounds*, with Wallace Beery, took a humorous look at the armored divisions of the U.S. Army during peacetime maneuvers. It highlighted the new high-tech equipment of the period: tanks, dive bombers, and jeeps. "In one scene," reported *Lion's Roar*, MGM's lavish in-house magazine, "with several thousand soldiers as hilarious witnesses, Beery eluded twenty tanks in a mad escape across the rutted ground. He dropped a suitcase, scattering laundry to be pressed by the careening steel fortresses, and when one of them passed him by a matter of inches, he lost his coat."

When America entered the war, such hilarity would disappear from MGM's films. Following the bombing of Pearl Harbor, such established stars as Robert Montgomery, Robert Taylor, Clark Gable, James Stewart, and director Woody Van Dyke would leave to join the war effort. Despite his patriotism, Mayer tried to get several of his employees deferred or at least given frequent leaves from training to finish projects in progress. However, he did fire Lew Ayres,

who as a conscientious objector refused to fight, declaring, "I'll praise the Lord, but I'll be damned if I'll pass the ammunition." Rather than replace him as the popular Dr. Kildare in the continuing series, the writers simply shifted the focus to Dr. Gillespie.

While it was primarily the male stars who went off to war, certain actresses also interrupted their careers, notably Myrna Loy, who took a leave of absence to work for the Red Cross. MGM briefly played with the idea of replacing her as Nora Charles but then decided to suspend the series instead. In 1944, Loy returned to costar with William Powell again in *The Thin Man Goes Home*, and then made her series swan song in *The Song of the Thin Man* in 1947.

Even with the MGM family of stars breaking up and going off to war, the studio's approach to war-related films focused mainly on the families at home rather than on the soldiers in battle. One such eloquent production was *The Human Comedy*, in which Mickey Rooney, playing a telegraph messenger who brings messages of death from the War Department to loved ones at home, gave one of his finest dramatic performances. Another was *Mrs. Miniver*, which depicted a thoroughly decent English couple suffering through the London blitz. The film was calculated to engender sympathy for the isolated island nation, fighting alone, though by the time it was released in the summer of 1942, America had also become enmeshed in the war. President Roosevelt was so impressed by the film's propaganda value that, in addition to requesting its hurried

release, he had millions of leaflets containing the vicar's speech from the end of the film scattered over occupied Europe by Allied warplanes.

Mrs. Miniver became the most popular film made in 1942, capturing seven Oscars; it also gave MGM a new leading lady in the person of Greer Garson. Mayer had discovered her five years earlier during a trip to London. He had gone to see a dramatic play called *Old Music* one evening and was deeply impressed by the red-headed, green-eyed actress with an aristocratic bearing. Mayer quickly signed her to a contract. It was at a time when films based on English subjects, both classic and contemporary, were popular, and MGM was just setting up its operations in Britain. For her first MGM film, Garson returned to England to play Mrs. Chips, the wife of James Hilton's idealized schoolmaster. Then, for MGM's version of Helen Jerome's stage adaptation of *Pride and Prejudice*, Garson was given the role of Elizabeth Bennett over Vivien Leigh, who was desperate to play opposite Laurence Olivier.

Garson almost didn't play Mrs. Miniver, her greatest role. First, it was offered to Norma Shearer, but Thalberg's widow felt she was too young at thirty-nine to be cast as a mother with a grown son. Garson accepted the part, even though she was equally opposed at first. She anxiously pressed director William Wyler about whether she should age herself with makeup. (Ironically, during the making of the picture, she was to fall in love with Richard Ney, the twenty-four-year-old actor playing her son; under pressure

ON THE
HOME FRONT

Sunlight streams through the shattered roof of a country church. There are empty places in the pews where, only a few weeks earlier, parishioners had sat—the local stationmaster, a choirboy, the young daughter-in-law of a much loved family. They are gone now, dead from the bullets or the bombs of an enemy they didn't know, in a war they hardly understood.

Framed by the wreckage of his church, the vicar delivers a ringing sermon: "Why, in all conscience, should these be the ones to suffer? I shall tell you why! Because this is not only a war of soldiers in uniform. It is a war of the people—of all people—and it must be fought not only on the battlefield but in the cities and in the villages, in the factories and on the farms, in the home and in the heart of every man, woman, and child who loves freedom....This is a people's war! It is our war! We are the fighters!"

The camera pans upward, through the sundered roof of the church. "Onward Christian Soldiers" rises on the soundtrack as British fighter planes—like a gathering flock of graceful birds—wing overhead, toward the enemy.

So ends *Mrs. Miniver*, MGM's most popular and award-winning film of World War II. Moviegoers around the world thrilled to it, and with good cause. MGM was at its best during the war years, making movies to build the morale of fighting men and women, and the families awaiting their return.

It was a time of pure patriotism, the fan club, the screen magazine, and the star system. MGM's male stars traded costumes for khaki and marched off to war. Clark Gable, James Stewart, Robert Taylor, Gene Kelly, Jackie Cooper, Stewart Granger, Van Heflin, Robert Montgomery, and Robert Sterling all served in

the armed services. Other stars of both sexes went overseas to perform in USO shows; some washed dishes, served food, or danced with lonely GIs in the Hollywood Canteen. And still others traveled around the United States, selling war bonds by the thousands, sometimes quite creatively. MGM, for instance, conducted a "Tanks for Yanks" campaign that featured Johnny Sheffield, the "Boy" in the *Tarzan* series, touring the country and speaking, from the turret of a tank, about "A Boy's Place in America."

In another promotion, MGM conducted a contest in several cities to pick seven girls who were "...doing the most to promote the war effort on the home front." Their prizes were corsages and dinner with seven sailors, all paid for by MGM.

Meanwhile, back at the studio, the sound stages busily produced war-related short subjects, such as *National Defense*, a documentary honoring all of the Rosie the Riveters and Max the Mechanics in the country. One of Pete Smith's

TOP LEFT: *Judy Garland gives a studio tour to a marine.* ABOVE: *The Minivers (Greer Garson, Walter Pidgeon, Teresa Wright, and Richard Ney) survey the remains of their bombed-out home in* Mrs. Miniver *(1942).*

TOP LEFT: *(Left to right) Donna Reed, Mickey Rooney, Dorothy Morris, and Fay Bainter in* The Human Comedy *(1943), a film that focuses on the American home front and is said to have been Louis B. Mayer's favorite film.*

TOP RIGHT: *June Allyson works for the Red Cross.*

ABOVE RIGHT: *Enlistees Clark Gable and James Stewart chat in 1942.*

lighthearted short subjects, *Victory Vittles*, advised home-front housewives to make do with leftovers, while an intriguing series on the medieval prophet Nostradamus revealed his provocative predictions for the advent and end of the war. *Don't Talk* and *Mr. Blabbermouth* warned home-front warriors about the consequences of rumor-mongering and spilling war secrets to unsuspected spies.

For the young and the young-of-heart, the studio's cartoon department penned, among others, *The Blitz Wolf*, in which Adolph the cartoon wolf, who bore a "striking resemblance to Adolph the Phewrer," was ultimately defeated by the three little pigs of Pigmania—once they abandoned isolationism and fought together for the common good.

Still, MGM's most effective weapons were its stirring home-front feature films. "Motion pictures are of the utmost importance to…build up morale," said General Dwight Eisenhower in 1942, "…feature productions bring home their

country vividly to the memories of soldiers. Let's have more motion pictures!" And MGM obliged, with multistar musical extravaganzas such as *Thousands Cheer* (1943), family musicals such as *Meet Me in St. Louis* (1944), comedies such as *Swing Shift Maisie* (1943), and, most movingly, tributes to the family values the Allied forces were fighting to defend.

MGM's *Mrs. Miniver* gently dissolved class distinctions in England and celebrated the enduring power of the family—itself a miniature world at peace. Its American counterpart was *The Human Comedy* (1943), William Saroyan's semi-autobiographical story about the Macauley family of Ithaca, California. In his own, spun-glass way, Saroyan created a town and a family with whom practically every American could identify and sympathize.

The Macauleys are poor in terms of money but affluent in the abundant, boundless love they have for each other. Since his father is dead and brother Marcus (Van Johnson) is in the army, young Homer Macauley (Mickey Rooney) works at a postal telegraph office to support the family. At the beginning of the film, Homer is a boy; by its end, the war has made him a man, as it has the American soldiers overseas. The telegraph office where he works receives and delivers wires from the War Department announcing the deaths of sons on the battlefield. Inevitably, it receives the news of the death of Homer's brother Marcus. As Homer tries desperately to cope with his terrible loss, the voices of Marcus and his father—like the vicar's words in *Mrs. Miniver*—comfort him, and the theater audience, too: "You are what we're fighting the war for. You are what we have left behind—to live the hopes we only dreamed."

from the publicity department, they postponed getting married until *Mrs. Miniver* was safely launched.)

Years later, Norma Shearer would look back on her decision to turn down Mrs. Miniver as the second-greatest missed opportunity of her career, the first being the chance to play Scarlett O'Hara (if, indeed, Selznick had seriously wanted her for the part). Without Thalberg to guide her career, she served out her MGM contract in three ill-chosen, inconsequential comedies. After the dismal failure of the third, *Her Cardboard Lover*, the former leading lady of the MGM lot married a ski instructor twenty years her junior and retired from Hollywood.

Shearer was not the only star to leave MGM. In 1942, after appearing in *Cairo*, a low-budget spoof about spies, Jeanette MacDonald's contract was terminated. Her last costarring role with Nelson Eddy in *I Married an Angel* occurred that same year, but public tastes had shifted away from these oversweetened operatic musicals.

Greta Garbo's career had begun to stall even before the war. Although *Ninotchka* had been considered a success, it had been her first movie in two years, and she waited two more years before making another. But it was the studio's attempts to update and reshape her image that proved the most damaging. In *Two-Faced Woman*, made in 1941, she played a ski instructor who pretends to be her own twin sister in an attempt to rekindle her husband's sexual interest. *Time* magazine called the movie "almost as shocking as seeing your mother drunk." George Cukor, who directed the film, thought it was "lousy." He did not, however, believe that Garbo retired because of its poor reviews, but rather because she became so wary that she could never decide on a project again.

Around the same time, Joan Crawford, who had been at MGM for eighteen years and proved to be the hardest working of the great female stars, also left. Despite being

TOP: *Hunt Stromberg's sumptuous production of* Pride and Prejudice *(1940) is based on Helen Jerome's stage version of Jane Austen's novel. (Left to right) Heather Angel, Marsha Hunt, Edmund Gwenn, Greer Garson, Ann Rutherford, Maureen O'Sullivan, and (seated) Mary Boland.*

ABOVE: *Greta Garbo dances the rumba in the unsuccessful* Two-Faced Woman *(1941), her last film. It is an ill-suited role that attempts to "Americanize" her since the war makes it impossible for the studio to reap its usual European profits from a Garbo film.*

ABOVE: *Although Greer Garson is known for "legitimate" lady roles at MGM in 1943, she is still a popular star who must pose for glamour portraits.*

OPPOSITE: *Greer Garson and Ronald Colman in* Random Harvest *(1942). Mervyn LeRoy's production of James Hilton's novel is one of the most fondly remembered romances of all time.*

OPPOSITE:

TOP: *Directed by Mervyn LeRoy,* Johnny Eager *(1942) stars Robert Taylor as a big-time criminal and Lana Turner at her hottest and best.*

LEFT AND CENTER: *In* Ziegfeld Girl *(1941), Lana's attire for the "You Stepped out of a Dream" number is first made in the costume department, and then is worn by Lana as she prepares to shoot on the set .*

RIGHT: Dr. Jekyll and Mr. Hyde *(1941) stars (left to right) Lana, Spencer Tracy (as Jekyll), and Ingrid Bergman. Originally cast as saloon singer Ivy, Lana plays Jekyll's sweet fiancée after Bergman asks that the roles be switched.*

TOP LEFT AND RIGHT: *A portrait of sweater girl Lana at the time of* Ziegfeld Girl *(1941), the film that makes her a sex symbol. By 1943, Lana has become* Slightly Dangerous*.*

ABOVE: *Lana visits her mentor, director Mervyn LeRoy, on the set of his film* Thirty Seconds Over Tokyo *(1944). LeRoy had directed Turner in Warner Bros.'s* They Won't Forget *(1937) and brought her with him when he signed with MGM.*

White Cargo *(1942) presents Hedy Lamarr as Tondeleyo, a sultry native for whom "no man could find a cure." Here, Lamarr is seen with costar Richard Carlson. Censorship prevents the film adaptation from capturing all the steaminess of Leon Gordon's play from the 1920s.*

labeled "box-office poison," she had continued to play a variety of roles, intent on fighting an increasingly indifferent studio, in an effort to keep her career from declining. She appeared, against Mayer's advice, in *The Women*, a 1939 film version of Clare Boothe Luce's Broadway comedy about the machinations surrounding a wealthy woman's struggle to keep her husband from a conniving shopgirl. The movie brought Crawford together for the only time with Norma Shearer. She took advantage of this opportunity to demonstrate the resentment she had felt every time Thalberg had given his wife a juicy role. When George Cukor tried to rehearse Shearer's lines for the one scene that the two stars had together, Crawford sat furiously clicking away with her knitting needles. Finally, Cukor—who had to manage 134 other women in the all-female cast—asked Crawford to leave and to apologize to her costar (Crawford sent Shearer a telegram rather than abase herself in person). "I love to play bitches," she later acknowledged, "and she helped me in this part."

After *The Women*, Crawford appeared in another half dozen MGM films, including *Strange Cargo*, her eighth and last teaming with Gable. And once more disregarding Mayer's advice, she worked with Cukor again, this time in *A Woman's Face*, the remake of a Swedish film starring Ingrid Bergman. Playing a criminal with a disfigured face, she won some of the best reviews of her career. When Carole Lombard died in a plane crash in 1942, Crawford sought and won L. B. Mayer's permission to go over to Columbia and replace her in *They All Kissed the Bride*. When she returned to MGM, Crawford portrayed a Parisian fashion designer (the studio took the opportunity to show off some of Adrian's latest creations), surrounded by wartime intrigues, in Jules Dassin's *Reunion in France*. Crawford then took a honeymoon in Germany in *Above Suspicion*, as the bride of Fred MacMurray, who was improbably cast as an Oxford don spying for Britain. When Conrad Veidt, in the role of a German nobleman, gives Crawford a tour of medieval instruments designed to extract fingernails, she exclaims: "A totalitarian manicure!"

Over the years, Crawford had matured from an image-conscious star into a committed actress interested in strong, meaty parts. Rather than suffer the torture of seeing Mayer lavish his attention on newer, younger talent, she left the studio and accepted a financially low offer from the unglamorous Warner Bros. studio, which was having problems of its own with Bette Davis and Olivia de Havilland. There, under the talented direction of the Hungarian-born Michael Curtiz, who had made *Casablanca*, Crawford captured the prize that had eluded her all those years at MGM: an Oscar for her performance in *Mildred Pierce*.

If Greer Garson represented Louis B. Mayer's idealized view of womanhood, Hedy Lamarr, one of the great beauties of the age, held a more sensual appeal. When director Max Reinhardt introduced Hedwig Kiesler to him, Mayer was aware of the notoriety she had gained after appearing nude in the 1933 Czech film *Ecstasy*. Meeting her in London, four years later, Mayer did not hesitate to profess his disgust with the picture; nevertheless, he offered her a six-month contract but would not pay her travel expenses to California. Initially, Lamarr refused. On the advice of an American agent, however, she wrangled her way aboard the ship on which the Mayers were sailing from Southampton back to New York, disguised as a governess to a boy-violinist, Grisha Goluboff. By the time the ship reached New York, both she and Grisha had contracts with MGM. To erase any connection with her infamous past, Mayer renamed her Hedy Lamarr, allegedly on Mrs. Mayer's suggestion, and also perhaps because her great beauty reminded him of Barbara La Marr, an early Metro star.

OPPOSITE: *Hedy Lamarr on the cover of the January 1939 issue of* Photoplay. *This issue is famous for Sheila Graham's article, "Hollywood's Unmarried Husbands and Wives," which reveals that several unwed couples— including Gable and Lombard, Robert Taylor and Barbara Stanwyck, and Constance Bennett and Gilbert Roland— are living together. A rash of 1939 marriages follow.*

PHOTOPLAY

25¢

JANUARY

HOLLYWOOD'S UNMARRIED HUSBANDS AND WIVES

Four Pages of Hilarious Star Caricatures by WALT DISNEY

Great Features by ELEANOR ROOSEVELT · LOUIS SOBOL · RETTA PALMER

THREE'S COMPANY

From its very beginnings, MGM realized that the formula of "three for the show" was sure-fire box office. *He Who Gets Slapped* (1924), the first film generated entirely by the infant studio, revolved around a threesome—John Gilbert, Norma Shearer, and Lon Chaney (Sr.). Chaney portrayed a brilliant scientist-turned-clown who loses a sublimely configured bareback rider (Shearer) to a younger, more poetic rival (Gilbert). Directed by Victor Seastrom, this film launched MGM, did nothing to damage the reputation of Chaney, and ignited the careers of Shearer and Gilbert. It was so successful that, in 1928, MGM tried the whole idea again with *Laugh, Clown, Laugh*. Chaney once more played an aging Pagliacci who lost out to a younger, handsomer man. This time, the winner was Nils Asther, and making her debut as the woman he won was a fifteen-year-old starlet named Loretta Young.

Other studios used the formula, but it rarely shone quite so brightly as it did at MGM, mainly because this studio had the stars to make it shine. At MGM, even the losers lost with class.

In the 1930s, the studio replaced Chaney with Clark Gable in the triangle. In *Dancing Lady* (1933), Joan Crawford played a dancer who had to choose between the monetary riches of playboy Franchot Tone and the romantic riches of Broadway director Clark Gable. Romance won, of course.

The next year, MGM capitalized on both the Crawford-Gable magic and the solidity of the triangle by casting them in two films involving a

Three's company, but subtraction to two often occurs by the last reel, when the heroine makes her final choice.
ABOVE: *Robert Montgomery, Joan Crawford, and Clark Gable in* Forsaking All Others *(1934).*

threesome. *Chained* provided Crawford with ninety sizzling minutes in which to leave her married paramour Otto Kruger for Gable and his ranch in South America; in *Forsaking All Others*, she forsook Robert Montgomery at the altar twice, instead becoming Gable's woman.

Also in 1934, Gable was again cast in a triangle, this time in *Manhattan Melodrama*. William Powell, in his first role for MGM, played a hard-fighting district attorney who not only prosecuted the pencil-mustached man who had been his boyhood chum but won his girl, too. The girl, Myrna Loy, was adept at creating her own kind of charisma both in this film and in the *Thin Man* series, which began later that year.

Now, MGM had two triangle regulars, one male and one female, and it capitalized on its good fortune. In 1938, the year Loy and Gable were voted king and queen of the screen in a national poll, MGM starred them in two triangle epics. In *Too Hot to Handle*, Gable and Walter Pidgeon played newsreel cameramen who fought over Loy. Gable won, as all kings do, and, later that year, in *Test Pilot*, he again ended up with his queen. This time, Loy, as Gable's adoring wife, kept him alive with her love, while Spencer Tracy, whose only real love was airplanes, died in a fiery crash.

And so it went. MGM's trios con brio proved that three could be company, as long as at least one man was a superstar, and the other could take losing gracefully.

ABOVE: *Clark Gable, Myrna Loy, and Spencer Tracy are a happy trio in* Test Pilot *(1938), one of MGM's biggest hits ever.*
RIGHT: *The Philadelphia Story (1940) may look like a four-some, but the real battle for Katharine Hepburn is between Cary Grant and James Stewart. John Howard is the husband-to-be, but he doesn't stand a chance.*

1942

◆ Carole Lombard dies when her plane crashes during a war-bonds tour. Clark Gable, her husband, is devastated and writes President Roosevelt, saying he wants to fight for his country and doesn't care where or what branch. Roosevelt replies that he's more valuable for morale in the movies. He joins the Air Force.

◆ John Barrymore dies, age sixty. Gable's presence at the funeral is his first public appearance since Lombard's death.

◆ *Mrs. Miniver*, the story of a brave British family in the Blitz, wins awards for best picture, best director for William Wyler, and best actress for Greer Garson.

◆ Norma Shearer completes her six-picture contract, signed shortly after Irving Thalberg's death, and retires.

◆ Esther Williams debuts in *Andy Hardy's Double Life*.

◆ Tex Avery creates his first MGM cartoon, *The Blitz Wolf*, a morale-boosting satire on Hitler and based on Disney's *Three Little Pigs*.

◆ *Woman of the Year* is a smash. Joe Yule, Mickey Rooney's father, plays the building superintendent.

◆ MGM makes $12 million.

Swimming champion Esther Williams screen-tests with Clark Gable. The result is a long-term contract.

202

Mayer, however, was uncertain how to use the most decorative newcomer he had signed in years. He charged Walter Wanger $1,500 a week on a loan-out for her appearance in *Algiers*. After that film's success, he announced that he would make her the studio's "most important star." To achieve that goal, he hired Josef von Sternberg, famous for having "created" Marlene Dietrich, to direct Lamarr in *I Take This Woman* with Spencer Tracy. The picture soon acquired the sobriquet "Mayer's Folly"—a succession of directors, writers, and actors came and went, while the studio boss tinkered personally with it for eighteen months. Generally considered one of the worst films MGM ever made, it came to be known as *I Re-Take This Woman*.

After its failure and despite a few popular encounters with Clark Gable in *Boom Town* and *Comrade X*, Mayer lost interest in seriously developing Hedy Lamarr, and while she continued to receive star-billing, her more noteworthy roles were mainly exotic ones. The actress said of her half-caste role in *White Cargo*, "I thought with some interesting makeup, a sarong, and some hip-swinging, I would be a memorable nymphomaniac." In certain instances, she sabotaged her own career, with a little bit of help from MGM. Lamarr was offered Ingrid Bergman's parts in both *Casablanca* and *Gaslight*. In the case of the former movie, the studio refused to loan her out to Warner Bros.; she turned down the role in the second. But MGM's publicity machine continued to exploit her beauty—during one of the patriotic drives to raise money for the war effort, each purchaser of a $25,000 government bond was offered a kiss from Hedy Lamarr.

Katharine Hepburn became the only major star at MGM in the forties to achieve critical success on a par with Greer Garson's. Both were talented women, but they had totally different personalities and did not vie for the same roles. Hepburn began her career on the stage and did not come to Hollywood until 1932, when she signed a contract with RKO. She experienced successes and failures at an early point in her career: after winning an Academy Award for *Morning Glory* and a Cannes Film Festival prize for *Little Women*, her third and fourth pictures in 1933, she bombed in a Broadway play called *The Lake*. Dorothy Parker wrote, in one of her most memorable one-liners, that Miss Hepburn "ran the gamut of emotions from A to B." It would be several years before RKO discovered her special talent for comedy, by which time her name was listed on the Brand Index as "box-office poison."

Hepburn's remarkable endurance as a star for almost sixty years is neither the result of circumstance nor of raw talent. She figured out the secret of success in show business and was willing to share her formula: "I am a personality as well as an actress," she once declared. "Show me an actress who isn't a personality, and I'll show you a woman who isn't a star." A Connecticut Yankee to the core, she enjoyed playing tomboy and rebel, determined to keep her own unconventional good looks rather than project the image of a glamorous, fashionable Hollywood star. Her frankness or sometimes gaucherie would often be perceived as combativeness. The writer-director Garson Kanin saw evidence of this trait when the actress first encountered Spencer Tracy on the set of *Woman of the Year*. Hepburn stood so much in awe of the man who had already won two Oscars and was worshiped as an actor's actor that she cooed with a nervous laugh, "Oh, Mr. Tracy, I'm really much too tall for you." Tracy appraised her coolly and replied with an

TOP LEFT: *In the Oscar-winning screenplay for* Woman of the Year *(1942), Katharine Hepburn and Spencer Tracy play married journalists at odds with each other. Tess Harding (Hepburn) agrees to attempt domesticity, and the result is comic disaster.*

TOP RIGHT: *Preparations are made for the scene in which Tess is made "Woman of the Year."*
ABOVE: *Director George Stevens (pointing his finger) instructs Hepburn and Tracy.*

OPPOSITE: Woman of the Year *marks the first time that Hepburn and Tracy work together, after which they become one of the screen's most enduring couples.*

1943

◆ Leslie Howard is killed in plane crash.

◆ Mickey Rooney is listed as "1-A," giving him his first shot at being drafted.

◆ Joan Crawford leaves MGM after eighteen years for a new start at Warner Bros.

◆ Katharine Hepburn signs a new MGM contract.

◆ A fourteen-year-old singer named Suzanne Burce is spotted and signed up by an MGM scout. She is renamed Jane Powell.

◆ Mickey Rooney gives his strongest performance to date in *The Human Comedy*. Saroyan's portrait of small-town America was Louis B. Mayer's favorite movie. Rooney received his second nomination for best actor.

◆ Van Johnson begins his climb to leading-man stardom with *A Guy Named Joe*.

◆ Gable returns to the top-ten list of stars. Only a world war could interrupt his record twelve appearances on the annual list.

◆ Greer Garson makes her second appearance on the top-ten list, one of only two women.

◆ An eleven-year-old British evacuée named Elizabeth Taylor is signed to a long-term contract.

On the set of Madame Curie, *Dame May Whitty congratulates Greer Garson on her best actress award for* Mrs. Miniver.

206

TOP: *Marie and Pierre Curie (Greer Garson and Walter Pidgeon) try to isolate the elusive element radium in* Madame Curie *(1943).*

ABOVE: *Director Mervyn Leroy sprays "perspiration" on Greer Garson for a tense laboratory session.*

edge to his voice, "That's all right, dear, I'll soon cut you down to size." Their teaming in five more MGM films during the next ten years would bring many benefits to both of them, in their professional and private lives.

Katharine Hepburn was an unlikely star to fit into MGM's patriarchal system. She was at a distinct advantage when she arrived there, however, because she chose the studio for her own purposes rather than the usual way around. Although she was a top star at RKO in the mid-thirties, Hepburn had grown disenchanted with the parts she was being offered. In search of good roles, she even went to Columbia, then considered the bottom of the barrel among the studios, to star in the film adaptation of Philip Barry's play *Holiday*, which George Cukor directed in 1938.

Next, the independent-minded Miss Hepburn bought out her contract from RKO and went back to Broadway, where she scored a major triumph in *The Philadelphia Story*. She played the socialite "virgin goddess" Tracy Lord, a part that author Philip Barry had written especially for her. When several studios tried to buy the screen rights, they discovered that Kate Hepburn had already beaten them to it.

The actress shrewdly selected MGM as the most high-profile studio to make the stylish comedy. Not only did she sell the rights to the play to Mayer for the steep price of $250,000, but she also wrangled herself a deal rare under the studio system: contractual clout to choose with whom she would work. First, Hepburn picked her director, George Cukor, and then her leading men: she wanted Tracy and Gable, who were unavailable, and had to settle for Cary Grant, with whom she had first acted two years before, and

the young James Stewart, who would win his first and only Oscar in the role of the newspaper reporter Macaulay Connor. Mayer reluctantly acquiesced to the headstrong star's demands, partly because he knew and respected acumen when he saw it, and partly because Hepburn was now enjoying tremendous success, just as the studio was losing Garbo, Shearer, and Crawford. MGM desperately needed a new larger-than-life personality. Like Harlow and Loy, Hepburn had great comic talent, which enhanced her dramatic skills and helped rejuvenate her popularity.

After adjusting to the loss of foreign markets during the war years, Hollywood found a steady stream of new customers in the U.S. government and the troops overseas, while providing the people at home with not only one of the few commodities not under rationing but also an escape from the stress of anxiety caused by the absence of loved ones. The film industry prospered as it had never done before as domestic audiences developed the habit of going to the movies two or three times a week.

The huge profits flowing into the studio's coffers during this period blinded Loew's leadership to the studio's internal problems. The executive committee of yes-men, through which Mayer governed, had allowed management to grow by leaps and bounds without a corresponding increase in productivity. By 1941, forty producers did the work that five or six had accomplished in the 1920s. Without the coordinating vision of a production chief like Irving Thalberg, or the creative guidance of an executive producer like David O. Selznick, the cost of producing quality pictures increased in direct proportion to the decrease in the talents and skills of

Irene Dunne, Spencer Tracy, and Van Johnson in A Guy Named Joe *(1944). Victor Fleming directs the story of a dead fighter pilot (Tracy) sent to earth to aid a young airman (Johnson). Dunne's appearance marks her first MGM film since 1933.*

1944

◆ *Gaslight* marks the debut of seventeen-year-old Angela Lansbury. Her defiant act of lighting a cigarette in one dramatic scene had to wait, by law, until her eighteenth birthday. After a celebration on the set, the scene was shot. Lansbury is nominated for best supporting actress, the youngest actress, at the time, ever to be so honored.

◆ Seven-year-old Margaret O'Brien wins a special miniature Academy Award as outstanding child actress. Her MGM films that year include *Lost Angel, The Canterville Ghost, Meet Me in St. Louis,* and *Music for Millions.*

◆ Ingrid Bergman wins her first Oscar for best actress for *Gaslight.*

◆ Myrna Loy returns from the Red Cross for *The Thin Man Goes Home,* the fifth installment in the still-popular series.

◆ MGM produces *Meet Me in St. Louis,* starring Judy Garland. It was on the set of this film that Garland fell in love with the man who was to become her second husband, Vincente Minnelli.

◆ Laurel and Hardy make their last MGM film, *Nothing But Trouble.*

Hair designer Sydney Guilaroff works with Marlene Dietrich to create an exotic look for Kismet.

207

STAR APPEAL

When it came to a film's success or a star's growth, MGM was the master of promotion. It was not unusual for stars to become spokespeople. For example, they advocated beauty products, and print ads were created linking such actresses as Rosalind Russell with Jergen's lotion, Lana Turner with Woodbury powder, and Ava Gardner with Lustre-Creme shampoo. Each endorsement was timed to coincide with the opening of a new film, which was usually also promoted in the ad. Thus, Myrna Loy touted DeSoto automobiles along with her *Thin Man* series, while Robert Montgomery did the same with cigarettes and *Lovers Courageous*.

MGM frequently offered a product that was related either to the star, the film, or both. Celebrity paper dolls flourished—so much so that for a while *Screen Life* magazine featured one each month and even included male stars such as Clark Gable and Mickey Rooney. There was even a Judy Garland paint book. At other times, the publicity department instead chose a movie or a character as the inspiration for a new item, thus giving rise to such wonders as *Ben-Hur* perfume, *Queen Christina* bookmarks, and Scarlett O'Hara gloves. Celebrity merchandising probably reached an all-time high at MGM with child star Margaret O'Brien, before tapering off in the fifties.

FROM TOP: *Products are often created based on a personality or popular movie. At MGM, Margaret O'Brien's popularity allows the studio to sell over twenty licenses for O'Brien dresses, hats, shoes, dolls, and other items.*
LEFT: *With* The Wizard of Oz, *MGM first attempts to exploit the tie-in market with such products as the handkerchief shown here.*

Some products receive endorsements tied to the release of a star's new film. Robert Montgomery plugs Lucky Strike cigarettes, Joan Crawford sells refrigerators, and Lana Turner, Judy Garland, and Myrna Loy promote various beauty products.

209

National Velvet *(1945) is based on Enid Bagnold's story of a little girl who enters and wins the Grand National horse race. Mickey Rooney and Elizabeth Taylor each play one of the most memorable roles of their careers.*

ABOVE: *Anne Revere, who wins an Oscar for best supporting actress, plays a former swimming champion who sees in her daughter (Taylor) the same determination and longing she experienced as a young woman.*

LEFT: *Taylor with her* National Velvet *costar, King Charles. After wrapping production, the studio presents Taylor with the horse for her thirteenth birthday.*

MGM's producers. Only a few of Thalberg's former production supervisors were still at MGM. Hunt Stromberg left in 1941 to produce independently; the following year, Bernie Hyman died of a heart attack. Only Lawrence Weingarten and Harry Rapf remained from the old guard, but neither of them had the dynamism or the independence to produce great films. Mervyn LeRoy, the man Mayer had hired to provide such vision and guidance, produced only four films before deciding he preferred directing, his first love.

There were few alternatives to finding another Thalberg open to Mayer. At all times, he remained on the lookout for in-house talent whom he hoped to groom into producers. One promising candidate was writer Joseph L. Mankiewicz, who started his career at Paramount, as had his older brother Herman, the famous wit and writer. Joseph learned the screenwriting trade under the tutelage of Ernst Lubitsch, and went to MGM in 1933, where he worked on the screenplays for *Manhattan Melodrama* and a couple of Crawford films, *Forsaking All Others* and *I Live My Life*. When he told Mayer that he wanted to direct, Mayer insisted, "No, you have to produce first. You have to crawl before you walk." Mankiewicz would always say that he never heard a better definition for a producer.

One of his early assignments was the production of *Fury*, a daring examination of lynching in a midwestern town, by the great German director Fritz Lang, whom Selznick had invited to MGM in 1934. Continuing his affiliation with Crawford, Mankiewicz produced six more of her films between 1936 and 1940 and also earned himself a solid reputation for handling many of the studio's female stars, including Katharine Hepburn in her early MGM successes.

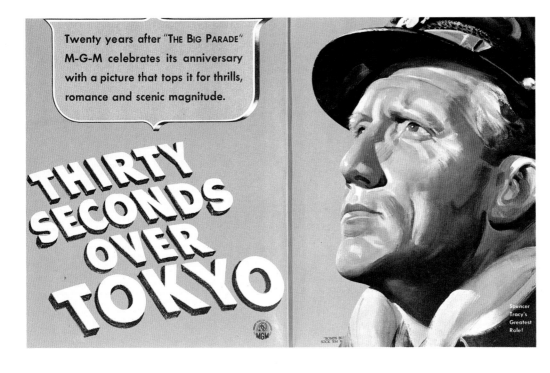

Twenty years after "THE BIG PARADE" M-G-M celebrates its anniversary with a picture that tops it for thrills, romance and scenic magnitude.

THIRTY SECONDS OVER TOKYO

Spencer Tracy's Greatest Role!

Thirty Seconds Over Tokyo *(1944), starring Spencer Tracy, Van Johnson, and Robert Walker, is a vivid and detailed account of the preparation, execution, and aftermath of the U.S. bombing of Tokyo in 1942.*

But Mankiewicz hated being a producer, referring to the ten years he was employed by Mayer ("the Great Cajoler") as his "black years." He sometimes took out his frustration on fellow writers by rewriting their scripts with astonishing speed, even though the Screen Writers Guild, which he helped found, denied him credit for such contributions.

In 1942, Mankiewicz became romantically involved with Judy Garland, who since 1938 had been working almost exclusively on musicals and Hardy films and was becoming affected by an increasing reliance on prescription drugs. Alarmed at her condition and her low self-esteem, the producer advised her to consult Karl Menninger, the celebrated psychologist, who, in turn, recommended that she see a German colleague in Los Angeles. Ethel Gumm, whom Judy once called "the real-life Wicked Witch of the West," found out about her daughter's secret appointments and complained to Mayer. The patriarch—affronted because he considered himself father confessor to his stars, especially those who had grown up under his care—called Mankiewicz on the carpet and scolded him. The young man resigned, having had enough both of Mayer and of being a producer. In truth, he had learned all the crawling he needed, and now moved on to 20th Century-Fox and a distinguished career as a writer-director.

Another writer, who would become an even more important name in the annals of MGM, began his checkered career in the thirties. When Dore Schary got his first job in Hollywood, a story editor at Columbia was impressed by the toughness of his writing sample, especially as it was thought to be the work of a woman named Dora. Schary, whose first name is an abbreviation of Isadore, was hired in 1933 by MGM as a writer at a salary of $200 per week. But he and his boss, Harry Rapf, who was in charge of low-budget operations, often quarreled, and so Schary left to free-lance. Three years later, MGM hired him to write *The Big City*, starring Spencer Tracy. While fashioning the script, Schary came up with the story for *Boys Town*. But Tracy was tired of playing priests, and the project languished for almost two years.

Meanwhile, Schary had another run-in with Rapf and left the studio for the second time. Eddie Mannix brought him back again after seeing *Boys Town*, for which Schary would share an Oscar for best original story in 1938. After working diligently in the writers' building for a number of years, Schary asked producer John Considine if he would let him write and direct the screenplay of a story by Paul Gallico about a munitions factory worker who is abducted by a group of Nazi spies. *Joe Smith, American*, Schary argued, could easily be made on a modest budget. The request went up the line, and one day Schary received a summons from the studio boss, whom he had never met. "Why do you want to direct?" Mayer asked. "Anybody can direct." He suggested that instead of wasting his time on one low-budget picture, perhaps Schary might want to consider running his own unit, which could turn out lots of meaningful and inexpensive pictures of the kind he liked.

Flattered, Schary was reluctant to become a producer, a position that generally enjoyed the worst reputation in Hollywood, especially among writers. There was also a catch: Mayer wanted Schary's old nemesis, Harry Rapf, to be the administrative head of the unit. The writer allowed himself to be seduced by a large increase in salary and the

opportunity to make pictures that had something to say, which appealed to him as a pro-Roosevelt New Dealer.

In early 1941, Dore Schary began to oversee a steady flow of features, produced at the rate of about one a month, covering a wide range of genres that included war themes, domestic dramas, westerns, and thrillers. The financial success of *Joe Smith, American*, his first endeavor, demonstrated the soundness of his production approach. It also drew upon the sympathies of an American audience increasingly consumed with the events in Europe. In fact, Harry Rapf was so moved following a preview of the movie that he grabbed Schary's arm and said, with a penchant for mangled metaphors not unusual among Hollywood producers, "Believe me, this is going to be a feather in our eye."

Although Schary preferred to make films with strong contemporary themes rather than escapist fare, it was his versatility that most impressed Mayer. For example, he produced *Pilot No. 5*, which raised the issue of American fascism through a fictional character based on Huey Long, while he encouraged Sam Marx to produce *Lassie Come Home*, an enormously successful Technicolor film that created a lineage of canine stars and inaugurated eleven-year-old Elizabeth Taylor's long tenure at MGM. Child performers became increasingly important to the studio as various adult stars left to join the war effort. Schary's *Journey for Margaret*, the story of an English war orphan adopted by an American couple, also launched five-year-old Margaret O'Brien as a child star on a par with Shirley Temple in her heyday. After performing with the youngster in *Dr. Gillespie's Criminal Case*, Lionel Barrymore professed that O'Brien was "the only actress besides Ethel [Barrymore] who's made me take out my handkerchief in thirty years."

In 1943, Dore Schary commissioned Nobel laureate Sinclair Lewis to write *Storm in the West*, an allegory that

TOP LEFT AND RIGHT: *Publicity art for* Gaslight *(1944), in which Charles Boyer plays a villainous husband and Ingrid Bergman his tortured wife.*
ABOVE: *Dore Schary, executive producer of MGM's B-picture operation from 1941 to 1943.*

OPPOSITE: Gaslight, *an eerie drama directed by George Cukor and produced by Arthur Hornblow, Jr., wins Oscars for Bergman and for its Victorian sets.*

◆ President Roosevelt dies in April. The country is plunged into mourning. Most of the country's 116,000 theaters are closed until 6:00 P.M. on the Saturday following his death.

◆ The industry receives a "well done" plaque from the Secretaries of War, Navy, and Treasury for its war efforts.

◆ *The Picture of Dorian Gray* is released. Angela Lansbury receives her second Oscar nomination, making her two-for-two in films made and nominations received.

◆ Fred Astaire makes his first screen appearance with Gene Kelly in *Ziegfeld Follies*. Their second teaming—and last—occurs thirty years later.

◆ During the filming of the navy patrol boat drama *They Were Expendable*, director John Ford falls off a scaffold and star Robert Montgomery replaces him for the final two weeks of filming.

◆ After moving to Warner Bros. two years earlier, Joan Crawford finally wins an Oscar, for *Mildred Pierce*.

◆ Judy Garland weds Vincente Minnelli, and Louis B. Mayer gives the bride away.

Clark Gable, back from the war and making Adventure *with Greer Garson, shares a smile with Margaret O'Brien.*

would treat the struggle between good and evil in Europe within the framework of an American western. One of the bad guys, for example, called Hyatt (for Hitler), would die in a burning building while his buddy Mollison (a thinly veiled Mussolini) was to be shot by his own men. Mayer was enthusiastic about the idea at first but did not like the way the script turned out. He referred the project to the New York office, where it was rejected. Schary, who had laid his job on the line in an effort to get it produced, resigned in November 1943 and went to work as production chief for David O. Selznick, who was just setting up a new independent company called Vanguard.

With both Joseph Mankiewicz and Dore Schary gone, Mayer abandoned his search for a central producer, at least for the time being. To outsiders, as well as to Nicholas Schenck, the sudden departure of these men demonstrated that creative producers or independent spirits no longer could fit in at MGM. Indeed, these were signs that Mayer, even if he could have found a new Thalberg, might not have been able to hold onto him.

While MGM did its part to satisfy the country's natural interest in the activities of American men and women away at war, with films like *Bataan*, *Thirty Seconds Over Tokyo*, and *They Were Expendable*, a major part of the studio's output remained geared toward the production of sunny, undemanding domestic comedies, principally the *Hardy* family films, the adventures of *Maisie* or *Lassie*, and the *Dr. Gillespie* series. And beginning in the early forties, MGM's profile would become increasingly identified with musicals, mainly through the efforts of producer Arthur Freed, along with the talents of Judy Garland, Mickey Rooney, and the numerous Broadway songwriters, choreographers, and directors whom Freed gathered around him. His unit became one of the busiest on the lot, gradually comman-

deering a growing percentage of the studio's resources while bringing in the lion's share of its revenues.

Even before *The Wizard of Oz* was ready to go before the cameras, Freed had won Mayer's approval to purchase the rights for the Rodgers and Hart musical *Babes in Arms*. Freed then diverted screenwriters Florence Ryerson and Edgar Allan Woolf from their work on the final stages of *Oz* to write the script. The first of several Broadway hits that Freed would turn into pictures, *Babes in Arms* became the prototype of a series in which Mickey Rooney, Judy Garland, and their friends all get together and put on spectacular Broadway-like shows. *Strike Up the Band, Babes on Broadway*, and *Girl Crazy* followed in quick succession. (There would be a final wistful reprise of this "let's put on a show" genre in Judy Garland's last MGM picture in 1950, *Summer Stock*.) The musical equivalent of the *Hardy* films, they represented a significant departure from both the MacDonald-Eddy operettas, with their European roots, and the backstage musicals, which usually dealt with the professional and private lives of show business folk.

Since *Babes in Arms* had originated on Broadway, its direction and choreography were placed in the hands of an accomplished showman. By the time Busby Berkeley came to MGM in 1939, his name had already become a part of the everyday language—the *American Thesaurus of Slang* defined a Busby Berkeley as "a very spectacular, elaborate, and original number." Berkeley came to Hollywood almost a decade earlier, after successfully directing stock theater and choreographing plays on Broadway. Samuel Goldwyn had first hired him, on the recommendation of singer Eddie Cantor, to direct the musical sequences for *Whoopee!*

Early musicals were essentially filmed stage productions. One of the first things Berkeley did when he arrived on the set was to get rid of three of the four cameras used

OPPOSITE:

TOP LEFT: Lassie Come Home *(1943), with Pal the dog and Roddy McDowall, is the first in the successful collie series.*

TOP RIGHT: *Jackie Jenkins, Margaret O'Brien, and Edward G. Robinson, as a Norwegian farmer, in the popular* Our Vines Have Tender Grapes *(1945).*

BOTTOM: *(Clockwise from upper left) William Severn, Robert Young, Margaret O'Brien, and Laraine Day in* Journey for Margaret *(1942).*

TOP LEFT: *John Wayne (bottom) and Robert Montgomery (on step) in* They Were Expendable *(1945), director John Ford's film about the crew of a torpedo boat fighting the Japanese in the Pacific.*

ABOVE: Weekend at the Waldorf *(1945) is an updated* Grand Hotel *set in New York City. The characters include a movie star (Ginger Rogers), a jewel thief (Walter Pidgeon), and a secretary (Lana Turner) who befriends a sickly war hero (Van Johnson).*

215

In Lady Be Good *(1941), chore-ographer Busby Berkeley rehearses the "Fascinatin' Rhythm" number with Eleanor Powell.*

216

THE FREED UNIT

"My own little Camelot," was the way Arthur Freed referred to his fiefdom within the greater kingdom of MGM. Indeed, the Freed Unit was a special group of creative individuals who worked wonderfully together and, as such, were appreciated and left alone by the studio. Most of its members came from Broadway and the reason was logical: Arthur Freed got his start in the theater. "I could tell Arthur an idea," Gene Kelly said recently, "and any other producer might say, 'You don't know what you're talking about.' But Arthur did. As somebody who was in the theater, as a songwriter himself, he could understand."

As a former performer in vaudeville, writer of special material for cabaret and Broadway shows, and manager of the Orange Grove Theater in Hollywood, Freed was a logical choice to join MGM at the precise moment that sound came to Hollywood. For ten years, he and composer Nacio Herb Brown reigned as MGM's resident songwriting team. But that period of lyric writing was just a step toward a larger destination for Freed. "Arthur was a strange and touching man; filled with contradictions, idiosyncrasies, and surprises," said Alan J. Lerner. "By any standard he was an original." By 1938, Freed had begun to acquire properties for MGM such as *The Wizard of Oz*, a fantasy by L. Frank Baum that had already been made into a Broadway musical in 1903. It would become one of MGM's most memorable musicals. By the time the profits began to roll in from *The Wizard of Oz*, Freed had become a full-time producer of contemporary musicals. And "contemporary" was important. No retreading of operettas for him. Those he would leave to the Pasternak Unit, which made them eagerly and beautifully.

Arthur Freed was a contemporary songwriter, and he wanted to bring a modern feeling to his musicals. He stocked his staff with talented theater people, starting with composer, arranger, and musical director Roger Edens, who became his longest-lasting partner. "Whatever taste Freed lacked," said vocal arranger Saul Chaplin,

ABOVE: *Producer Arthur Freed (at piano) with director Vincente Minnelli.*

CENTER: *The two stars of the Freed Unit—Gene Kelly and Judy Garland.*
BELOW: Meet Me in St. Louis *(1944), Freed's first great musical classic.*

"Roger Edens supplied." Together, while they were inventing what would become the Freed Unit, they originated the so-called "barnyard musical," a formula movie inspired by Mickey Rooney's idea to transform a falling-down building into a spiffy theater, so he, Judy Garland, and the rest of the kids can put on a show, as in *Babes in Arms* (1939), *Strike Up the Band* (1940), and *Babes on Broadway* (1942).

Meanwhile, the trains from New York to Pasadena began to deliver more and more theater people to the Freed Unit. Among them: Vincente Minnelli; costume designer Irene Sharaff; writers Fred Finklehoffe, Jack McGowan, and Guy Bolton; and musical directors Adolph Deutsch and Lennie Hayton. In 1942, the studio limousine drove to Pasadena to pick up Gene Kelly, who arrived with an address book full of talented acquaintances; among them, his mentor, the great Robert Alton; Betty Comden and Adolph Green; Hugh Martin and Ralph Blane. Freed hired them all.

By the middle of 1942, the Freed Unit was in place and ready to make its first memorable classic, *Meet Me in St. Louis,* which Gene Kelly, to this day, pronounces "my favorite musical." Like *The Wizard of Oz*, its main theme revolved around five words: "There's no place like home." The movie celebrated family values; it had scenes to make you weep and scenes to make you gasp; it was opulent, but it recognized a simple, happy, human time.

Behind all of these seemingly simple sentiments were savvy Broadway creators: the screenplay was by Fred Finklehoffe and Irving Brecher, the majority of the musical score was by Hugh Martin and Ralph Blane, who contributed three timeless standards: "The Trolley Song," "The Boy Next Door," and "Have Yourself a Merry Little Christmas"; the film was directed by Vincente Minnelli; the musical adaptation was by Roger Edens; the musical direction by Georgie Stoll and Lennie Hayton; the orchestrations by Conrad Salinger; the art direction by Cedric Gibbons; the costumes by Irene Sharaff; and the

dance direction by Charles Walters.

And so began the Freed Unit musicals that were to continue over the next twenty years. Other Broadway composers and lyricists passed through the unit: Irving Berlin, Ira Gershwin, Cole Porter, Alan Jay Lerner, Burton Lane, and Johnny Mercer among them. If the songwriters were unavailable, Freed made movies about them that featured copious quantities of their words and music, such as *Till the Clouds Roll By,* about Jerome Kern, and *Words and Music,* about Rodgers and Hart.

This special, show-business world, this Broadway–Hollywood connection, was never more apparent than in what many critics have called the best movie musical ever made, *Singin' in the Rain.* Even though it was an example of the supreme Hollywood musical, *Singin' in the Rain* had its roots on Broadway, in George S. Kaufman and Moss Hart's play *Once in a Lifetime,* the 1930 stage hit that skewered the early days of the talkies. Two Broadway writers, Betty Comden and Adolph Green, musicalized that idea and turned it into an inspired tribute to the adolescence of Hollywood. If *Meet Me in St. Louis* was the Freed Unit's beginning, *Singin' in the Rain* was its apotheosis, its major celebration of both the Broadway connection and MGM itself. Its "Broadway Ballet" was a tribute to all of the *Broadway Melody* films MGM made from 1929 to 1940, and its production team was the Broadway-bred unit in full force: Adolph Green and Betty Comden, Lennie Hayton, Roger Edens, Walter Plunkett, and Carol Haney (assisting Gene Kelly in his choreography for the last time before leaving for Broadway and her own bright and tragically short fame); and Gene Kelly and his sidekick from the theater, Stanley Donen, codirecting. The score was by those long-time collaborators, Arthur Freed and Nacio Herb Brown, with one interpolation by Roger Edens, and Comden and Green.

This team was a perfect fusing of the two coasts, as was the Freed Unit itself. But *Singin' in the Rain* was also, as was *Meet Me in St. Louis,* a tribute to the studio that gave it the freedom to function and even innovate.

And oh, did Freed and his fellow Camelot dwellers innovate. Gene Kelly and Stanley Donen were among the first to film musical production numbers on location, in New York, for *On the Town.* Most of *Gigi* was shot in Paris, another Hollywood first. And it was the Freed Unit which established, in *Yolanda and the Thief's* dream ballet, story ballets as the penultimate string of moments in a succession of movie musicals from the early 1940s onward, culminating in the magic sixteen minutes and thirty-seven seconds of the *An American in Paris* ballet.

The next-to-last truly great musical from the Freed Unit, *The Band Wagon,* became its valedictory. In the film, as in the history of the Freed Unit, the overblown, operetta-style artifice of Jeffrey Cordova (Jack Buchanan) was set straight by the salvation/direction of the no-nonsense, vaudeville-trained, practical but imaginative Tony Hunter (Fred Astaire, playing a cross between himself and Arthur Freed).

The Band Wagon's creative credits, like those of *Singin' in the Rain,* linked the coasts as securely as a transcontinental airline: the music and lyrics were by Arthur Schwartz and Howard Deitz; the book was by Comden and Green—who even managed to write themselves into the script in the personae of Lester (Oscar Levant) and Lily Marton (Nanette Fabray); the dances were by Michael Kidd; the musical direction by Adolph Deutsch; the set design by Oliver Smith; the orchestrations by Conrad Salinger, Skip Martin, and Alexander Courage; and the direction by Vincente Minnelli.

MGM fostered the Freed Unit. And, in return, the Freed Unit brought prosperity to MGM. When movie audiences thought about musicals in the 1940s and 1950s, they thought about MGM. And even when other films lost money, the Freed Unit musicals returned an average of 250 percent in profits to the studio. The Camelot-like world of the Freed Unit was so beautiful and so successful, it should have gone on forever. In 1963, Freed was still dreaming big: His last, unrealized project was to be a celebration of the music of Irving Berlin, but it was never filmed. Television came to stay in Hollywood, the dream faded, and the Freed Unit, like all families, gradually dissolved into memory.

"When I look back," Arthur Freed said, in one of his last interviews, "what I remember fondest is the people I worked with, Alan Lerner and Fritz Loewe, Betty and Adolph, Judy, Minnelli, all these great people I worked with. Those are the great moments."

TOP: Take Me Out to the Ball Game *(1949), with Gene Kelly, Esther Williams, Frank Sinatra, and Betty Garrett.* ABOVE: *Gene Kelly in* An American in Paris *(1951).* BELOW: *The Tin Man (Jack Haley) from* The Wizard of Oz *(1939).*

routinely to film musical numbers. He put himself behind the fourth. "I soon realized," Berkeley told an interviewer in 1969, "that in the theater your eyes are limited by the conventional dimension of the stage. In films, through the single eye of the camera I could go anywhere I wanted to and take the audience along." Liberating the camera from its fixed positions, where lighting focus and sound insulation had confined it, Berkeley devised an overhead monorail, enabling him to film the action directly from above. He also went below the stage and bored holes through the floor so that he could shoot dynamic and titillating angles of the hoofers from yet another perspective.

Despite these innovative filming techniques, Berkeley remained a quintessential showman of the twenties, when Broadway stages were filled with hundreds of long-legged chorines. This lavish style and taste were at odds with MGM's increased emphasis on middle-American family values. When he employed two hundred girls in the chorus of *Babes on Broadway*, another Rooney and Garland vehicle, Berkeley remarked wistfully that they "had to be pretty, typical American youngsters, not statuesque queens . . . the gorgeous showgirls of the past just wouldn't fit into such a setting."

In 1941, the choreographer did get his chance to demonstrate what he could do with statuesque queens in

LEFT: *Mickey Rooney and Judy Garland dance "La Conga," a Busby Berkeley number with a Latin beat staged for the school gym set of* Strike Up the Band *(1940).*

TOP: *Busby Berkeley (right) shows Mickey and Judy the fruit models that will become animated musicians in the "Our Love Affair" number of* Strike Up the Band. *Vincente Minnelli, a newcomer to the studio, conceives the idea.*

221

Ziegfeld Girl, an elaborate musical about the familiar vicissitudes of three showgirls, a plot that had served Hollywood well many times before. (A 1925 version of the story, *Sally, Irene and Mary*, featured Constance Bennett, Sally O'Neil, and Joan Crawford). *Ziegfeld Girl* was a huge production, starring Judy Garland, Lana Turner, and Hedy Lamarr, as well as Edward Everett Horton, James Stewart, and Jackie Cooper—all the leading talents who were available at the time.

Although Berkeley was slated to direct *Lady Be Good* in 1941, he was dropped from that position at the request of two of the film's stars, Eleanor Powell and Ann Sothern. He did choreograph the dance numbers, however, and relished the prospect of working with "The World's Greatest Feminine Tap and Rhythm Dancer," a title bestowed on Eleanor Powell by the Dance Masters of America in the mid-thirties. For the number "Fascinating Rhythm," Berkeley backed her up with a hundred dancers decked out in tuxedoes and eight pianos set on a stage measuring two thousand square feet and draped by sixty-five-foot-long chiffon curtains.

"She started the dance in front of a huge silver-beaded curtain," Berkeley recalled, "which circled to the left in a zig-zag course, disclosing, on five-foot-high platforms, one grand piano after another. Eleanor followed, and as the curtain circled each piano, a high-lift would move in, pick up the platform with the piano on it, and pull it back out of the way of the camera boom which was following Eleanor as she

TOP: *(Left to right) Virginia Weidler, Ray McDonald, Judy Garland, Busby Berkeley, Mickey Rooney, Annie Rooney, and Richard Quine on the set for the minstrel show finale of* Babes on Broadway *(1942).*

RIGHT: *In the same number, Mickey and Judy perform as the minstrels "Mr. Tambo" and "Mr. Bones." Arthur Freed (at left of center wearing a tie) looks up at Busby Berkeley on the camera boom.*

222

TOP: *A group recording session for the finale of* Babes on Broadway *(1942). In the foreground, Georgie Stoll (on the platform) conducts the orchestra, while in the back Roger Edens leads the chorus.*

ABOVE AND RIGHT: *Mickey and Judy prerecord sections for the film's finale and rehearse the "Hoe Down" number. Judy, in rehearsal moccasins, appears to be having trouble with the tricky Busby Berkeley steps.*

danced. All of this was filmed in one continuous shot until the last piano disappeared and the moving curtain revealed Eleanor in a huge circular set surrounded by the hundred boys, with a full orchestra in the background." Arthur Freed had allotted more than eighty thousand dollars to film this sequence. And he had given Berkeley three days to rehearse it and one day to shoot it. After more than twelve hours of work, Berkeley's cameraman quit at 10:00 P.M. At 2:30 A.M. the whole crew walked off the set. By that time, Miss Powell was covered with bruises, but according to Berkeley, she later thanked him after seeing the preview. Berkeley lasted only four years at MGM, though he would return at the end of the forties to make *Take Me Out to the Ball Game*, which featured Gene Kelly and Frank Sinatra.

As Mayer and his executive committee approved more and more musicals for production, Arthur Freed was joined by a number of other talented producers. With *Ziegfeld Girl*, Pandro S. Berman debuted at MGM, after a successful career at RKO producing the Fred Astaire-Ginger Rogers hits, and showed that he could handle a glossy MGM star spectacle as well as anyone. He followed this supermusical with a new version of *Rio Rita*, an RKO hit from 1929 based on an original Ziegfeld show, but in this case, Berman went outside MGM to borrow Abbott and Costello from Universal to star in the film.

Jack Cummings forever tried to live down the fact that he happened to be a nephew of Louis B. Mayer, and he made up for it by producing some of the studio's more successful musicals, including the last two installments in the *Broadway Melody* series. While Arthur Freed had a monopoly on the services of superstars such as Judy Garland, Cummings did very well handling MGM's specialized talents—Red Skelton, Esther Williams, and Howard

TOP LEFT, RIGHT, AND ABOVE:
In Babes on Broadway, *Mickey and Judy rehearse the scene in which their characters first meet. Mickey loves to clown, and Judy loves to laugh, and together they are infectious—as Busby Berkeley can attest!*

LEFT: *In* Girl Crazy *(1943), Busby Berkeley conceives the finale as a rodeo, complete with Mickey, Judy, the Tommy Dorsey Orchestra, dancing cowboys and cowgirls, whips, and canons. The song is Ira and George Gershwin's "I Got Rhythm."*

TOP: *Setting up a camera shot for the finale.*

ABOVE LEFT: *Smiling cowgirls line up for a shot.*

ABOVE RIGHT: *Judy awaits her cue.*

ABOVE: *Lena Horne performs "Honeysuckle Rose" in* Thousands Cheer *(1943), an all-star wartime musical produced by the Pasternak Unit.*

OPPOSITE: *As Lena performs, cameraman George Folsey and his assistants photograph her from the camera boom. Director George Sidney stands below, providing inspiration.*

The woman near Sidney closely watches Lena's lips to make sure she stays in sync with her prerecording.

Keel. In 1942, he produced *Ship Ahoy*, a tap-dancing vehicle for Eleanor Powell, in which a skinny kid called Frank Sinatra went all but unnoticed. Cummings produced well over a dozen musicals for MGM, the most famous of which were *Kiss Me Kate* and *Seven Brides for Seven Brothers*.

In the forties and fifties, Hungarian-born Joseph Pasternak became, after Freed, the busiest musical producer at MGM. He had come with an established reputation for having worked with Marlene Dietrich and for having brought Deanna Durbin over to Universal. He inherited the studio's operetta tradition, nurtured in the thirties, and specialized in light and often schmaltzy subjects. His first project was *Seven Sweethearts*, starring one of his perennial favorites, the singer Kathryn Grayson. Next, Pasternak cast practically every available MGM star in *Thousands Cheer*, a big wartime, morale-boosting musical of 1943. Throughout his long career, Pasternak's Central European charm worked wonders on a host of MGM female stars, from the compliant child-star Margaret O'Brien and the sweet-natured June Allyson to the more self-willed Esther Williams.

Williams, who would become known as the "million-dollar mermaid," came to the studio in the early forties after MGM executive Sam Katz had spotted her at the San Francisco Aquacade. She always had a firm sense of her own limitations and turned down the chance to replace Lana Turner in a Clark Gable picture, *Somewhere I'll Find You*, saying, "I am a swimmer, not an actress." Pasternak first worked with her and Van Johnson in the 1945 picture *Thrill of a Romance*. Williams, who could be extremely caustic about most of the top MGM brass, including Mayer, maintained a lifelong fondness for Pasternak, remembering him as "the only man I ever knew that ate spaghetti with his hands. It was such a sight to see, that everybody came to the commissary to watch."

THE GENIUS OF GENE KELLY

Think of a soaring camera, death-defying stunts, and heart-stopping tricks; of exuberance, comedy, tenderness, and surprise. Think of Gene Kelly and the world of dance he created onscreen: an exhilarating mix of reality and fantasy, fact and fiction, dances that were composed, as in all movies, of both the truth and the treated truth.

For Gene Kelly, like his friend and fellow dancer Fred Astaire, was the man in charge when he danced on film. No compromises; no doubles when the dance called for him to swing like an aerialist from the topmost reaches of a partially completed building in *Living in a Big Way* (1947). No double when he teetered on the edge of the real Loew's skyscraper on New York's Broadway in *On the Town* (1949). Or when he slid, at jet speed, down the halyards and across the decks of a flaming ship in *The Pirate* (1948).

His only concession to personal safety was when he allowed a circus performer to do his high wire walking in *Thousands Cheer* (1943). "I did the closeups on a wire about a foot off the ground," Kelly smilingly admitted, "but that was considered kosher in those days."

The stunts were the truth; the low wire was the treated truth, and that Gene Kelly used to perfection, too. He partnered the camera as skillfully as he partnered Cyd Charisse or Leslie Caron; he knew its ability to accelerate motion and increase excitement, and so he and his fellow dancer-turned-director Stanley Donen harnessed a

ABOVE: *Gene Kelly's best remembered number— "dancin and singin' in the rain!"*

BELOW LEFT TO RIGHT: *In Thousands Cheer (1943), Gene Kelly doesn't seem to notice that his dancing partner is not Cyd Charisse, Leslie Caron, or even Jerry the mouse.*

swooping, boom-mounted camera to add to the excitement of a spinning Gene Kelly at the end of his *Singin' in the Rain* (1952) dance.

That same sequence treated the truth in another way, too. Nobody can tap in loafers, but Gene Kelly did, all the time. And nobody can tap in water and make it sound like anything more than a splash. But in that sensational street dance on a rainy night, Gene Kelly did, or seemed to.

And it was all done in what he would call a kosher way. Until the advent of body mikes, every onscreen dancer tapped for the camera, then post-recorded the taps. This practice gave rise to various Hollywood myths, one of which had everyone from Gwen Verdon to Carol Haney recording the sound of Gene Kelly's taps-in-water for *Singin' in the Rain*.

Not so. Just as Kelly had done his own stunts, he did his own taps. He worked them out for the sequence, minutely, with Ms. Haney, who was his assistant. "We tried different shoes," he recalled, "soft shoes, ballet slippers, you name it. But in the end I did it myself with metal taps. MGM's ace soundman, Bill Saracino, produced exactly the right sound."

So, the genius of Gene Kelly was composed not only of imagination and brilliance but integrity, too. Doing his own stunts and his own taps gave him control. And using the camera to create the treated truth gave him both the power of illusion and the possibility of perfection.

Pasternak hit his stride at MGM with *Anchors Aweigh*, one of the big successes of 1945. Frank Sinatra and Gene Kelly played two sailors on leave, both in pursuit of Kathryn Grayson—a variation on the eternal threesome theme that MGM never seemed tired of using. During the three years since his brief appearance in *Ship Ahoy*, Sinatra had become an idol to bobby-soxers across the country. He still felt uncomfortable acting, but he had signed a seven-year contract with RKO and now came to MGM on a loan-out. On the set, Sinatra was becoming infamous for his confrontations with the press, just as Gene Kelly was acquiring the opposite reputation, as one of the most agreeable people in show business.

Mayer first spotted Kelly in the Broadway musical *Pal Joey*, in which he played the leading role as a show-business heel. The studio boss offered to sign him and asked him to come out to California. But when Kelly arrived, he was asked to make a routine screen test. The Broadway star then thought that Mayer had reneged on his offer, and within a few days he accepted a contract from David O. Selznick instead. Telling Kelly that he was wasting his talents in musicals, Selznick, nevertheless, could find no suitable parts for him, so he loaned him out to MGM for the Judy Garland musical *For Me and My Gal*, directed by Busby Berkeley.

No one, it seems, really knew what to do with Gene Kelly. He appeared in straight dramatic roles, such as the French prisoner of war in *The Cross of Lorraine*, and then he was loaned out to Columbia, where he starred with Rita Hayworth in *Cover Girl*. That movie provided him with the opportunity to choreograph his own dance numbers with Stanley Donen, a pal from the cast of *Pal Joey*. When Kelly returned to MGM to do *Anchors Aweigh*, Joe Pasternak gave him not only a more sympathetic role to play but also his first credit as a choreographer.

TOP LEFT: For Me and My Gal *(1942) is Kelly's first feature with Judy Garland, and both are right at home with the film's vaudeville theme. Kelly is forever grateful to Garland for being so generous in helping him make his transition to moviemaking.*
TOP RIGHT: *Kelly rehearses for* Du Barry Was a Lady *(1943).*

BELOW: *Kelly and Garland rehearse the "Ball the Jack" number from* For Me and My Gal.

231

ABOVE: *In the finale of* Presenting Lily Mars *(1943), Judy performs the "Where There's Music" number with dancers and pipe organ show-girls. It soon breaks into* "Broadway Rhythm" *with the Tommy Dorsey Orchestra play-ing and Judy dancing with choreographer-director Chuck Walters. The original finale, called "Paging Mr.* Greenback," *was shot and recorded in late 1942, but cast and crew were reassembled when it was decided that a more rousing finish was needed.*

TOP RIGHT: *Judy sings with the Bob Crosby Orchestra in* Presenting Lily Mars.

Next, Arthur Freed put Gene Kelly into *Ziegfeld Follies*, a plotless revue built around a succession of musical numbers. George Sidney, who directed some of them, called the picture "just a big cream puff." In it, however, Kelly appeared in a number called "The Babbit and the Bromide" with Fred Astaire—the first time they danced together. For all practical purposes, it was also their last: their only other appearance together occurred some twenty years later, when they hosted *That's Entertainment, Part Two*.

With Pasternak and Cummings handling a good portion of MGM's slate of musical productions, Arthur Freed was free to do what he did best: gather talent. One particular director Freed lured to MGM in the spring of 1940 was Vincente Minnelli, after Freed saw his staging of the Kern-Hammerstein musical *Very Warm for May*, which ran only fifty-nine performances. Born into a family of circus performers, the young man had studied painting and had worked as a photographer's assistant and window decorator. He started in show business as a costume designer and, in 1933, was appointed art director of Radio City Music Hall, where he staged huge spectacles. All these experiences would contribute to making him the most important director of musicals at MGM during the forties and fifties.

Minnelli almost did not come to MGM. Initially, he turned down Freed's invitation to work for the studio because he had once wasted eight months at Paramount under a contract he could not break. The producer suggested a solution to that problem: perhaps Minnelli would come to the studio without a contract, look around for a few months, and if he did not like it, he could just leave. In the meantime, Freed would pay his expenses and assign some writers to adapt *Very Warm for May* into a screenplay. It was a clever approach and reflected Freed's confidence that his unit would come up with something to interest Minnelli.

233

Upon arrival, Minnelli wandered around the studio and onto the set of *Strike Up the Band*, the Gershwin musical that Busby Berkeley was filming with Mickey Rooney and Judy Garland. The story focused on friends in a high school band who put together a swing band and try to raise money so they can enter a radio contest in Chicago. Berkeley was having problems choreographing a song called "Our Love Affair," when Minnelli appeared and pointed to a bowl of fruit, suggesting that Mickey Rooney create an orchestra out of various pieces of fruit: for example, a pear could be used for the violinist's head, and half a pear for the violin; a pineapple could serve as a double bass; and a bunch of grapes could be substituted for the conductor's head. (Some people said this clever-looking doll reminded them of Leopold Stokowski from the back.) Not only did the results enchant Freed, but even his boss took notice when a critic in *Variety* remarked that the sequence was "an outstanding example of imaginative entertainment." Taking visitors around the studio lot, Mayer pointed to Minnelli as "the genius who took a bowl of fruit and made a big production number out of it."

Minnelli assisted Berkeley on another Rooney-Garland musical, *Babes on Broadway*, and finally got his first credit as musical director on *Panama Hattie*. In the Broadway production, Cole Porter had written several songs for Ethel Merman, who played the role of a nightclub owner in Panama. The play had also given June Allyson her proverbial big break, when she was asked to step in to take over for Betty Hutton, who had the measles. In the film version, however, Ann Sothern, queen of MGM's highly successful *Maisie* series, did not measure up to Merman. Indeed, she was so miscast that Mayer frequently had to give her pep talks just to keep her going. After a dispiriting sneak preview in mid-November 1941, Freed began a massive rescue operation. When the picture, finally released in September 1942, made more than three million dollars' profit, part of the credit for the salvage went to Minnelli. Still, Freed considered it one of his failures, though it did not prevent him from adapting another Cole Porter musical, *Du Barry Was a*

OPPOSITE:

TOP: *Frank Sinatra, Kathryn Grayson, and Gene Kelly in* Anchors Aweigh *(1945). The Pasternak Unit production is a top grosser and receives a nomination for best picture.*

BOTTOM LEFT: Kismet *(1944) is a Technicolor spectacle of the Arabian Nights story. Ronald Colman stars with Marlene Dietrich, who performs a hypnotic dance choreographed by Jack Cole.*

BOTTOM RIGHT: *A Jacques Kapralik rendering of Mickey and Judy in* Girl Crazy *(1943).*

ABOVE LEFT AND RIGHT:

Judy Garland and George Murphy in Little Nellie Kelly *(1940). It is Judy's first adult role and the only time she bears a child or has a death scene on film. She plays two characters, a mother and a daughter.*

ASTAIRE'S WOMEN

red Astaire made his screen debut at MGM, playing himself and dancing with the first of a passel of partners. The year was 1933, the lady was Joan Crawford, and the film was *Dancing Lady*, a gloriously successful, *Forty-Second Street*-inspired back-stage musical that also included, among its several blessings, Nelson Eddy, and Clark Gable, doing a Warner-Baxter-as-Broadway-director imitation. But it was the nimble feet of Fred Astaire achieving the nimble feat of maneuvering Crawford around a dance floor, that provided the movie with its most magical moment, and earned the debonair dancer his reputation as the man who could make any woman look graceful.

"Partners are very important to me...." Astaire said, in his self-effacing autobiography. "The main thing is to make sure they're doing something they like...." And that he did, right from the beginning, looking on mostly with bemusement, at the hops and skips of Crawford and, then, effortlessly drawing the audience's attention toward his own airborne antics.

It was a revolution in screen dance, a dynamiting of the geometry-as-choreography of Busby Berkeley, and the introduction of class to cinematic choreography. And class was to be Astaire's trademark for the rest of his long career, during which he would be accompanied by a long parade of sometimes-panting partners—nine at MGM alone.

The women of MGM would, however, have to wait seven years after *Dancing Lady* for Astaire to return to the studio of his cinematic beginnings. And even then, they'd have to fight the cemented-in-stardust image of the partnership of Fred Astaire and Ginger Rogers. Aware of this, the studio teamed him, in *Broadway Melody of 1940*, with Eleanor Powell, arguably his most exhilarating partner, demonstrably the only one who could match his seamless dancing skill. The two burned up the black-and-white screen in what some have called his most exciting several minutes of partnering on film: the circular tap to Cole Porter's "Begin the Beguine."

Five more years passed before Astaire made his next film at MGM. Fresh from *Meet Me in St. Louis* (1944), the elegant, enigmatic Lucille Bremer was a perfect foil for him, most successfully in *Ziegfeld Follies* (1946), in which the two floated romantically and weightlessly to the Arthur Freed-Harry Warren ballad "This Heart of Mine," and then faced each other down in the pseudo-story ballet "Limehouse Blues."

The other Astaire-Bremer coupling was less triumphant. *Yolanda and the Thief* (1945) had some extraordinarily inventive and surrealistic dream dances, which retained the team's distinctive lighter-than-air look, but their airborne quality barely survived the counterweight of a ten-ton story line.

Three years later (and two years after he had announced his retirement from show business), Astaire, who was called in at the last minute when Gene Kelly broke his ankle, teamed with Judy Garland in the jovial Irving Berlin songfest, *Easter Parade* (1948), with its memorable vaudeville-scented bum rap, "A Couple of Swells." In the same film, Astaire had a chance to widen his horizons by sweeping, in Fred-and-Ginger style, a remarkably subdued, nontapping Ann Miller through Berlin's ecstatic "It Only Happens When I Dance with You."

The public loved the new partnership of Astaire and Garland. MGM signed the two for an immediate follow-up, *The Barkleys of Broadway* (1949). But her erratic behavior triggered a last-minute replacement, who turned out to be none other than Ginger Rogers. Ten years of removal from each other melted before the Astaire-Rogers magic, which expressed itself in "Manhattan Downbeat," their seminal swan song.

Once more, MGM tried to couple Astaire and Garland, and she again delayed rehearsals, this time, ending her career at MGM and giving up the part (and the partnership) to Jane Powell in *Royal Wedding* (1950). And once more, Astaire let his partner do her own thing, which was to

TOP LEFT: *Fred and Ginger feel the "Manhattan Downbeat" in* The Barkleys of Broadway *(1949)*.
ABOVE: *Astaire debuts in* Dancing Lady *(1933) with Joan Crawford*.
OPPOSITE:
CENTER: *A song rehearsal with Eleanor Powell for* Broadway Melody of 1940.
BOTTOM: *Fred and Cyd Charisse "Dancing in the Dark" in* The Band Wagon *(1953)*.

sing and move her feet gracefully, while he soared rapturously around her.

But Powell was the last nondancing companion with whom Astaire would appear at MGM. His last four musicals featured two exquisite and seasoned ballet dancers, Vera-Ellen and Cyd Charisse.

Vera-Ellen filled yet another Garland-vacated role in *The Belle of New York* (1952). Transcending yet another earthbound book, she and Astaire danced in whirling abandon atop a turn-of-the-century New York skyline.

In 1953, Astaire partnered the long-stemmed wonder of MGM, Cyd Charisse. Slightly taller than Astaire, she donned flats and floated with him through the ballroom-born, elegantly magical "Dancing in the Dark" (and in the park) in *The Band Wagon*; four years later, with a slightly Russian accent and the music of Cole Porter's "All of You," she duplicated the scene on a deserted soundstage in *Silk Stockings*.

Charisse's was the last in a long line of partnerships without parallel or precedent, populated by the lovely women made somehow more lovely by dancing with Fred Astaire.

Lady, in which he substituted Lucille Ball for Ethel Merman. The redhead turned out to be a sharp comic parry for Red Skelton, Rags Ragland, and Zero Mostel. The film became an enormous hit in 1943, the same year that Vincente Minnelli finally directed his first musical at MGM.

One of the saving graces of *Panama Hattie* had been the presence of singer Lena Horne, whom Minnelli had planned to cast in a stage musical that did not materialize before he left New York. Now an ideal opportunity to use her came with his first directing assignment for the studio. It was to be *Cabin in the Sky,* an all-black, musical reworking of the Faust story, about a man caught between his good wife and his scheming mistress, paralleled by the more cosmic struggle between Lucifer and the Lawd's General. The Broadway show, directed and choreographed by George Balanchine, had enjoyed a modest success. Freed's decision to do a film version was fairly brave, at least in commercial terms. Since many theaters were segregated, black films tended to be made by blacks. With a few exceptions, the major studios avoided what they perceived to be a specialized market. (Back in 1929, King Vidor had received permission from Nicholas Schenck to make the only other all-black film at MGM, *Hallelujah,* but Vidor, in return, had to invest his salary in the picture.)

Initially, Arthur Freed's plans to produce *Cabin in the Sky* also sparked fears in the black community. There was concern that Hollywood would give the film the patronizing treatment that some felt had befallen *The Green Pastures,* produced by Warner Bros. a few years earlier. Freed went straight for the best performers in the business. He hired Louis Armstrong, Duke Ellington and his orchestra, and the Hall Johnson Choir. He also had the foresight to forestall criticism by showing the script to Hall Johnson, who analyzed it for authenticity. "At the moment," he wrote

back to Albert Lewis, the associate producer, "the dialect in your script is a weird but priceless conglomeration of pre-Civil War constructions mixed with up-to-the-minute Harlem slang and heavily sprinkled with a type of verb which Amos and Andy purloined from Miller and Lyle, the Negro comedians; all adding up to a lingo which has never been heard nor spoken on land or sea by any human being, and would most certainly be 'more than Greek' to the ignorant Georgia Negroes in your play. . . ." But Johnson encouraged the producer to keep working on improvements and not to be afraid of adverse criticism: "We love nothing better than to laugh at ourselves on the stage—when it is ourselves we are laughing at."

Freed supported Minnelli's debut with his usual careful attention; he assigned Andrew Marton, an experienced director, as a resource and mentor. The production went smoothly, and the only trouble Minnelli encountered was with the two principal actresses. Ethel Waters objected to portions of the script on religious grounds: she had similarly disrupted rehearsals of the stage version, declaring that she had to confer privately with God about some of her lines. More routine clashes resulted from her jealousy toward Lena Horne, the young star who played the temptress, but these fitted in well with the premise of the story. Vincente Minnelli was now on his way to becoming a highly successful film director. *Cabin in the Sky* won high praise from the critics and made a million dollars' profit. On his next project, *Meet Me in St. Louis*, Minnelli would help Freed complete the liberation of MGM musicals from the stagebound conventions of Broadway, a process that Freed had begun with *The Wizard of Oz*.

Sally Benson's girlhood reminiscences about St. Louis at the turn of the century had appeared in *The New Yorker* between 1941 and 1942. Although evocative and charming in the Jane Austen manner, they lacked flamboyant characters, dramatic conflict, or a conventional plot. Arthur Freed asked Lillie Messinger, the studio's new Scheherazade, to "pitch" the stories to the studio's executive committee, but all were against it—except for the one person whose opinion

TOP LEFT: *Al Hirschfeld's poster for* Cabin in the Sky *(1943). Vincente Minnelli's first directorial effort employs an all-black cast and is a huge success.*

TOP RIGHT: *Eddie "Rochester" Anderson and Lena Horne in* Cabin in the Sky.
ABOVE: *Lena Horne.*

mattered most. Louis B. Mayer was enchanted: he felt they told a clean, sentimental tale about simpler and happier times. Freed's choice of Garland, as star, and Minnelli, as director, also appealed to the mogul, whose faith in the Freed Unit grew with each success. The first hitch came when the twenty-one-year-old Garland, recently separated from her first husband, announced that she was tired of playing teenager parts, even though the role of Esther Smith offered a different character and milieu from her previous parts. Garland appealed to Papa Mayer to let her off the project, but he insisted that Garland's name was needed to carry an expensive picture such as *Meet Me in St. Louis.* Her initial lack of enthusiasm as well as her personal problems certainly helped to make the production more expensive, but Mayer's judgment, in the end, proved to be sound.

Freed took infinite care, as always, with the music itself. He asked Hugh Martin and Ralph Blane to write the songs, which had to be integrated into a script that was being written and rewritten by half a dozen writers. Freed specifically chose these relatively obscure newcomers, rather than any of the great Broadway tunesmiths, to avoid the show-stopping conventions of a stage musical, which required the reaction of a live audience. Every time Martin and Blane came up with a big number, he would simply say, "You know what, I'll use it in the *[Ziegfeld] Follies*," the musical Freed and Roger Edens were readying at the same time.

The man responsible for the orchestration and arrangements, Conrad Salinger, shared the producer's desire to avoid the stagy belting of songs. Instead of working with a huge orchestra, whose sound would overwhelm the soundtrack, Salinger achieved all the color and texture the music required with about thirty-six players, or one third the number that was considered normal for a big musical. Then, since Leon Ames could not sing, Arthur Freed was persuaded to add his untrained voice to the dubbing of "You and I," a song which Freed had written with Nacio Herb Brown .

TOP LEFT: *Vincente Minnelli and Judy Garland share a moment between scenes.*

TOP RIGHT: *An early portrait of Vincente Minnelli.*
ABOVE: *In* Meet Me in St. Louis *(1944), Esther Smith (Judy) musically yearns for "The Boy Next Door."*

241

With his background as a lyricist, Freed knew the type of songs he wanted. For the famous trolley scene, Martin and Blane wrote what they considered a great song to sing while riding a trolley. But the producer wanted a song about the trolley itself. After several attempts, frustration drove Blane to the Beverly Hills Public Library. There, in a book about St. Louis at the turn of the century, he found a photograph of a double-decker trolley, with a caption that ran: "Clang, Clang, Clang, Went the Trolley." After that, it took him and Martin only about ten minutes to write one of the best-known songs in the picture.

It was Judy Garland herself who offered suggestions for improving another famous song, "Have Yourself a Merry Little Christmas." Originally the opening line, a reprise of the title, led to a downbeat lyric: "It may be your last/Next year we will all be living in the past." The singer felt the line was too sad, so Blane recast it. The revision was more in keeping with the mood of the whole picture, which, it was hoped, would raise audiences' spirits as America approached its third Christmas of the war. The main score of *Meet Me in St. Louis*, as in many Freed-Edens productions, was buttressed with a number of old and new songs from other sources. The title song was vintage Sterling and Mills; Nacio Brown sent a new song from New York to his old collaborator; and Freed included "Boys and Girls Like You and Me," a song Rodgers and Hammerstein had written for *Oklahoma!* (the song did not make the final cut).

Freed brought the Broadway designer Lemuel Ayres, who had just done the sets for *Oklahoma!*, to Hollywood and set him to work with unit art director Jack Martin Smith and the art department. Their job was to design miniatures for a "St. Louis Street," and the inside of the Smith family residence, down to the last detail. These would enable Minnelli to plan the camera setups and shots in advance. To give the costumes in the production a unified look, Freed

THE FILM DAILY

ABOVE LEFT AND RIGHT: *Studio art for* Meet Me in St. Louis *(1944). Al Hirschfeld's caricature shows Margaret*

O'Brien's character pestering Esther (Judy), but another artist chooses to depict their camaraderie.

"THE BIGGEST THING TO HAPPEN TO THE MGM MUSICAL"

MGM provided Judy Garland with the initial opportunity to garner what the *National Observer* once described as her almost absurdly far-reaching "eternal fame." And, although Garland's natural genius and unparalleled talent for musical comedy had been honed in eleven years of stage work before she arrived in Culver City, it was the resources of MGM that polished and refined that talent and presented it to the world.

From the starlet's screen beginnings, her impact had led even the most blasé and inured critics to refer to the Garland "magic." By 1938, when she was cast in *The Wizard of Oz* (her seventh feature film), her ability and power had burgeoned to the extent that she spearheaded the formation and rise of the Freed Unit. Composer-arranger Roger Edens later commented that Garland was "the biggest thing to happen to the MGM musical," a statement that was accurate even by the most stringent standards.

From *Oz*, she graduated to the "backstage" musicals with Mickey Rooney; their pictures together established Freed and his professional associates at MGM. Gene Kelly's screen debut in *For Me and My Gal* (1942) was the direct result of Garland's lobbying to get him the part, and his success in the film and at MGM grew out of her selfless help in easing him into a working style far different from that of his Broadway background. Five years later, when Kelly broke his ankle, the then-retired Fred Astaire delightfully accepted the chance to appear with Garland in *Easter Parade* (1948), the beginning of a nearly ten-year professional reunion between Astaire and Freed.

MGM was, of course, profoundly adept at showcasing the specific gifts of its stars. In Garland's case, however, the studio often best served the situation by letting her be herself. As a result, the "baby vaudevillian" they had signed in 1935 played a fledgling or professional entertainer in twenty-one of her twenty-seven features for MGM. And, as one journalist wrote when providing an overview of the

ABOVE: *Garland by Sotéro.*

golden years of Hollywood, Garland's rise to fame in those screen stories often gave the films a conviction they would otherwise have lacked.

Whether or not playing the performer, Garland also revealed other noteworthy aspects of her personality. Her energy, warmth, sincerity, buoyant enthusiasm, and alternately wry or baggy-pants humor provided additional justification for her popular and critical appeal.

Unfortunately, the artistic soul and seemingly limitless vulnerability that made Garland unique also left her increasingly unable to keep pace with the mounting demands of the studio, the requisite personal appearances, outside commitments to radio and recording work, and other responsibilities that went with her professional triumphs and her personal life. After fifteen years, making movies came to mean more of a strain than she could withstand on a regular basis. Fortunately, her roots in the theater, coupled with the image created by her MGM films, led to other options.

As a result, when Garland's Metro contract was terminated in 1950, she was able to return to the stage with a reputation, a repertoire, and a recognition from mass audiences that garnered for her not only adulation and acclaim but veneration by people of all ages as the world's greatest entertainer. Her incomparable talent was the foundation, but the cornerstone of her legend was supplied by MGM.

Garland would, in 1968, quite simply and earnestly tell Johnny Carson that the studio had been the greatest influence on her career. And, although her later history is replete with reports that she sometimes (and with some justification) railed against MGM for causing a number of her personal difficulties, her own artless intelligence and professionalism could also provide a more positive outlook. In January 1969, just six months before her untimely death, she commented to a British reporter, "We all did well out of Metro, and Metro did well out of us. There were lots of good times, too...."

Judy Garland and Robert Walker are quickly married by a justice of the peace in The Clock *(1945), the first non-musical produced by the Freed Unit.*

ABOVE AND RIGHT: *This die-cut advertisement by Kapralik from a 1945* Lion's Roar *opens to reveal the rest of the Judy Garland and Robert Walker caricatures seen through the "O" in "Clock."*

employed Irene Sharaff, another New Yorker. MGM's chief costume designer, Adrian, was in the process of leaving the studio to open his own boutique in Beverly Hills. He used to design all the gowns for the studio's leading ladies but usually left wardrobes for the men and actors playing smaller roles to others in his department. Sharaff, on the other hand, was used to designing all the costumes for a stage production and gradually introduced this practice at MGM, first in *Madame Curie*, and especially in *Meet Me in St. Louis*. Freed was shocked when he saw her first sketches of buttoned-up dresses. "How can you have a star with no cleavage?" he asked Sharaff, who later recalled, "When I explained the mono-bosom look of the period, he replied that it would be fine for the mother, but Judy Garland could not possibly wear it."

Clothes were the least difficult of the problems that Freed encountered with Garland. At her first meeting with Vincente Minnelli, the two clashed over the merits of the script. Once shooting began, she was continually sick, blaming her habitual lateness and absences on her chronic insomnia and sleeping pills. The morning that she kept the cast and crew waiting for the big Christmas-party scene reportedly cost the studio thirty thousand dollars. Minnelli showed great patience toward Judy, and they gradually fell in love during the filming of the picture. *Meet Me in St. Louis* became one of the studio's greatest hits, and Judy Garland later wrote a note to Arthur Freed in which she said she would never again tell him what kind of picture to make.

The growing trust between the producer, the star, and the director led to successive collaborations. Garland appeared briefly in *Ziegfeld Follies*, as Madame Crematon singing "The Great Lady Has an Interview," a satiric spoof of Greer Garson. The film was an extravagant recreation of the era of the great Broadway show, featuring almost every star whom the war had spared at MGM.

In 1943, Arthur Freed bought a short story, "The Clock," by Paul and Pauline Gallico. The romantic tale, about a woman who pursues and marries an ordinary soldier on forty-eight-hour leave in New York, was to be the first dramatic picture produced by Freed. Judy Garland was to play the female lead, and young Fred Zinnemann was scheduled to direct. But these two failed to hit it off, and before long there was little communication between them. After three weeks of shooting, Minnelli took over as director, and Judy became the model of good behavior. The part gave Judy a chance to stretch herself in a nonsinging adult role. Film critic James Agee, in his review, said, ". . . there is more ability, life, resource, and achievement in it than in any fiction film I have seen for a long time." Despite such praise, audiences—like Mayer—did not want to see their Judy change. Soon she was back playing a more familiar role, this time in *The Harvey Girls*, a Freed confection that provided a sanitized version of the settling of the West, directed by George Sidney. In the meantime, Vincente Minnelli was working on one of his few failures, *Yolanda and the Thief*, a musical based on Ludwig Bemelman's whimsical fairy tale and starring Fred Astaire and Lucille Bremer. Both of these films began shooting early in 1945 but would not be released until a year later, when the war was over.

In June 1945, after *Yolanda and the Thief* and *The Harvey Girls* were almost finished, Judy Garland and Vincente Minnelli married. Ira Gershwin was best man, and Minnelli cites his recollection of an incident: "Ira swears that at the end of the wedding ceremony, the minister brought out a symbolic wooden staff. He asked Betty [Asher, the maid of honor] to grasp it first, then Ira, followed by Judy and me. Then out of nowhere came an alien hand and grasped the staff by the knob on the top. It was Louis B. establishing his territorial imperative."

TOP: *Louis B. Mayer watches Judy Garland and Vincente Minnelli cut their wedding cake, June 15, 1945.*

RIGHT: *Fred Astaire, Lucille Bremer, and MGM dancers in the "Limehouse Blues" number from* Ziegfeld Follies *(1946).*

The end of the war brought a feeling of euphoria to America, the only major country to emerge with both its economy and its military power stronger than they had been before 1939. Hollywood studios posted record revenues as the nation indulged its habit of moviegoing. Loew's, too, seemed to be riding the wave of prosperity and in 1946 offered audiences a selection of films brightened by children and animals—*Gallant Bess* and *My Brother Talks to Horses* as well as a fresh installment in the *Lassie* series, *Courage of Lassie*, starring Elizabeth Taylor. The young actress had made her breakthrough two years earlier as Velvet Brown in *National Velvet*, a film based on a story about an English girl and her horse that wins the Grand National. These were mostly low-budget features that did well at the box office. *The Yearling*, a family saga about a dirt-poor husband and wife, their son, and his pet fawn, did even better, but its production delays were illustrative of the kinds of problems that continued to beset MGM.

The Yearling took five years to complete. When production began, Spencer Tracy and Anne Revere were cast as the parents, but by the time it ended, Gregory Peck and Jane Wyman had the leading roles. Billy Grady, the MGM casting director, interviewed more than five thousand young boys and their mothers in an attempt to find the right candidate for the part of Jody. A year later, he was dismayed to

LEFT: *Gene Kelly and chorus in the "Broadway Ballet" dream sequence of* Singin' in the Rain *(1952). The Freed Unit film borrows from the studio's library of songs accumulated over twenty-eight years.*
TOP: *Eddie Mannix, Dore Schary,* *Cyd Charisse, Greer Garson, Jane Powell, Pier Angeli, Lana Turner, Ann Miller, Jeff Richards, Carlos Thompson, Louis Calhern, Kurt Kasznar, Keenan Wynn, Walter Pidgeon, and John Ericson celebrate* MGM's 30th birthday in 1954.

find that his choice, Gene Eckman, had grown a foot and gained fifteen pounds. And so, Grady was forced to start his search all over again. Claude Jarman, Jr., finally got the part and was rewarded with a juvenile Oscar for his performance.

Victor Fleming was the first of three directors to work on *The Yearling*. While shooting on location in Florida, he received one telegram after another from his producer, Sidney Franklin, asking for footage or other evidence of progress. He finally wired back: "JUST SAT DOWN AND READ SCRIPT AND YOUR TELEGRAM TO DEER + FEEL SURE HE WILL DO BETTER HEREAFTER." Soon after King Vidor took over as director, he received a call from an assistant production manager in Ocala, Florida, mentioning 45,000 plants of corn growing in tin cans. As it happened, there were another 30,000 plants of varying sizes growing in Culver City. All this was needed solely for the scenes in which the pet deer wanders into the cornfield and eats up the poor family's only source of livelihood. Since films are not shot in sequence, the production department had to be prepared for scenes involving cornfields at various stages of growth.

The animals needed for the film presented yet another problem for the production crew. George Emerson, the MGM zookeeper for many years, had little difficulty providing raccoons and a family of bears, but his biggest headaches came with the herds of deer. "To accomplish a growth-stopping miracle," Vidor recalled wryly in his memoirs,

"a production line of fawn-bearing does had been established both in Florida and at the studio. But nature has its own timetable. In late spring each year Madame Doe becomes disinterested in the advances of Mr. Buck, and the great MGM fawn production line would come to a standstill. Therefore, we would have to start production by April 15th or postpone the film another year. By this time it had become apparent that many script revisions were necessary."

The Yearling was postponed for three years, and another veteran, Clarence Brown, took over the direction. In the meantime, the studio workers consumed the corn.

The year 1946 marked the last of seven years of high profits for MGM, a period that had begun in 1939 with *The Wizard of Oz* and *Gone with the Wind*. Movie attendance began to fall sharply soon after the war. As the exodus to the suburbs drained profits from Loew's city theaters, people sought out newer forms of entertainment. Dropping ticket sales hurt the whole industry, but it held a more specific warning for the people who ran Loew's. Dissatisfaction with the studio's product began to show at the box office. In the two decades since the Academy Awards were inaugurated, 1947 was the first year that an MGM film did not receive a nomination for best picture. To make things worse, the long-running sequels that had been the studio's staple for years—the *Hardy* family, the *Thin Man*, *Lassie*, *Dr. Gillespie* (formerly *Kildare*), and *Maisie*—were all

Gregory Peck, Jane Wyman, Claude Jarman, Jr., in MGM's prize picture, "The Yearling".

VOL. VI, NUMBER 1, Spring Number, 1947

winding down, leaving the MGM lion increasingly identified with big, splashy Technicolor musicals. Although many of these were memorable and successful, they were also expensive to produce.

As for the rest of MGM's product, the public was growing tired of aging stars and clichéd formulas. "Gable's back and Garson's got him!" proclaimed the movie posters when Gable returned from the war. Audiences, however, were disappointed with *Adventure*, a dull romance that even Joan Blondell's humor could not save. Gable continued to make the top-ten lists, but the appeal of Garson's sweet, proper image was wearing thin. Her reputation was further damaged by films such as *Desire Me*, a romantic triangle in which her husband, presumed dead, returns from the war to find her in love with another man. Robert Montgomery, the original star, walked out and was replaced by an unknown, Richard Hart; during the following eighteen months of reshooting and cutting, two successive directors, George Cukor and Mervyn LeRoy, disowned the film. *Desire Me* proved to be so undesirable that it became one of the few MGM features released without a director's credit.

These disasters were not isolated ones. Since 1916, the *Exhibitors' Herald* had run a column called "What the Picture Did for Me," in which theater exhibitors across the United States and Canada reported their audiences' reactions to the latest releases. A typical sample from March 1946 thrashed major stars such as Tracy and Hepburn in

Without Love: "You would think that Metro would have learned that the public doesn't want to see Miss Hepburn at any price, although Spencer Tracy is co-starred. Very, very poor. . . ." Their next collaborative effort, a western entitled *The Sea of Grass*, fared no better. Hepburn's work with other actors (she was tormented by Robert Taylor in the thriller *Undercurrent* and portrayed Clara Schuman opposite Paul Henreid in *Song of Love*, a film more memorable for Artur Rubinstein's piano playing than for its actors' performances) was similarly disappointing.

During the postwar years, moviegoers began turning to other genres, such as westerns and film noir, provided by rival studios that seemed to be more in touch with prevailing tastes. Although MGM experimented with film noir, the genre's gloomy pessimism clashed with the studio's glossy style. The love scenes between John Garfield and Lana Turner lit up *The Postman Always Rings Twice* and made the movie a popular hit, but many thought the film blunted the edges of James M. Cain's best seller. Less popular was Raymond Chandler's *Lady in the Lake*, starring Robert Montgomery as private eye Philip Marlowe, his last role at MGM. Montgomery also directed the film and made the camera the equivalent of a first-person narrator. The story is told as if Marlowe is actually viewing it, with the audience catching glimpses of him only when he is reflected in a mirror. During shooting, Montgomery would squat just under the camera to help the other actors remember where he was.

1946

◆ *The Yearling* is released, starring Gregory Peck, Jane Wyman, and Claude Jarman, Jr. Filming had begun in 1941 with an entirely different cast headed by Spencer Tracy. The intervening war and clashes between Tracy and original director Victor Fleming led to a complete overhaul of the project by Louis B. Mayer.

◆ Robert Montgomery stars in and directs *Lady in the Lake,* based on a Raymond Chandler novel. It is his last MGM film.

◆ *The Cat Concerto,* featuring Tom and Jerry, wins an Oscar for best short subject cartoon.

◆ "On the Atchison, Topeka and the Santa Fe," from *The Harvey Girls,* wins composer Harry Warren and lyricist Johnny Mercer an Oscar for best song.

◆ *Ziegfeld Follies* is released, filled with stars from the MGM firmament. Lucille Ball appears riding a familiar-looking white horse, who is better known as the Lone Ranger's Silver. His trainer almost sues MGM for "sissifying" Silver by braiding his tail and decorating him with pink satin bows.

◆ Mickey Rooney, back from the war, stars in *Love Laughs at Andy Hardy.*

Katharine Hepburn presents Vincente Minnelli with a birthday gift on the set of Undercurrent.

But they had a difficult time because they tended to follow him instead of looking straight into the lens, something actors are trained never to do.

In 1947, MGM ranked fourth in profitability among the major film companies. By 1948, it was heading toward a twenty-year low of $4.2 million in profits, whereas only two years before the studio had achieved a record high of $18 million. And since its rivals were prospering, Nicholas Schenck could no longer blame MGM's decline on external or industry-wide causes. Inevitably, Schenck began to focus his attention on management. Under Louis B. Mayer, unit producers enjoyed a good deal of autonomy. His freewheeling style allowed all departments to spend money lavishly on sets, costumes, and the sundry elements involved in picture making; most films ran over budget. As long as these films made money, their hefty budgets could be accommodated, but too many MGM films were failing at the box office. And there were fewer films. Annual output was at around twenty-six pictures—down almost 50 percent from 1942.

Louis B. Mayer, for many years the highest-paid executive in the United States, did not seem to have a clear strategy for dealing with MGM's problems. He had been at the studio's helm for almost twenty-five years, but there was no successor on the horizon. While it was unthinkable to retire the man who had become synonymous with MGM, Nicholas Schenck recalled the days when Thalberg was production chief and decided that what the studio needed again

ABOVE: *Hepburn takes one of her famous constitutionals on the MGM lot.*

1947

◆ For the first year ever, MGM fails to receive an Oscar nomination for best picture.

◆ Greer Garson receives a new seven-year contract guaranteeing her $30,000 a year for life—whether she stays at MGM or not.

◆ William Powell and Myrna Loy complete the sixth and last Nick and Nora Charles movie, *Song of the Thin Man.* Two other MGM series, *Maisie* and *Dr. Gillespie,* also take final bows with *Undercover Maisie* and *Dark Delusion.*

◆ *Green Dolphin Street* is the only MGM film to receive multiple Oscar nominations, in the categories of cinematography, sound recording, film editing, and special effects. It wins for special effects.

◆ The postwar boom is on as American cinemas take in over $1.5 billion for the year, about $500 million more than a decade earlier.

◆ *Good News,* a Technicolor remake of a 1930 musical, marks the directorial debut of choreographer Charles Walters as well as the debut of screenwriters Betty Comden and Adolph Green.

Elizabeth Taylor walks to the set of Julia Misbehaves.

256

ABOVE: *Clark Gable and Deborah Kerr in* The Hucksters. *The film marks Kerr's Hollywood debut.*

RIGHT: *The stars of* The Hucksters *(1947). Based on Frederic Wakeman's best-selling novel, the story exposes the corruption of Madison Avenue ad agencies.*

was someone with central authority to guide MGM's selection of projects and production operations.

For once, Mayer agreed with Schenck, but he did not think that any of the current MGM producers had the executive ability to oversee the studio's entire schedule, and his attempts to find somebody to fill Thalberg's shoes in the dozen years that had passed since the producer's death had been fruitless. David O. Selznick, virtually bankrupt after producing *Duel in the Sun*, was also in the process of divorcing Irene Mayer. He respected his father-in-law but had no desire to work for him again. The other candidates Mayer considered had all previously left MGM after conflicts involving the studio boss: Walter Wanger, Joseph Mankiewicz, and Dore Schary. The first two were not interested, at least not while Mayer continued to hold sway. Schary, currently the production chief at RKO, had demonstrated both executive efficiency and creative gusto while running the Schary-Rapf Unit at MGM during the war, and had the advantage of already knowing most of the key members of MGM's exclusive family. In fact, from the point of view of Loew's management, there seemed to be only one drawback to hiring Schary: he held political views that were too liberal for archconservatives such as Mayer and Schenck; in other words, he was a Democrat.

Their ideological differences would not have mattered much if the political climate had been normal. But in May 1947, the House Un-American Activities Committee moved into Los Angeles's Biltmore Hotel to hold a secret session investigating communism among members of the film industry. This meeting was followed in October by open congressional hearings in Washington, during which witnesses were subpoenaed. Those who refused to cooperate with the committee, questioning its constitutionality and methods, were cited for contempt of Congress. And some of these "unfriendly" witnesses, who came to be known as the Hollywood Ten, were sent to jail. Scores of others, denounced before the committee either as Communists or as sympathizers, were driven from their jobs. Long-standing relationships, built on hard work and play, were destroyed virtually overnight. The period of the blacklist, which lasted informally until years after the demise of Senator Joseph McCarthy in 1954, changed the atmosphere in Hollywood from one of charmed innocence to one of fear and distrust.

The majority of studio executives did not support HUAC out of conviction, although some perceived an opportunity to curb the power of the guilds and unions, which had been growing stronger since the thirties. During the war, Hollywood had even made a number of pro-Soviet films to support a wartime ally. MGM, for example, produced *Song of Russia*, cowritten in 1943 by Paul Jarrico, who later became one of the more prominent figures to oppose the committee. Yet the top leaders should have been influential enough to resist the committee's defamation campaign, had it not been aimed to press on the one spot where they felt psychologically most vulnerable. By adopting the kind of un-American tactics of intimidation it was established to stamp out, the House Un-American Activities Committee reminded Hollywood's moguls of centuries of oppression in Eastern Europe and of anti-Semitic discrimination in America. So rather than fighting, as many journalists and newspaper owners did, for those constitutional rights that define Americans, the handful of frightened studio bosses instead chose a path of appeasement. As Lillian Hellman wrote, "It would not have been possible in Russia or Poland, but it was possible here to offer the Cossacks a bowl of chicken soup."

Among those accused of being Communists were some of the most talented employees of MGM. Men such as Louis B. Mayer bristled at the idea of pressure groups dictating whom they could hire and whom they should dismiss. Lester Cole, one of the subpoenaed writers, recalled Mayer telling him at the time, "Your kind don't grow on trees. I don't want to lose you." He implored Cole to break with "them goddamn Commies that you're tied up with. . . . Stick with us. With me . . . you'll do what you want. Direct your own pictures? Say so. I believe you'd do great. Dough means nothing. We'll tear up the contract, double your salary. You name it, you can have it. Just make the break." Cole refused and eventually went to prison.

Dalton Trumbo, one of the Hollywood Ten, had scripted such patriotic war movies as *Thirty Seconds Over Tokyo*. At the time of the hearings, he was one of the highest-paid writers at MGM. But when the blacklisting began, his contract to adapt *Lust for Life*, a best-selling

SYDNEY GREENSTREET ADOLPHE MENJOU AVA GARDNER

novel about van Gogh, was broken by the studio. Abraham Polonsky, who wrote and directed *Force of Evil*, one of MGM's rare ventures into film noir, would be driven from Hollywood for two decades; John Garfield, one of its stars, was hounded into an early grave.

Dore Schary, a classic liberal, appeared before HUAC in late 1947 to defend RKO against charges of harboring Communists. Producer Adrian Scott and director Edward Dmytryk had worked on a film for RKO, called *Crossfire*, that depicted a war veteran who was anti-Semitic. Given the historical bias of the committee and its most ardent supporters, even this premise was considered thoroughly un-American. In addition, investigation into Scott and Dmytryk's backgrounds revealed that they had previous left-wing affiliations. Schary supported them, declaring that until "it is proved that a Communist is a man dedicated to the overthrow of the government by force or violence or by any illegal methods, I cannot make any determination of his employment on any basis except whether he is qualified best to do the job I want him to do." The Hollywood community generally applauded Schary's vigorous defense of *Crossfire*. But less than a month later, Adrian Scott and Edward Dmytryk were fired by RKO's board of directors, and industry leaders, gathered at New York's Waldorf-Astoria Hotel, declared that no studio would "knowingly employ a Communist." Schary helped to draft that statement.

LEFT: *June Allyson, Peter Lawford, and the chorus perform the "Varsity Drag" number in* Good News *(1947).*
TOP: *Allyson and Lawford rehearse a dance step.*

1948

◆ *The Pirate*, the second of three Garland-Kelly pairings, is released.

◆ Another hit is *The Three Musketeers*, a lavish costume picture starring Gene Kelly, Lana Turner, Angela Lansbury, and Van Heflin. Turner wears slacks and street shoes underneath her bodices and cloaks. Kelly performs his own stunt-work and spends two months learning to fence but still loses half of his fake mustache when a blade nicks him on the set.

◆ MGM releases *Easter Parade*, starring Judy Garland, Fred Astaire, Peter Lawford, and Ann Miller. Gene Kelly is originally slated for the lead, but he breaks his ankle two days before filming begins, so MGM calls on semi-retired Astaire, who has not danced for two years. *Easter Parade* catapults Astaire through another twenty years of stardom. Ann Miller is a replacement for Cyd Charisse, who is also injured.

◆ MGM's gross hits a new high of $185 million for the year, but excessive studio overhead lowers profits to below $5 million. Mayer brings in Dore Schary to remedy matters.

Judy Garland, between scenes of The Pirate, *holds a bouquet in the shape of a pirate ship, a gift from her husband, the film's director, Vincente Minnelli.*

TOP: *Gene Kelly charms the village lasses in "Nina," a number from* The Pirate *(1948).*
ABOVE: *Judy Garland, on a break from* The Pirate, *spends a moment with her baby, Liza Minnelli.*
OPPOSITE: *Judy Garland and Fred Astaire as "A Couple of Swells" in* Easter Parade *(1948).*

After one of the early HUAC hearings, Nicholas Schenck happened to meet Dore Schary on a train going from Washington to New York. They got on very well, and not long afterward, Mayer put out feelers to determine if Schary was interested in becoming MGM's production head. With almost total autonomy at RKO, Schary felt no particular enthusiasm about returning to fight Mayer and his men for every decision. In fact, he saw MGM's problems as managerial; the same tired, entrenched group of people had been running the studio for the past quarter-century. He had no reason to think that they would act any differently now from when he had fought them in the early part of the decade.

He changed his mind, however, after Howard Hughes bought RKO in May 1948. The eccentric millionaire had a phobia about communism almost as great as his fear of germs. Despite initially reassuring Schary that he would not get involved in production details, Hughes soon began to interfere. The two men disagreed on a number of issues, including Schary's desire to make a war story called *Battleground*. When Hughes nixed the producer's plans for the film, Schary found that Schenck and Mayer's proposal did not seem like such a bad idea.

Dore Schary returned to MGM on July 1, 1948. Although never officially dissolved, the "college of cardinals," as Mayer's executive committee was known, was reduced to an advisory board. Technically, Schary would still be answerable to Louis B. Mayer, but the old lion was relegated to the largely honorific position of Vice-President in Charge of the Studio. The senior administrative figures, such as Mannix, Thau, and J. J. Cohn, would stay on their

TOP LEFT: *John Hodiak (aiming gun) and Van Johnson as soldiers in* Battleground *(1949). Paul C. Vogel's cinematography and Robert Pirosh's script, about American forces besieged by Nazis in Belgium, win Oscars.*

TOP RIGHT: Battleground *opens at the Astor in New York City.*

ABOVE: *Colonel Harry Kinnard (standing), who serves as a technical advisor, looks toward director William Wellman (at the head of the table), who presides at a script reading for* Battleground. *Wellman will be nominated for best director.*

jobs to provide continuity. Schary had no objection, as he had always gotten on well with these men, particularly Mannix. But Sam Katz and Al Lichtman resigned. And Schary's old enemy, Harry Rapf, would die a year later. Finally, Arthur Freed, Joe Pasternak, and Jack Cummings would be allowed to operate their musical units semi-independently. Since he had a limited expertise with that genre, Schary readily agreed to this arrangement.

Schary immediately froze all productions for six weeks while he decided which projects were worthwhile enough to be given the green light. At the same time, he bought the screen rights to *Battleground* from Howard Hughes and now planned to produce the gritty story, about GIs surviving the Battle of the Bulge, at MGM; it would be his personal statement about the kind of pictures he wanted to make. Mayer did not like the idea any more than Hughes had, arguing that war pictures released so long after the war had ended would fail at the box office. But he had no mind to quarrel with his new production chief; let him learn by experience.

Schary was determined to do without the usual MGM gloss for *Battleground*. He hired William Wellman, who had taken an unsentimental approach to a similar theme in *The Story of G.I. Joe*, to direct. Wellman cast practically all the male contract players at the studio in the film, including James Whitmore, John Hodiak, and Jim Arness, as well as Van Johnson, Ricardo Montalban, and veteran actor George Murphy. He brought *Battleground* in under budget and twenty days ahead of schedule. The picture was MGM's first contender in three years for an Oscar for best picture; Robert Pirosh won one for his screenplay, as did Paul Vogel for cinematography. The film's commercial success became a personal vindication for Schary, who had successfully stood his ground against Mayer.

THE SEARCH FOR PAST MAGIC

There is no better assurance of a future hit, it seems, than the remaking of a past one. Throughout its period of preeminence, Metro-Goldwyn-Mayer employed this rule with great confidence, particularly with respect to its own films, often taking the same story back before the cameras not just once but twice. *The Merry Widow*, which was based on a comic operetta by Franz Lehar, was first produced by the studio as a silent film in 1925, and then twice more, with sound, in 1934 and 1952. Another musical, *Rose Marie*, followed the same path, appearing in 1928, 1936, and 1954. *The Last of Mrs. Cheyney* was also thrice produced, as a vehicle for stars Norma Shearer (1929), Joan Crawford (1937), and Greer Garson (in a version retitled *The Law and the Lady* in 1951).

Some remakes were intended not only to capitalize on past successes but also to breathe continuing life into the careers, and earning power, of MGM's stars. *Grand Hotel* (1932) featured the best talent of the studio—Garbo, Crawford, Beery, and the Barrymore brothers. Its remake, *Weekend at the Waldorf* (1945), offered little improvement on the story but showcased current favorites Van Johnson, Lana Turner, Ginger Rogers, and Walter Pidgeon. *Libeled Lady* (1936) was a crisp, fast-paced comedy hit that packed as much star punch—with Harlow, Tracy, Loy, and Powell—as any other MGM film. *Easy to Wed* (1946), if less brilliant than the original, seemed sure to feed off the popularity of Van Johnson and Esther Williams, as well as the comic antics of Lucille Ball.

Remakes were also employed as launching pads for newer talent. *A Free Soul* had sent

Clark Gable rocketing toward stardom back in 1931, so it was thought that perhaps the remake, *The Girl Who Had Everything* (1953), would do the same for Fernando Lamas (it didn't). *The Trial of Mary Dugan* had helped Norma Shearer establish her position as a Hollywood queen in 1929, so when Laraine Day was voted the most promising new star of 1940, the studio gave her the challenge of reprising Shearer's role.

Then, there were the remakes that involved the same actors as in the originals, but in different roles. Mickey Rooney appeared in both *Ah, Wilderness* in 1935 and *Summer Holiday* thirteen years later (the real story was that Eugene O'Neill's tender comedy was turned into a full-blown Technicolor musical in the mold of *Meet Me in St. Louis*).

Perhaps the most interesting remakes of all are those in which actors reprise roles they had played before, and MGM had a bunch of these. Lon Chaney (Sr.) did two versions of *The Unholy Three,* one silent and the other with sound. Ramon Novarro performed the same switch as both *The Arab* (1924) and *The Barbarian* (1933), and was followed by Garbo in *Love* (1927) and *Anna Karenina* (1935). Clark Gable outdid them both, waiting twenty-one years after *Red Dust* (1932) to return to the jungle in *Mogambo* (1953). Even the fading of Gable's youthful good looks had taken away nothing from his distinctive charisma.

Screenwriter William Goldman wrote recently: "Movies are always a search for past magic." MGM knew the truth of this idea only too well, and in 1959, with its glory days seemingly well behind, it returned to the epic tale that had heralded its rise to power back in 1925: *Ben-Hur.*

In February 1949, Metro-Goldwyn-Mayer celebrated its silver anniversary by throwing a lavish luncheon on one of its largest sound stages. The menu featured, of course, Papa Mayer's chicken soup, followed by stuffed squab, and finished with chocolate ice cream in the shape of Leo the Lion. Fifty-eight stars—almost three quarters of the top contract players—sat on a tiered dais set against a sky blue backdrop. MGM could still boast that it had more stars than there were in heaven; the other film studios had yet to match it in having so many famous names under contract. On the third and highest tier, the top brass and visiting studio heads surrounded L. B. Mayer, who gazed down benevolently at the eighty-one national sales managers assembled from all over the country. Sitting to one side with his own armchair, Lassie put one of his paws discreetly on his fully laid table.

The sales force, unimpressed by the stars, waited to hear how MGM was going to pull itself out of its long creative and financial slump. They listened eagerly when Dore Schary outlined a schedule of sixty-seven pictures going into production in 1949-50, compared to twenty-four the year before. He promised to promote a more varied diet but also to keep tested recipes on the menu. MGM still had the capacity to create new stars, he said, but it would not abandon box-office favorites. Referring to an upcoming Clark Gable vehicle, Schary cracked, "If we can't make money with this one, fellows, we all better go back to vaudeville!"

In fact, Gable had already regained his star footing in *Command Decision*, an unusual war drama adapted from

LEFT: *An ornate set for* That Forsyte Woman *(1949), based on John Galsworthy's novel,* A Man of Property. *The film is one of a dozen literary adaptations MGM releases in 1949. The oil portrait is of Harry Davenport,* a character actor who appears in the film.
TOP: *Greer Garson is* That Forsyte Woman, *the wife of a wealthy man who falls in love with her niece's fiancé.*

1949

◆ MGM celebrates its 25th Anniversary with the largest gathering of famous stars ever controlled by one organization.

◆ Clark Gable marries Sylvia Fairbanks Stanley, the former Mrs. Douglas Fairbanks, Sr.

◆ *Gone with the Wind* director Victor Fleming dies in January.

◆ *Adam's Rib*, starring Tracy and Hepburn, is a hit. Judy Holliday debuts as the husband-shooting defendant. As usual, Tracy receives top billing; when asked if he's ever heard of "ladies first," he replies, "This is a movie, not a lifeboat."

◆ Fred Astaire and Ginger Rogers take their last curtain call as a team in *The Barkleys of Broadway*. Though she hasn't worked with Fred in ten years, Ginger is a late replace-ment for an ailing Judy Garland. Their swan song is "Manhattan Downbeat."

◆ *On the Town* is the first of three collaborative efforts between Gene Kelly and Stanley Donen. After *Anchors Aweigh*, Frank Sinatra vowed never to don a sailor suit again, but Kelly manages to persuade him otherwise.

◆ MGM improves its profit margin to $6.75 million.

Frank Sinatra and Gene Kelly play Gay Nineties song-and-dance men in Take Me Out to the Ball Game.

TOP: *In* Intruder in the Dust *(1949), Claude Jarman, Jr. (far left), is a witness to a small southern town's simmering racial tensions. The film is adapted from William Faulkner's novel and directed by Clarence Brown.*

ABOVE: *In Mervyn LeRoy's* Quo Vadis? *(1951), set in ancient Rome, Robert Taylor and Deborah Kerr play lovers who are thrown to the lions. The film is MGM's first to be shot in Italy since* Ben-Hur *(1925).*

William Wister Haines's Broadway play, which questioned the choices officers faced during the war. Spencer Tracy and Katharine Hepburn also recaptured their magic when, in *Adam's Rib*, they played married attorneys fighting over the case of a woman who tried to kill her husband. The role of the murderess marked Judy Holliday's film debut; she had been recommended by Garson Kanin, who had written the script with his wife, Ruth Gordon. Under the direction of George Cukor, who attended a real murder trial in order to gain insight, *Adam's Rib* was enriched by sequences shot on the streets and subways of New York.

The successful return of MGM's seasoned veterans was accompanied by the rising status of an assortment of new-comers, such as Jane Powell, Cyd Charisse, and Janet Leigh (the personal discovery of Norma Shearer). Also, Elizabeth Taylor was making the difficult transition from child to adult roles in a series of films, including *Little Women* and *Conspirator*. Among the men, there were young hopefuls such as Peter Lawford, Ricardo Montalban, and Glenn Ford, as well as reliable character actors such as Keenan Wynn.

By the end of 1949, Loew's income had bounced back over 50 percent from the previous year's low. The lot was energized by new hope. Many on the creative staff wel-comed Schary's more centralized decision-making and collegial style. Sam Marx, MGM's story editor and producer, even wrote a fan letter to the new boss, thanking him for restoring in just over a year "a lonely, frightened studio . . . back to a thriving, exciting place," such as it had been under his old friend Irving Thalberg.

LEFT: *Gene Kelly, Jules Munshin, Frank Sinatra, and part of the army of technicians hired to film on location in New York for the musical,* On the Town *(1949). A boom mike takes a sound level of Sinatra's voice.*

Once again, MGM looked to prestige pictures to set it apart from the other studios. Movie spectaculars were coming back into vogue, as filmmakers tried to give people a reason to leave their new black-and-white television sets. *Quo Vadis?*, a biblical story by the Polish novelist (and Nobelist) Henryk Sienkiewicz, had been floating around the studio in various versions since the Thalberg era. Dore Schary tentatively authorized producer Arthur Hornblow, Jr., and director John Huston to proceed with a script that paralleled the oppression of the Christians in imperial Rome with the Nazi persecution of the Jews, but Louis B. Mayer disliked this approach. Rather than trying to iron out their differences, which might have given Mayer the satisfaction of exerting some control over him, Schary went directly to Schenck, who approved the project.

Quo Vadis? was to be shot overseas in Italy, one of several European countries whose postwar currency regulations trapped Loew's foreign distribution income, forcing the company to spend it there financing new films. The production had all the earmarks of another *Ben-Hur*. Eddie Mannix went to Rome to arrange for the rental of Cinecittà studios. Enormous sets were built while some two million dollars went down the drain with little usable footage to show for it. More delays led to personnel changes: Sam Zimbalist took over as producer from Arthur Hornblow; and Mervyn LeRoy, as director from John Huston; these replacements inevitably led to the hiring of new writers. While the screenplay was being revised, various actors had to be replaced due to illness or schedules. Robert Taylor and Deborah Kerr succeeded Gregory Peck and Elizabeth Taylor as the principal stars.

Before leaving for Rome, Mervyn LeRoy sought counsel from Cecil B. De Mille, but even the master of the spectacle had not encountered such problems as fifty "hungry" lions that refused to eat Christians. "We had to fake the scene," LeRoy recalled in his memoirs. "I wound up having the propmen stuff empty clothing with meat so it looked like a Christian lying on the ground, and we brought the lions out forcibly, and they ate those 'bodies.' I augmented that with close-ups of fake lions, which the technicians built, jumping on real people. . . . I still don't know how the ancient Romans staged their bloody circuses."

Quo Vadis? became one of MGM's all-time box-office hits. A young Peter Ustinov ran away with the film in a ham's dream of a role as the emperor Nero. The movie, along with adventure stories such as *Kim* and *King Solomon's Mines*, inspired a series of big-budget spectacle films shot in Europe. Similarly, the response to *The Three Musketeers*, produced back in 1948, led to later swashbucklers like *Scaramouche*, *Ivanhoe*, and *Knights of the Round Table*. Encouraged by its success with these films, MGM even brought the Bard back to the big screen.

John Houseman, who had cofounded the Mercury Theatre in 1937 with Orson Welles, became a producer at MGM in 1951. He introduced the idea of adapting *Julius Caesar*. Both Dore Schary and Joseph Mankiewicz, whom Houseman had lured back to direct the film, thought it should be done with an English cast. Houseman had staged a

ENCORE! ENCORE!

Audiences loved series films because the plots were so predictable and they featured a common cast of characters with familiar traits. The studios loved them because they were steady moneymakers. They kept the film units busy, used the same sets over and over, and their plots were easy to devise since the characters were already defined. Series films served as a training ground for novice directors, such as Fred Zinnemann, Jacques Tourneur, and George Sidney, as well as vehicles for actors who were no longer big box-office attractions. They also exposed newcomers, such as Kathryn Grayson, to mass audiences for the first time.

Series films covered a wide range of genres: comedy, jungle adventures, animal stories, mysteries, medical dramas, and westerns. All the major studios produced them. Although they were generally second-rate in terms of production, none of them had as much polish as the series that emerged from MGM. And that was because none of the other studios had Louis B. Mayer. Cameraman Harold Rosson told Joel W. Finler, the author of *The Hollywood Story*, that "naturally you didn't have as much time to spend on one of the Dr. Kildare films, but I remember Mr. Mayer saying to me, 'If it's an MGM film, it has to look like an MGM film,' regardless of the fact that it was officially a B-picture."

A Family Affair, in 1937, launched the most popular and successful of all MGM series. It featured the adventures of the Hardy family and, most importantly, a young actor named Mickey Rooney. He played the cocky, wise-cracking but affable son of a small-town judge. All of the sixteen *Hardy* movies were sentimental comedies about the virtues of domestic tranquillity and the simple life. They were particular favorites of Mayer because they exalted virtue, patriotism, and family life. Mayer was known to scrutinize every detail of their production. His faith in the series proved itself at the box office. In 1938, *Love Finds Andy Hardy* out-grossed other films at the studio that had cost ten times as much to produce.

After the success of *Young Dr. Kildare*, in 1938, a new series was launched that would

BELOW: *The three stars of* The Thin Man Goes Home *with open books—William Powell, Asta, and Myrna Loy. The series' fifth entry finds Nick and Nora visiting Nick's parents and breaking up a crime ring. Loy takes a hiatus from her war relief work to make the film.*

produce fifteen sequels. The series boosted the careers of Lionel Barrymore and Lew Ayres, who played Dr. Kildare. Ayres starred in nine *Kildare* movies but then was dropped by the studio when he was blackballed from the industry for refusing to fight in World War II.

In 1934, Mayer had another surprise hit on his hands with *The Thin Man*. The movie was the brainchild of director Woody Van Dyke, who had bought the rights to the Dashiell Hammett detective story because he was fascinated by the relationship between Nick and Nora Charles. Van Dyke was a happily married man and he felt that most movies unfairly emphasized the negative aspects of long-term relationships, stressing jealousy and infidelity over compatibility and love. The director wanted to make a movie that showed a married couple actually enjoying each other's company.

In 1934, Van Dyke directed William Powell

and Myrna Loy in *Manhattan Melodrama* and noticed the strong chemistry that existed between the two actors. He eventually cast them as Nick and Nora Charles in *The Thin Man*, which was a huge hit when it opened in 1934. Depression audiences loved the sophisticated couple and, as a result, over the course of the next few decades, Loy and Powell made eleven more MGM movies together, five of them as Nick and Nora Charles.

Another MGM series began with a B-movie called *Maisie* (1939). The film was originally intended for Jean Harlow, but when she died unexpectedly in 1937, the project was shelved until Ann Sothern was put under contract by MGM in 1938. Playing a hard-boiled adventuress with a heart of gold, Sothern rescued the mediocre *Maisie* plots with her high-spirited performances. The second entry in the series, *Congo Maisie* (1940), was a remake of Harlow's *Red Dust* (1932). In all, Sothern starred in ten *Maisie* films, from 1939 to 1947. Although they were relatively popular in their day, most of the films suffered from poor production values and a lack of continuity.

And, finally, there was *Tarzan*, king of the series film. Since the character first appeared onscreen in 1918, more than forty *Tarzan* films have been made, featuring eighteen different actors in the leading role. Swimming champion Johnny Weissmuller was certainly one of the most popular Tarzans. He starred in six *Tarzan* adventures for MGM and six more for RKO.

After WW II, the popularity of series films declined and then virtually disappeared by the late 1950s. Series were, however, the forerunners of almost every situation comedy or drama show on television. (In fact, *The Thin Man*, *Dr. Kildare*, and *Lassie* were all successful as television shows.) The series format survives in movies featuring James Bond, Superman, and Rocky, although these are generally promoted as sequels rather than series films.

number of Shakespearean plays with American actors and argued that if none were to be used, then the production should be made overseas. In the end, he assembled an Anglo-American cast, with John Gielgud and James Mason playing opposite Marlon Brando, who had never done a classical role. With patient coaching from Gielgud, "the Great Mumbler" turned in a superlative performance as Mark Antony.

Drawing on his theatrical experience, Houseman allowed the cast of *Julius Caesar* to have an unusual amount of time—three weeks—for rehearsals before any cameras rolled. Mankiewicz then shot the film in sequence. MGM would have preferred that the picture be made in Technicolor, but Mankiewicz opted for black and white, claiming he had "never seen a good, serious, dramatic movie in color, except maybe *Gone with the Wind*." He also thought Technicolor would make Caesar's murder too gory. Though by no means as resourceful or splashy as Orson Welles's 1952 version of *Othello*, MGM's adaptation of *Julius Caesar* drew respectful notices and respectable box-office receipts. It opened in the Booth Theatre, a legitimate Broadway house, but MGM had to blow up the 35mm print to a wide-screen ratio, inadvertently cutting off the actors' heads and feet, which led to a screaming match between an enraged Mankiewicz and Nick Schenck.

The profits on these elaborate spectacles were slim, and they served only to draw attention away from more serious problems developing at the studio. Except for the productions that distinctly reflected the tastes of Dore Schary and the mixed bag of westerns, light comedies, and thrillers, MGM's major efforts during this period were echoes of its past rather than heralds of the future. Along with epics and musical spectacles, updated remakes of MGM's hits from the twenties and thirties became something of a fashion at the studio. With rare exceptions, they were disappointing.

Clark Gable repeated his *Red Dust* role with aplomb in *Mogambo*, a big-budget production directed by John Ford.

Emma Bovary (Jennifer Jones) contemplates adultery with Rodolphe (Louis Jourdan) in Vincente Minnelli's film adaptation of Flaubert's Madame Bovary *(1949).*

Words And Music

MGM had them by the dozen, sometimes for several pictures, sometimes for only one. Most of them came from Broadway, and after a few years in Hollywood, most of them went back. But they kept Beverly Hills addresses because Hollywood was a tempting place, a Lorelei's lair, and all that was wrong with it was the distance the composers and lyricists seemed to be from the actual moviemaking. On Broadway, they were there in the rehearsal hall, in the theater, in the middle of the action. In Hollywood, they wrote their songs, delivered them, and that, unfortunately, was that; they went on to the next picture. This method was efficient and probably the reason that Nacio Herb Brown and Arthur Freed were able to write the songs for forty-seven films at MGM.

From "You Were Meant for Me" in *The Broadway Melody* (1929) and "Alone" in *A Night at the Opera* (1935), to the oft-used "Singin' in the Rain," Arthur Freed's lyrics sounded from MGM films for forty-three years, even after he became a full-time producer with his own unit.

The legendary Cole Porter wrote more scores for MGM than for any other single studio, which gave him many an occasion to become involved in studio politics. His classic confrontation with L. B. Mayer came in 1937, when he wrote the score for the Eleanor Powell-Nelson Eddy extravaganza *Rosalie*. In a letter to bandleader Paul Whiteman, Porter poured out his frustrations over the title tune, one that was eventually filmed on sixty acres of backlot by twenty-seven cameras grinding away at 2,000 extras. "It was very important that [it] should be good," wrote Porter, "I wrote six before I handed one in, but I was very proud of No. 6. Louis B. Mayer asked me to play the score for him and when I was finished, he said to me, 'I like everything in the score except that song "Rosalie." It's too high-brow....' So I took 'Rosalie No. 6' home and in hate wrote 'Rosalie No. 7.' Mayer was delighted with it.... Six months later, when the song became a hit, I saw Irving Berlin and he congratulated me on it. I said to him, 'Thanks a lot but I wrote that song in hate and I still hate it.' To which Irving replied, 'Listen, kid, take my advice. Never hate a song that's sold a half million copies.' "

Irving Berlin himself hovered on the fringes of MGM, even though he was the first composer-lyricist to have his music in feature films when Al Jolson picked his 1926 hit "Blue Skies" for *The Jazz Singer* (1927). Two years later, Berlin wrote his first song specifically for the movies, "Waiting at the End of the Road," for the critically acclaimed MGM black drama *Hallelujah*. And although the studio used some of Berlin's old songs in new movies—*The Great Ziegfeld* (1936), which featured "A Pretty Girl is Like a Melody," and *The Big City* (1947), in which "God Bless America" was heard—it was twenty-one years after *The Jazz Singer* was released that Berlin wrote an original score for the studio. *Easter Parade* (1948) included a cornucopia of seventeen Berlin songs, seven of them new.

Deep in My Heart (1954) was a semibiographical tribute to Sigmund Romberg, a composer who had supplied the studio with three smash musicals for Nelson Eddy and Jeanette MacDonald: the film versions of his stage operettas *New Moon* (1940), *Maytime* (1937), and *The Girl of the Golden West* (1938).

One of MGM's most popular biographies, however, celebrated the work of a composer who hardly ever worked at the studio. Jerome

LEFT: *In 1929, lyricist Arthur Freed (standing) and composer Nacio Herb Brown publicize their song, "Singin' in the Rain," with starlet Sally Starr.*
ABOVE: *Roger Edens (at piano) with Judy Garland, Mickey Rooney, and conductor Georgie Stoll (far right) at a rehearsal for* Babes on Broadway *(1942).*
BELOW: *Composer Jerome Kern and Jean Harlow on the set of* Reckless *(1935).*

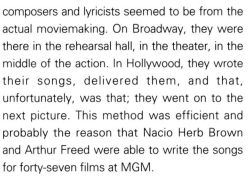

TOP LEFT: *Judy Garland and Louis B. Mayer with Irving Berlin, who plays music from* Easter Parade *(1948).*
TOP RIGHT: *(Left to right) Lyricist Alan Jay Lerner, Arthur Freed, and composer Frederick Loewe at work on* Gigi *(1958).*
ABOVE: *Cole Porter plays from the score of* Kiss Me Kate *(1953) as musical director André Previn and producer Jack Cummings (in the dark jacket) look on.*

Kern's lavish screen biography, *Till the Clouds Roll By* (1946), featured no less than forty-one of his standards. Yet, though Kern had four of his Broadway shows—including *The Cat and the Fiddle* (1934) and *Show Boat* (1951)—transferred to film by MGM, he had only two new songs filmed there. The birth of one of these, which was composed by Kern and Oscar Hammerstein II for themselves on the spur of the moment, became an MGM legend.

Shortly after the fall of Paris in World War II, the story goes, Hammerstein called Kern with a memory lyric he had written about the city of love and light. Kern listened, then paused for a moment; he always wrote melodies before the lyrics were written and always for a particular place in a particular show. But Kern broke both rules for the only time in his life. The result was "The Last Time I Saw Paris." Later that same year, the song was interpolated into the screen adaptation of Gershwin's *Lady Be Good,* and it won the Academy Award for best song of 1941.

Like Richard Rodgers, composer George Gershwin never wrote a song specifically for MGM, although his Broadway hits *Lady Be Good* and *Girl Crazy* both evolved into successful MGM films. In 1951, the studio used eleven Gershwin songs, the third movement of his Concerto in F, and his orchestral suite for the movie of the same name, *An American in Paris.*

Although lyricist Howard Dietz churned out delightful words to the dreamy music of Arthur Schwartz while serving as the chief of advertising and publicity at MGM, the lot of most lyricists was peripatetic and unpredictable. Alan Jay Lerner's first job at MGM was not as a lyri-cist but as a screenwriter for such films as *An American in Paris.* Also in 1951, he wrote the screenplay for *Royal Wedding.* When *Gigi* (1958), the last of the great MGM musicals, was planned, Lerner was hired as both screenwriter and lyricist.

Betty Comden and Adolph Green also served double duty at MGM, writing more screenplays than lyrics. Still, their rhymes managed to find their way to the music of Roger Edens in *Take Me Out to the Ball Game* (1949), of Leonard Bernstein and André Previn in *On the Town* (1949), and of André Previn alone in *It's Always Fair Weather* (1955).

E. Y. ("Yip") Harburg was a Broadway lyricist who, while he served at MGM, was most consistently associated with Burton Lane—the hugely talented composer responsible for "Everything I Have is Yours" in *Dancing Lady* (1933). But to millions, Harburg's most warmly remembered lyrics are the ones he wedded to Harold Arlen's melodies in *The Wizard of Oz* (1939). The troubled odyssey of the now classic song "Over the Rainbow" has become one of the most often-told tales of Hollywood. It was among the last songs Arlen wrote for the film; its theme came to him, he said, "as [my wife and I] drove by Schwab's Drugstore on Sunset." Three times, the heads of the studio tried to pull it from the picture, arguing that the song slowed the film down, and it was over the heads of children, or, as Jack Robbins, the head of the music publishing division moaned, "Nobody will sing it—who'll buy the sheet music?" But associate producer Arthur Freed prevailed, and the rest, as they say, is history.

1950

◆ *The Asphalt Jungle* is a major hit. Endlessly imitated, it gives birth to a whole new cinema genre: the big heist picture. It is also Marilyn Monroe's breakthrough film, though she is not listed in the original screen credits. She later claims that her small but climactic scene is one of the best she ever gave.

◆ After many setbacks and cast changes, *Annie Get Your Gun* finds its way to the screen and becomes one of the biggest musical moneymakers of all time for MGM. Howard Keel achieves instant stardom in his leading role.

◆ Another hit is the Spencer Tracy-Elizabeth Taylor comedy *Father of the Bride*, with Joan Bennett making her first film for MGM opposite old friend, Tracy, who receives his fourth Oscar nomination.

◆ Elizabeth Taylor marries and divorces hotel-heir Nicky Hilton.

◆ Judy Garland makes her last MGM film, *Summer Stock*.

◆ Although industry business is down, with the lowest theater attendance since 1933, MGM's net income rises $1 million from 1949.

> Although it won't be released for another year, filming in Rome ends for the cast of thousands in Quo Vadis?

TOP AND ABOVE: *In* Royal Wedding *(1951), Fred Astaire dances up the wall and across the ceiling to "You're All the World to Me." At top, he holds a photograph of Sir Winston Churchill's daughter, Sarah, an actress, who appears in the film in the largest role of her career.*

OPPOSITE: *Judy Garland in the "Get Happy" climax of* Summer Stock *(1950). The number, added after shooting is completed, finds Judy at the height of her powers and marks her final MGM appearance.*

Ava Gardner, who had succeeded Hedy Lamarr as the studio's siren, performed Jean Harlow's orginal role with self-assurance but was upstaged, as in the story, by the elegant Grace Kelly. *In the Good Old Summertime*, starring a healthy Judy Garland, proved to be a charming musical version of *The Shop Around the Corner*. These films made money. But pictures such as *Watch the Birdie* (from *The Cameraman*), *The Law and the Lady* (filmed twice before as *The Last of Mrs. Cheyney*), and the third versions of *The Merry Widow* and *Rose Marie* failed to impress a new generation of moviegoers.

Many of the stars who had assembled at the studio's silver anniversary a few years before began to leave. Greer Garson seemed particularly afflicted by MGM's remake syndrome. She was cast in *The Miniver Story*, which failed, as did *The Law and the Lady*. The actress also had a small part in *Julius Caesar*, but following *Her Twelve Men*, a weak attempt to duplicate the appeal of *Goodbye, Mr. Chips*, she left MGM. Her Hollywood career lasted five more movies, but her days as a leading lady were essentially behind her.

When Mickey Rooney returned from the army in 1945, he found a changed atmosphere. Fans who had once made him the box-office champion of the world now were tired of seeing him in the fifteenth rewarming of the *Andy Hardy* series. But audiences, it seems, were also unprepared to see Mickey play a new kind of role. The studio continued to pay Rooney a minimum of $200,000 a year, even as he fought for better parts. After his portrayal of the sad lyricist Lorenz

Hart in *Words and Music* in 1948, Rooney and MGM parted ways. The actor remained a celebrity—especially in the divorce courts—and returned frequently to make pictures for MGM, including *Andy Hardy Comes Home* in 1958, the final installment of the series.

After years of enduring Judy Garland's emotional roller-coaster rides, the studio finally cancelled her $5,000-a-week contract in 1950. Her problems were so closely interwoven with MGM's output that they almost seemed to parallel its decline. Following her marriage to Vincente Minnelli in 1945, Garland enjoyed a year of domestic happiness with him and their newly born daughter Liza. Following a cameo appearance in *Till the Clouds Roll By*, Garland did not appear again until *The Pirate*, in 1948, in which she and Kelly had the lead roles that Alfred Lunt and Lynn Fontanne had played on Broadway. Set in the Caribbean, its location was far removed from the American heartland that audiences had come to identify with Garland. During filming, the actress showed signs of great stress and was often close to hysterics. During the many months of rehearsals, shooting, and retakes, Garland was often absent due to illness. Despite being critically acclaimed for its surrealistic use of color, Garland's sophisticated comedy, and Kelly's athletic dancing, *The Pirate* failed to score a profit at the box office.

Overwork, pills, weight problems, and domestic strains began to overwhelm Garland's career in 1949. Since projects were often carefully tailored for Garland and nurtured over years, her unpredictability caused havoc with schedules. First, she ceded her part opposite Fred Astaire in *The Barkleys of Broadway* to Ginger Rogers, but then she came back to make a guest appearance in *Words and Music* with Mickey Rooney and to star in *In the Good Old Summertime*. These parts were followed by a nervous collapse that forced her out of *Annie Get Your Gun*. Once more she returned to the studio and costarred again with Gene Kelly in *Summer Stock*. Joe Pasternak, the producer, recalled the loving patience that surrounded the stricken star on the set: "How many days the director, Charles Walters, and the cast and the crew showed up for work at nine (that would be eight o'clock in Makeup) and waited. And waited. And waited. At eleven or twelve, with nothing else to do, the order was given to knock off for the day. . . . Never once did I hear a cross word, a tart comment, a bitter crack, on the part of any member of the crew or cast. They all understood. . . . Gene said: 'I'll do anything for this girl, Joe. If I have to come here and sit and wait for a year, I'd do it for her. That's the way I feel about her.' " In fact, Pasternak felt so desperate at times that at one point he asked Mayer to have the picture shut down. The studio boss persuaded him to carry on.

Garland's most famous number in the picture, "Get Happy," was shot several weeks after the production was finished. By then, she had had a chance to lose fifteen pounds and to get herself into better emotional shape. The improvement in her health did not last, nor did the studio's patience. Though she replaced a pregnant June Allyson in *Royal Wedding*, Arthur Freed was forced to drop her from the cast when her absences began to recur. On June 17,

1950, Judy Garland was suspended by the studio, even though there were plans for her to appear in other projects currently being developed. Later that summer, after a fifteen-year partnership that earned MGM millions of dollars, Garland's contract was finally canceled. Although Garland made several comebacks on the stage, records, television, and in films (*A Star Is Born*), she never returned to MGM.

For a brief period following *Battleground*, Schary seemed to have the answers to MGM's problems, and Nicholas Schenck, seeing parallels between the success of *Battleground* and that of *The Big Parade* back in 1925, began to sense the emergence of another Thalberg. "It made my first two years easier," Schary wrote of the film in his reminiscences, "much easier than if it had failed." And there were many who wanted him to fail. Despite MGM's reinvigorated morale and improved balance sheet, the studio divided into political camps over the new production chief. Many among the old guard, having been shunted aside into niches of reduced responsibility, waited for the messiah to fall. Howard Dietz sent out Christmas cards in 1948 with a personal note: "Watch out, or you'll get Dore Schary for Christmas." And the wife of Howard Strickling openly bemoaned the fact that "*Battleground*, alas, was a success."

The conflict between Schary and Mayer was the most obvious one and generally involved the subject matter of the movies Schary wanted to make. His tastes and methods ran completely counter to Louis B. Mayer's idealized view of small-town America. One of the first productions Schary authorized was based on William Faulkner's *Intruder in the Dust*, about a young boy who saves a black man from being lynched in a Mississippi town. Originally vetoed by Mayer, Clarence Brown's project received Schary's enthusiastic nod. The film's critical success was due, in large part, to Brown's expert handling of a difficult subject, but his competence did not help to fill the movie theaters with audiences. If *Battleground* had vindicated Schary, *Intruder in the Dust* gave Mayer some artillery of his own.

Dore Schary continued to pursue stories for their own sake rather than as vehicles for stars. He encouraged realism and committed the studio to producing suspense

(On the platform, left to right) Benay Venuta, Edward Arnold, Howard Keel, Betty Hutton, and Louis Calhern after a sharpshooting match in Annie Get Your Gun *(1950).*

277

ABOVE: *In* Father of the Bride *(1950), Elizabeth Taylor plays Kay Banks, the bride. Also a bride in real life, her marriage to Nicky Hilton is brief.*

BELOW: *Spencer Tracy as Stanley T. Banks, Kay's overwhelmed father. Tracy, the film, and screenwriters Frances Goodrich and Albert Hackett all receive Oscar nominations.*

thrillers. Among the first of these films made during his regime was *Act of Violence*. Directed by Fred Zinnemann, it was highly praised by the critics. Others of this genre included such descriptively titled films as *Scene of the Crime*, *Tension*, and *Shadow on the Wall*. Many of them enjoyed commercial success, and a few would become influential. *The Asphalt Jungle*, cowritten and directed by John Huston, about a lawyer planning a burglary with a gang of criminals, would often be imitated and remade. Marilyn Monroe had an important, if small, role in it, as the lawyer's mistress; Schary later wrote that he would never live down failing to recognize her star potential and allowing her subsequent departure to 20th Century-Fox.

As it turned out, John Huston played an indirect role in the constant friction between Schary and Mayer. The myriad problems associated with the production of *Quo Vadis?* exacerbated the differences between the two men. Mayer later claimed that he had "rescued" the picture from John Huston, whose films he disliked. Referring to *The Asphalt Jungle*, Mayer told an associate, "I wouldn't walk across the room to see a thing like that." Huston's political leanings also did not sit well with Mayer. The director had refused to take the loyalty oath that studio heads were advocating to divert HUAC's witchhunters. When John Huston proposed a film version of *The Red Badge of Courage*, Stephen Crane's classic story about a young recruit's struggle with his fears during the Civil War, Mayer was immediately opposed to its grim realism and marshaled a number of senior executives and influential members of Loew's sales force against it. This tactic put Schary on the defensive. He admitted that the story had no romantic element, no female leads, and no single incident around which a plot could be built, but he had faith in Huston and in his own instincts about the national mood. Schary appealed to Schenck, who was not overly enthusiastic about the project but felt he had to back up his production chief. The picture, written and directed by Huston and produced by Gottfried Reinhardt, proved to be no *Battleground*, except between Schary and Mayer. This time, Mayer's instincts had been entirely vindicated. Audiences at sneak previews had trouble following the plot. Unfortunately, Huston was already on location, shooting *The African Queen*, and Reinhardt and Schary were left to tinker with the film. They added a narrative framework and began cutting scenes, in the interest of clarity, until the picture's length was only sixty-nine minutes. Though *The Red Badge of Courage* was treated respectfully by the critics, it never made back its $1.65 million cost.

More significantly, the film marked the first time that Schary had been given his way and then stumbled badly. Jokes about the production chief selling the studio's soul "for a pot of message" filtered from the executive dining room down to the ranks. In fact, Schary did have a predilection for films with a message, sometimes literally. *The Next Voice You Hear*, which he produced in 1950 and later wrote a whole book about, featured God delivering His message through the radio. (The film did poorly, though it gave Nancy Davis her biggest break until she became better known as Mrs. Ronald Reagan.) Mayer, of course, had not been adverse to movies that depicted his own view of America and the world, but he had not built or staked the studio's image on realism. He would have agreed with Samuel Goldwyn, who once told a writer that if he wanted to send a message, he should use Western Union.

But Mayer's final showdown came with Nicholas Schenck. Each man tried to use Dore Schary as a point man against the other. Mayer expected to command the loyalty of his former producer and had even advised Schary to hold out for a better deal during his negotiations with Schenck. But Mayer greatly underestimated their differences in temperament and managerial style. Like so many first-generation moguls, Mayer was quick to anger when he did not get his way and was usually just as quick to forget. Schary wanted to be considered a nice guy even by those whom he had to hurt. Rather than argue with Mayer or quote the terms of his contract, which gave him power over creative decisions, Schary would annoy Mayer by completely sidestepping him. The production chief often appealed directly to Schenck, who frequently sided with him, though not for the artistic reasons Schary might have imagined. Instead, Schenck used these opportunities to assert control over an ever-weakening Mayer.

Dore Schary's projects became pawns in an end game between his two masters. In the final clash between Schenck and Mayer, he remained a fairly innocent bystander. Predictably, the showdown came over money and recognition, always the most powerful forces in the motion-picture industry. As Loew's financial situation improved, at least temporarily, Schenck announced in early 1951 that stock options would be given to several key executives in the organization. Mayer submitted his list of candidates but was not consulted on the final distribution. He expressed anger over not being the one to bestow the largesse upon his executives and asked Schenck for an explanation. More likely, his anger was the result of Schenck's decision to reward Schary with

TOP: *Louis Calhern and Marilyn Monroe in* The Asphalt Jungle *(1950). Director John Huston receives an Oscar nomination.*

ABOVE: *Two Union soldiers (the one on the right played by war hero Audie Murphy) in* The Red Badge of Courage *(1951), also directed by Huston.*

FROM AFRICAN JUNGLES
TO ANDY HARDY STREET

An aerial view of the MGM backlot in the early fifties. At bottom right is the paddle-wheel steamer built for Show Boat *(1951).*

During MGM's "golden years"—from 1924 to 1954—the studio was like a small city, self-contained and very powerful. Whole lives were spent behind its walls, where many films—some classic and some forgotten—were produced with an artistry and expertise that contributed to one of America's most important industries, as well as to the City of Los Angeles. The studio buildings have been witness to cinematic history, and they stand as a monument to the many people who dedicated their lives to the industry.

At the turn of the century, the area southwest of Los Angeles was unnamed, unincorporated, and unpopulated, making it perfect for location filming. East Coast companies had been sending production units regularly to the western metropolis. Nebraska-born Harry Culver, a real-estate developer, bought acreage there and, on July 25, 1913, announced the birth of "Culver City."

Early in 1915, Thomas Ince, a director and the western manager of the New York Motion Picture Company (NYMPC), was scouting the region for locations. His studio, known as "Inceville," was located up the coast and shot mostly westerns; when it began making more "civilized" films, the location became unsuitable, since it was too difficult to move people in and out, and the terrain was too rugged.

On July 20, 1915, a new division of the NYMPC was formed. In recognition of its three directors—D. W. Griffith, Mack Sennett, and Thomas Ince—it was named Triangle. At this time, Culver owned eleven acres in La Ballona Creek, part of the original Macedonio Aguilar La Ballona Rancho. He convinced the NYMPC to lease this land with an option to buy it, and even financed the construction of the buildings on the new site.

The first buildings, army-surplus barracks, were designated as production offices and dressing rooms. They officially opened in January 1916, making the company and studio the first in Culver City. By February, eight new stages had been built, featuring glass enclosures positioned to receive the sun's rays for most of the day. Other buildings, which fronted on Washington Boulevard, were also completed.

Although Triangle films found an audience, it was in financial trouble after only one year. The three directors abandoned ship, and the plant turned into a ghost town for a while.

By 1918, Samuel Goldwyn's company had plans to expand its operations from the East Coast, where it had been formed the year before. After assuming the lease for the Triangle studio, Goldwyn settled in and began making films. After a contract dispute in 1921, he left the studio, with at least two major films—*Greed* (1924) and *Ben-Hur* (1925)—still in production.

On April 18, 1924, Goldwyn Pictures, Metro Pictures Corporation, and Louis B. Mayer Productions merged into the Metro-Goldwyn-Mayer Studio, which was controlled by Loew's Incorporated, with Louis B. Mayer in charge of the studio. Mayer and his chief of production, Irving Thalberg, proceeded to expand the studio property and upgrade all facilities.

Between 1924 and 1930, a monumental expansion and modernization program was instituted. New buildings and departments were built to satisfy the demand for increased film production. With the advent of sound, the glass-enclosed stages of the silent era were dismantled, and new sound stages were constructed. In 1928, an area for outdoor sets was created across from Overland Avenue. Outdoor sets from Lot No. 1 were moved to the new Lot No. 2, which over time became a massive area of settings representing architecture from all over the world. In 1930, while making *Billy the Kid*, director King Vidor created Western Street on newly acquired land on

Jefferson Boulevard and Overland, an area that became known as Lot No. 3.

Between 1930 and 1940, many new stages were completed, with new facilities dotting the entire lot. The press later referred to this transformation as the building of "the film factory." Indeed, the studio was becoming a large and modern factory, with its own industrial area and police force. By 1934, there were 4,000 employees at MGM, with sixty-one stars, seventeen directors, and fifty-one writers under contract. After Irving Thalberg died in 1936, MGM erected its most impressive structure, the "Irving Thalberg Building."

In October 1938, when *The Wizard of Oz* began filming on Stage No. 27, the studio was at its height, and, in order to meet the demands of increased production, new buildings and sets were constructed on Lots No. 2 and No. 3. By 1945, MGM had six outdoor location lots. No. 1, the main lot, held all the facilities and stages. No. 2 contained outdoor sets: a train station, a nursery, Verona Square, a French courtyard, New England Street, New York Street, a lake, a small town street, Quality Street, Copperfield Street, Wimpole Street, Andy Hardy Street, and many others.

By 1940, the exterior lots were becoming small communities. Lakes, rivers, tanks, barracks, a fort, film vaults, stables, Salem Waterfront, and several new streets were added to Lot No. 3. Lots No. 4, No. 5, and No. 6 were used for the zoo, the stables, storage, parking, and occasional filmmaking.

But the golden years were coming to an end. By the end of the 1960s, most films were being shot on location out of the country, and many Hollywood studios were suffering from high overhead and decreased production. At MGM, as elsewhere, employees were slowly being let go. Many of the departments that had once served the features and short subjects produced on the lot were also cut. In 1970, MGM auctioned off much of its prop, costume, and set inventory. In 1971, it sold off Lot No. 3, and the following year, Lot No. 2. In the "new Hollywood" of the 1980s, the studios primarily produced for television and even rented their facilities to independent producers in order to help pay for their large overhead.

TOP LEFT: *A "western town" built in 1930 and used in the 1930 and 1941 versions of* Billy the Kid.

TOP RIGHT: *The Cotton Blossom, better known as* Show Boat, *docks in the MGM backlot river.*

BOTTOM LEFT: *Called "Tarzan River" because of its use as a location for the* Tarzan *series, this backlot site also appears in other films.*

BOTTOM RIGHT: *The backlot of the frequently used "little old New York" set.*

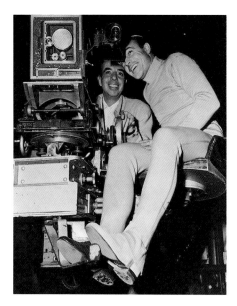

options for 100,000 shares, more than any other MGM employee received, without consulting him. Mayer took this as a challenge. The studio boss hinted to a reporter of *The New York Times* that he might resign. This time it was Schenck who wanted an explanation, and Mayer played what he thought his strongest card: "It's either Schary or me," he told his president.

Robert Rubin tried to mediate between the two men, but Schenck clearly saw an opportunity to get rid of Mayer, whom he felt had served out his usefulness to the company. He made it certain that Schary was essential to the future of MGM, leaving Mayer no room to maneuver. The studio announced Mayer's resignation on June 22, 1951. "I am going to be more active," Mayer told the Associated Press, "than I have at any time during the past fifteen years." But he said pointedly that he sought to pursue his projects "at a studio and under conditions where I shall have the right to make the right kind of pictures—decent, wholesome pictures for Americans and for people throughout the world who want and need this type of entertainment." It was a bold display coming from a man nearing seventy who really had never made plans to leave the organization he had dominated for twenty-seven years. Such was his surprise and bitterness at the ouster that Louis B. Mayer, the man who loved sentimental occasions and ceremonies, quit without expressing any formal farewells to his family of thousands, to whom he had been boss, father, and legend.

With Dore Schary now in full charge of the studio, "the General," as Schenck was called, moved to assume total control of Loew's operations. He reinstated the executive committee on the West Coast, consisting of old-timers Eddie Mannix, Benjamin Thau, J. J. Cohn, and also Louis K. Sidney, who had the title of general manager of the studio. These men considered themselves on an equal, if not higher, level with Schary and thus answerable only to Schenck. They also

TOP LEFT: *Vincente Minnelli and Gene Kelly ride the camera boom during production of the ballet sequence for* An American in Paris *(1951).*

The Romantic/Early Modern style of the ballet sets is inspired by French artists of the late nineteenth and early twentieth centuries. Henri de Toulouse-Lautrec is emulated for the Achilles Bar sequence (above); Vincent van Gogh for the Place de l'Opéra locale (opposite left); and Henri Rousseau for the carnival segment in a park (opposite right). In each scene, Gene Kelly dances with Leslie Caron.

THE DIRECTOR'S CHAIR

Late in his life, when he was confined to his bed, John Ford was told that a retrospective of his films was being screened at UCLA. He reviewed the films, stopping at one title: "*Flesh*—tell them not to run that. It's not my picture. They changed it. They put someone else on it. It's not my picture." Nearly forty years after having directed *Flesh* (1932), Ford retained strong feelings about the way they made movies at MGM—where directors were considered akin to efficient traffic cops.

For the same reason, Victor Fleming still has only a negligible critical reputation, even though he directed two of the most beloved films of all time, *The Wizard of Oz* (1939) and *Gone with the Wind* (produced by Selznick International and released by MGM, also in 1939), not to mention such classics as *Red Dust* (1932), *Bombshell* (1933), *Treasure Island* (1934), and *Captains Courageous* (1937).

Richard Thorpe—who directed *Ivanhoe* (1953), *The Prisoner of Zenda* (1952), *Knights of the Round Table* (1954), and *Jailhouse Rock* (1957)—refused to speak about his career in his later years. Thorpe had made most of his best films at MGM, and was bitter that his accomplishments as a director had been largely ignored by critics and historians.

Clarence Brown, who was Greta Garbo's favorite director, spent over twenty-five years at MGM, yet he always said his best working experience was when he was on loan to 20th Century-Fox for *The Rains Came* (1939). "At Fox," declared Brown, "all of the departments—art direction, camera, costumes—they all blended with a single goal—to make the picture better. At MGM the individual department heads worked so hard to maintain their authority and power that I often felt I was making my pictures in spite of their help rather than because of it."

Such top-flight filmmakers as Erich von Stroheim, Cecil B. De Mille, John Ford, Howard Hawks, Frank Capra, and William Wyler flirted briefly with Leo the Lion, but the directors who had lasting careers at MGM were W. S. (Woodbridge Strong) Van Dyke II, Victor Fleming, Jack Conway, and Richard Thorpe.

ABOVE: *Sam Wood clowns with Jean Harlow on the set of* Hold Your Man *(1933)*.

BELOW: *Director Mervyn LeRoy on the set of* Blossoms in the Dust *(1941)*.

These men cut their teeth on B-westerns and low-budget quickies—but, to their more prestigious projects at MGM, they brought a vitality and a filmmaking savvy that delighted audiences, even if their contributions went largely unnoticed by film critics.

"Woody" Van Dyke came to MGM in 1926, after Louis B. Mayer had noticed his work at Fox on several Buck Jones westerns. Mayer hired Van Dyke to guide the studio's new cowboy star, Lt. Col. Tim McCoy. McCoy's pictures did little to advance Van Dyke's career, but the director's experience on distant locations led MGM to send him to the South Pacific to work with famed documentary filmmaker Robert Flaherty on *White Shadows in the South Seas* (1928). When Flaherty was fired in midproduction, Van Dyke took over and finished the picture. *White Shadows* was a tremendous hit, and Van Dyke quickly became known as a director of outdoor action pictures and docudramas such as *Trader Horn* (1931), *Tarzan, the Ape Man* (1932), and *Eskimo* (1934). The Depression brought an end to big-budget location expeditions, and Van Dyke found himself making modest star vehicles, but fortune struck again. *The Thin Man* (1934), which he churned out in a mere eighteen days, turned out to be one of the biggest hits of the year.

"People like Van Dyke and Richard Thorpe were ideal directors for a studio like Metro," recalls Lindsley Parsons, one-time production head of Monogram Pictures Corporation. "There wasn't a trick they didn't know about the mechanics of making pictures.... Van Dyke might shoot the equivalent of a rough sketch of a picture. Then they'd preview it, and if the love scenes needed a little punching up the studio would have the sets re-built and the scenes re-written and the actors brought back for retakes. Maybe Van Dyke would direct the re-takes, maybe the producer thought some other director could add a bit more romance or a touch more comedy. That's not to take anything away from Van Dyke, or Conway, or Thorpe. They were very talented men, but the way they made pictures under the studio system was entirely different from the way they make pic-

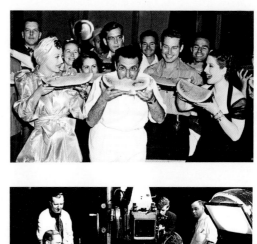

ABOVE: *W. S. Van Dyke directs technicians on the set of* Shadow of the Thin Man *(1941).*
TOP RIGHT: *The man behind* The Women *(1939) is director George Cukor, who stands between Joan Crawford and Norma Shearer.*
BOTTOM RIGHT: *Robert Z. Leonard directs Crawford and Gable in* Dancing Lady *(1933).*

tures today. The producer developed the properties, and the directors may or may not [have been] involved. By the time post-production came around, the director's salary was being charged to some other picture, and the producer saw the picture through to the final release print."

A former actor, Jack Conway was another of MGM's dependables. His most imposing directorial credits before he signed with Louis B. Mayer were a handful of Tom Mix westerns. But Conway was versatile, lending his talents with equal skill to producer David O. Selznick's literary adaptation of *A Tale of Two Cities* (1935) and to the comedy *Libeled Lady* (1936), which was produced by Lawrence Weingarten's unit. And when Howard Hawks was fired from the set of *Viva Villa!* (1934), Conway stepped in and seamlessly finished the picture.

Filmmakers such as King Vidor, Sidney Franklin, and Mervyn LeRoy made some effort to have more control of their projects at MGM. The box-office success of Vidor's *The Big Parade* (1925) allowed him to make such personal projects as *The Crowd* (1928) and *Hallelujah* (1929). Increasingly, however, Vidor found he had to leave MGM in order to pursue his most cherished projects. Franklin and LeRoy became producers in order to gain some control over their projects, though LeRoy also continued to direct.

Robert Z. Leonard came to MGM during the merger of 1924 and his craftsmanship was evident in such pictures as *Dancing Lady* (1933),

The Great Ziegfeld (1936), *Maytime* (1937), and *Ziegfeld Girl* (1941). Like Clarence Brown, Leonard stayed with Metro into the 1950s.

One of the most interesting directors to hang his hat at MGM was Roy Del Ruth, who started his career as a gagman with Mack Sennett and built his reputation directing hardboiled melodramas at Warner Bros. in the early 1930s. In 1935, Del Ruth switched gears and turned out two highly entertaining musicals—*Folies Bergère* (Twentieth Century Pictures) and *Broadway Melody of 1936* (MGM). Over the next several years, he played hopscotch with several Hollywood studios, but he made some of the best MGM musicals—including *Broadway Melody of 1938* and *The Chocolate Soldier* (1942)—before Arthur Freed's unit became established.

George Cukor may best exemplify the MGM director. He came to the studio in 1933 after working with David O. Selznick at RKO-Radio Pictures. Cukor's visual style was understated and unobtrusive, but performers came to life under his direction. With *The Women* (1939), *The Philadelphia Story* (1940), *Adam's Rib* (1949), *Les Girls* (1957), Cukor made solid entertainments that were appreciated at the time of their release but not considered especially extraordinary. In retrospect, Cukor's work looks much better—and the same can be said for the work of Victor Fleming, Jack Conway, Vincente Minnelli, and W. S. Van Dyke. In this day of inconsistent "auteurs," the dependable professionalism of these studio hired hands seems all the more remarkable.

1951

◆ Louis B. Mayer, the man who personified the success of MGM, leaves the studio after twenty-seven years.

◆ Nineteen-year-old French ballerina Leslie Caron makes her debut in *An American in Paris*. Discovered by Gene Kelly in 1948, Caron's casting is an onscreen breakthrough for nonconventional looking females. The trick-photo sequence where Oscar Levant plays all the instruments in an orchestra while he also conducts was filmed in one day. The seventeen-minute ballet sequence was rehearsed for eight weeks. The movie wins eight Oscars, including best picture.

◆ *Quo Vadis?* is released. Using 5,500 extras, twenty lions, two cheetahs and costing $7 million, it took six months to shoot. Filmed three times as a silent, this is the first sound version and it generates the largest cashflow for the studio since *Gone with the Wind* (1939).

◆ A new musical remake of *Show Boat* is released, starring Kathryn Grayson and Howard Keel. It is the third time the story has been filmed.

◆ Despite a declining industry, MGM maintains its profits of $7.6 million.

Gene Kelly and Louis B. Mayer on the set of An American in Paris, *the first musical to win an Oscar for best picture since* The Great Ziegfeld *(1936).*

TOP: *Stewart Granger, Deborah Kerr, and Richard Carlson on an African location in* King Solomon's Mines *(1950). The film wins Oscars for color cinematography and editing.*
ABOVE: *June Allyson's wholesome girl-next-door image makes her an American favorite during and after World War II.*

OPPOSITE:
TOP LEFT: *A Technicolor title card for* Show Boat *(1951).*
TOP RIGHT: *To* Photoplay *Ava Gardner is "sexsational," but her role as Julie La Verne in* Show Boat *brings her greater credibility as an actress.*

remained Mayer loyalists and kept in touch with him. Thau, who had run the studio while Mayer had busied himself with politics, social life, and horse breeding, remained particularly close to his former boss. Under the new business arrangement, Thau's authority remained strong. His office handled all the studio's contracts, and as a member of the executive committee, he was, in Schary's word, the chief "naysayer." And while the rest of the old guard established a *modus vivendi* with the new chief, Thau remained cold and aloof, biding his time.

Mayer was wounded, but the old lion did not intend to fade away. His settlement with Loew's left him financially secure. Although several moguls bid to buy out his stake in Loew's, Mayer was persuaded to sell the stock back to the company. He also received a lump sum of $2.6 million for his share of future profits from the approximately eight hundred pictures produced under his stewardship. This payment proved to be one of the few bad financial deals that Mayer ever made; within five years a new, never-ending stream of profits began to flow from television syndication of those films.

As no studio responded to his availability—some, like Paramount, had their own founders to take care of—Mayer decided to become an independent producer. It was a time when most studios were scrambling to cut back on overhead, and many stars were forming their own companies. Mayer would be joining a growing trend in Hollywood. *Quo Vadis?* was fast becoming MGM's biggest moneymaker since *Ben-Hur*, so Mayer looked around for biblical properties, hoping to exploit the fad for religious spectacles. He noted that Cecil B. De Mille had made an impressive comeback with *Samson and Delilah*; the Old Testament story of

Joseph and his brethren grew in appeal as Mayer pondered the wrongs his former colleagues had done unto him. Did not Joseph triumph over the treachery of his brothers, prosper in exile, and then stage one of the more spectacular comebacks of all time?

Meanwhile, MGM seemed to be thriving without Mayer. It must have hurt him to see the Academy, which had given him a special statuette only the year before, shower honors on his former studio and on his friend Arthur Freed on Oscar night, March 1952. Although *Quo Vadis?* had received eight nominations, it was *An American in Paris* that became the big winner of the evening, picking up six Oscars and three special awards for people associated with the film. Two serious dramas had been favored to win: *A Place in the Sun* and *A Streetcar Named Desire.* Immediately following the Awards, MGM placed large ads in the trade papers, depicting Leo the Lion as he bragged, "I was just standing in the Sun, waiting for a Streetcar. . . ."

It was only the third time a musical had won the top honors; appropriately enough, the first had been *The Broadway Melody*, which marked Arthur Freed's film debut as a songwriter. This time Freed was also the official producer of the twenty-fourth Academy Awards. Darryl F. Zanuck handed him the Irving G. Thalberg Memorial Award for his consistently high quality of production. "Turning out musicals can be a routine job," said Zanuck. "It isn't with Mr. Freed. In his hands the film musical has taken on a new scale. He has replaced mere prettiness of production with extraordinary beauty. He has brought a thorough knowledge of music and dancing to his job and learned to mix the elements of charm, humor, and melody in a production which makes an Arthur Freed musical completely

distinctive. . . . By his achievements he has added stature to the whole industry."

Freed stood, indeed, at the peak of his productivity, with *Show Boat* behind him and *Singin' in the Rain* already in the works. He continued to operate semiautonomously after Schary's appointment but missed Mayer's strong support. Nick Schenck did not see why *An American in Paris* needed Gene Kelly's famous seventeen-minute ballet sequence, which would add an extra half-million dollars to a film that had already cost two million dollars. In the end Dore Schary got authorization, but only because he believed in the principle of backing up his producer, who insisted on its inclusion. Still, after previewing the film for the board of directors in New York, Schenck called Schary and asked about reducing the length of the ballet, which would have meant butchering Gershwin's music, too. Vincente Minnelli, who had formal art training, used original paintings from his own and Arthur Freed's collection to make the picture a tribute to French artists. Schenck commented to an associate after the preview, "Am I wrong? It seems to me that I once saw some paintings on 57th Street that looked like certain sets in the ballet."

Mayer had left MGM just days after filming began on *Singin' in the Rain*, widely considered as the masterwork to emerge from the Freed Unit. Pauline Kael called it "perhaps the most enjoyable of all movie musicals—just about the best Hollywood musical of all time." The story satirized the tumultuous times of the first talking pictures. In fact, it was during the transitional period from silents to sound that Freed and Nacio Herb Brown wrote "Singin' in the Rain," which was used in *The Hollywood Revue of 1929*. In the spring of 1950, screenwriters Adolph Green and Betty

1952

◆ *This Is Cinerama*, shown on a curved screen six times the normal size, opens.

◆ MGM trots out *The Merry Widow* for a third time and stars Lana Turner and Fernando Lamas.

◆ Spencer Tracy and Katharine Hepburn make *Pat and Mike*, their last MGM film together. It is written by Ruth Gordon and Garson Kanin, who had coauthored *Adam's Rib* for the duo.

◆ Gloria Grahame wins an Oscar as best supporting actress for her role in *The Bad and the Beautiful*, one of five statuettes the film garners, including one for best screenplay.

◆ With the release of *Ivanhoe*, MGM has its first British-made box-office smash since before World War II.

◆ The hit *Singin' in the Rain* is Gene Kelly's third musical production with producer Arthur Freed and makes Debbie Reynolds a star.

◆ Two Rex Ingram silents from the twenties, *The Prisoner of Zenda* and *Scaramouche*, are remade. Lewis Stone, who appeared in both silents, also appears in both remakes.

In a promotional photograph for Singin' in the Rain, *Debbie Reynolds makes the best of a rainy day by splashing through puddles on the lot.*

TOP: *Gene Kelly and company give it their all in the "Broadway Ballet" sequence from* Singin' in the Rain *(1952).*

ABOVE: *Gene Kelly and Cyd Charisse, as a seductive flapper, in the "Broadway Rhythm" number of the ballet sequence.*

Comden began work on a film that would use as many of the old songs from the Freed-Brown catalogue as possible. Director Stanley Donen recalled that "now when we talk about 'Singin' in the Rain,' it seems like a wonderful title for the movie. But at the time . . . the only reason to call it 'Singin' in the Rain' is because the number turned out so well." The famous "Singin' in the Rain" dance took a day and a half to shoot. The only problem came when the water pressure that created the downpour suddenly turned into a drizzle in the late afternoon, as the people of Culver City began to water their lawns.

The "Broadway Ballet," another virtuoso sequence in the film by Gene Kelly, lasted fourteen minutes and cost the studio $600,000. Although Nick Schenck readily agreed to it, the creators had not forgotten his critique of their previous effort. In the movie, Gene Kelly and Donald O'Connor describe a ballet to their studio boss as the audience watches it on the screen. When they eagerly ask him, "Well, what do you think of it?" the mogul replies, "I can't really visualize it until I see it on the screen." *Singin' in the Rain* went over budget by almost exactly the amount it cost to film the ballet. Released in April 1952, it made back three times its original cost.

The early fifties saw Schary's revitalization program threatened by the larger financial problems faced by the whole film industry. The impact of television resulted in dwindling audiences and the closing of theaters. By the summer of 1952, Nick Schenck asked Loew's executives with salaries exceeding $1,000 a week to take a cut—up to 50 percent in some cases. During the Depression, such sacrifices had been made for a couple of months, but now the

THE LIFE OF A SONG

ABOVE: *The cover of the "Singin' in the Rain" sheet music for* The Hollywood Revue of 1929.
LEFT: *Buster Keaton and Jimmy Durante work out the melody in* Speak Easily *(1932).*
RIGHT: *Judy Garland swings the tune in* Little Nellie Kelly *(1940).*
BELOW: *A wet Gene Kelly takes the lyrics literally in* Singin' in the Rain *(1952).*

On a sunny afternoon in 1929, composer Nacio Herb Brown, with whom Arthur Freed had been writing songs for eight years, appeared at the Freed-Brown office at MGM with a tune he had written for a coloratura soprano. "All I could think of," Freed remembered in later years, "was that a vamp in the bass and a few minor changes would give it the zip for some lyrics I'd written." Over the course of the next forty-odd years, "Singin' in the

Rain," the transformed ditty, would be included in seven films.

In its first onscreen appearance, the song was featured several times in *The Hollywood Revue of 1929*, most notably by the ever-popular Cliff Edwards (Ukelele Ike), strumming and singing along with a gaggle of slicker-clad chorines.

Its next cinema incarnation came along three years later, in *Speak Easily,* an amiable show-business yarn starring Buster Keaton, Jimmy Durante, Thelma Todd, and Hedda Hopper. In it, Durante claimed "Singin' in the Rain" for himself, plunking out the first eight bars on a rehearsal hall piano to a disbelieving stage manager.

Eight years afterward, the tune found its way into *Little Nellie Kelly*, which was based on a minor George M. Cohan musical. Starring Judy Garland in her first adult role, it was a ten-hand-kerchief story about a young Irish immigrant who dies while giving birth, but who then

returns as the daughter, Little Nellie. The film included some Cohan tunes, the Roger Edens rouser "It's a Great Day for the Irish," and, in one of those grand organdy-and-tuxedo songs-on-the-stairs settings, "Singin' in the Rain."

In 1944, the song was loaned out to Universal for a slight programmer, *Hi, Beautiful.* Based on an even more obscure film, *Love in a Bungalow,* it starred Noah Beery, Jr., Martha O'Driscoll, Hattie McDaniel, and Walter Catlett.

"Singin' in the Rain" was buried among many songs in this story of a GI couple.

Eight years later, after convincing Betty Comden and Adolph Green that their MGM contract would cheerfully accommodate a film featuring the songs of Freed and Brown, Arthur Freed revived his musical moneymaker (with a trademark "doodle-oo-doo, doodle oodle oo doo" by Roger Edens) as the featured number in the nonpareil MGM musical *Singin' in the Rain.*

In 1971, the tune was given its most bizarre setting when Stanley Kubrick used it in a song-and-dance rape and mutilation scene in *A Clockwork Orange.* Sandwiched between Rossini and Beethoven, "Singin' in the Rain" served as the musical underpinning for a scene of syncopated sadism.

But that was an aberration; the song's original sweetness returned two years later in the MGM compendium, *That's Entertainment.* Here "Singin' in the Rain" showed its simple splendors in a final, joyful reprise.

chief executive outlined austerity measures lasting a whole year. And he set an example by giving up half of his own $300,000 salary. Contrary to Schary's optimistic forecasts three years earlier, MGM's annual output was declining again; the studio's production dropped from an average of forty films per year to below thirty. Moreover, because of foreign quotas and changing tax laws, American film companies were being forced to reinvest their earnings abroad in foreign productions. In 1949, MGM revived its London studios and invested in a chain of theaters. The studio made fewer films in Hollywood, which meant less work for production personnel.

The only way real economies could be achieved was through drastic reductions of the permanent staff at Culver City, still numbering over 4,000 people. Contract players, who made five or six pictures a year in former days, now were making only one or two. As for the high-priced stars, they might be loaned out if another studio wanted them. Otherwise, they mostly sat on their hands. When contracts expired, some were renewed, but only as short-term, nonexclusive agreements. Scores of familiar faces began disappearing from the studio lots, and some of the best-known inhabitants of the small city-state left. There had been many emotional scenes in the early forties when everybody went off to war; now everybody knew that this time they would not be coming back. By the mid-fifties, most of the great stars had completed their exodus.

Clark Gable's contract, guaranteeing him $10,000 a week, ran out in 1954. After he made *Betrayed*, a tired World War II spy drama set in occupied Europe, the king found himself without a kingdom. If he suffered at all from not having a studio system to pick his roles for him, Gable made up for it financially through the lucrative deals based on percentages that Hollywood now offered.

Spencer Tracy's last affectionate teaming with Katharine Hepburn at MGM occurred in *Pat and Mike*, a film that benefited from the experience of two studio veterans, director George Cukor and producer Larry Weingarten. Following Hepburn's departure from MGM in 1952, Tracy found himself in troubled waters. That same year he captained the Pilgrim Fathers in *Plymouth Adventure*, a big-budget disaster produced by Schary that came to be known as the "Thanksgiving turkey." Schary had to threaten Tracy with a lawsuit to make the actor show up for his last, and perhaps best, role at MGM, in the contemporary western *Bad Day at Black Rock*. His portrayal of a one-armed veteran, whose sudden arrival in a small desert town exposes a murderous secret, brought him an Academy Award nomination and a prize at the Cannes Film Festival. But after he quarreled with director Robert Wise, Tracy was replaced by James Cagney in *Tribute to a Bad Man*. He would not act at MGM again.

Throughout the fifties, there was a steady exodus from the studio of stars, including Van Johnson, Esther Williams, and Jane Powell. The demise of the twin phenomena of the seven-year contract and the studio system meant that top Hollywood actors such as Marlon Brando, Gregory Peck, Cary Grant, and Jean Simmons now signed contracts to appear only in a specific role. With a lack of commitment on both sides, MGM no longer had the interest or the time to

TOP: Million Dollar Mermaid *(1952) is Esther Williams's favorite role. She plays Australian swimming champion Annette Kellerman, who also acts in films and who revolutionizes the swimwear industry with her one-piece, form-fitting bathing suit.*

ABOVE: *Esther Williams as a starlet in a 1944 photographic study. She will entertain audiences in lavish water extravaganzas for over a decade.*

develop an actor. In its golden era, MGM spent almost as much of its resources grooming its stars as it did making pictures; at least, the two threads had been intertwined. Louis B. Mayer's greatest personal achievement may have been in making MGM the greatest star of all.

Dore Schary, less concerned with stars than his predecessors had been, wanted to be remembered for the content of his pictures. In fact, both he and Schenck tried to carry on the central producer system, which was more akin to Thalberg's type of creative control than Mayer's management-by-committee. Only now these two executives were operating under vastly less favorable circumstances. They were fighting a rearguard action against two of the biggest threats that the film industry faced in the postwar period: television and the government's Paramount Decree, which forced motion-picture companies to choose between producing films and exhibiting them. Some studios started to invest in television programming at the same time that they began selling their theater chains. Loew's Inc. took another decade to divest, which may explain its tardiness in entering television.

Visual images had been broadcast successfully in the mid-1920s, when the talkies began, but television did not become a viable medium until twenty years later. In 1946 and 1947, around seven thousand television sets were manufactured; three years later, a million homes in the United States had them; and by 1951, ten million sets had been sold. As early as 1948, David Sarnoff, the founder of RCA, went to see Nicholas Schenck to offer a strategic alliance between NBC and MGM. Schenck reputedly told him,

ABOVE: *Mario Lanza at his peak as* The Great Caruso *(1951), an enormous success. Under contract to MGM, the tenor's weight balloons along with his ego, and he walks out of production during the remake of* The Student Prince *(1954). The studio slaps him with a lawsuit, which is settled when MGM keeps his singing voice but uses Edmund Purdom in the role. In 1959, Lanza dies of chronic ailments at age thirty-eight.*

ON THE TECHNICAL SIDE

Over the years, MGM developed a reputation for superior technical quality, but it was never the first studio to put a new process on film. Even while waiting for systems to be proven by others, the company became an innovator in several fields.

TWO-COLOR TECHNICOLOR: Early color films were either tinted or, in special cases, hand colored. Herbert Kalmus founded the Technicolor Motion Picture Company by 1917, and, by 1922, Metro was the first to distribute a feature in two-color Technicolor, *Toll of the Sea*. MGM used this system in the 1925 *Ben-Hur*. The biblical scenes were in color, and the remainder in black and white, although extensive tinting was applied. MGM's first entire Technicolor feature, the silent film *The Vikings,* appeared in 1928.

The musical number, "The Wedding of the Painted Doll," in *The Broadway Melody* (1929) was filmed in Technicolor. The number is also considered to be the first shot to a prerecorded soundtrack, eliminating the need to make a perfect recording in front of the cameras.

The main drawback to the two-color system was that it could not truly reproduce the visible spectrum. Audiences soon tired of the unrealistic color, and, as a consequence, Warner Bros.'s *Mystery of the Wax Museum* (1933) was the last feature film to use the process.

THREE-STRIP TECHNICOLOR: By 1932, Technicolor introduced a three-color process to commercial motion pictures with Walt Disney's cartoon *Flowers and Trees*. The use of all three primary colors resulted in an image that could be completely true to the actual color of the object being photographed. It was first used for live action in the 1934 short, *La Cucaracha*.

Shortly thereafter, MGM experimented with the new technique in the final scenes of *The Cat and the Fiddle* (1934). They also made several short subjects that helped the studio photographic staff experiment with lighting techniques. Although Pioneer Pictures (whose owner was an investor in Technicolor) made the first full three-strip feature in 1935, MGM did not make one until *Sweethearts* in 1938, followed by the classic *The Wizard of Oz* the next year. Although *Oz* used black and white (processed in

sepia tone) for the Kansas sequences, it went into three-strip color once Dorothy arrived in Oz.

David O. Selznick's *Gone with the Wind,* also in 1939, marked an important breakthrough for Technicolor, as its use in a film of this calibre had a major impact on the film industry. MGM made increasing use of this three-color process in the 1940s. In fact, the studio made 115 features, more than any other studio, in the three-strip process before discontinuing its use in 1953.

THREE-DIMENSION: Three-dimension photography is almost as old as photography itself. Hand-held stereoscopic viewers were a common fixture in many living rooms. In order to produce a 3-D image, two photos must be taken, using two cameras with lenses about the same distance apart as the human eyes. Then these photos must be viewed with an instrument that allows each eye to see only the image intended for it.

This proved cumbersome for motion pictures, because it is not possible to have a viewer system for a large audience. So the separation of pictures was managed by printing one image with a red tone and the other with green. When a viewer put on special glasses with one red and one green lens, each eye saw only the image photographed with the corresponding camera, and the brain interpreted it as having depth.

MGM experimented with this process in three short subjects in 1938. These were successful as novelties, but never more than that. After the wide-screen revolution in 1952, experi-

ments with 3-D resurfaced, this time using Polaroid filters instead of the old red/green ones.

MGM's first 3-D production was *Kiss Me Kate* (1953). The addition of depth was used to good effect, but the cumbersome projection and audience resistance to wearing the glasses made the system short-lived. *Kiss Me Kate* ran only a short time in its original format but later achieved fame as a conventional "flat" film. (Either the left or right print of a 3-D pair could be projected normally in any theater.) The only other 3-D movie made by MGM was *Arena* (1953), which also had a short run.

CINEMASCOPE:

CinemaScope, a wide-screen system perfected in 1952 by 20th Century-Fox and the Bausch and Lomb Optical Company, used conventional cameras with a special lens that squeezed the image to half of its width in proportion to its height. Additionally, this process used stereophonic sound, recorded directly on the projection print by painting magnetic stripes on the film in the sprocket-hole area (in effect, a tape recording allowing four channels of sound, instead of the usual optical soundtrack, with only one channel). Fox licensed CinemaScope to other production companies, and MGM first used it with *Knights of the Round Table* (1954). With the exception of some modifications in the soundtrack—placing both a standard optical track and the stereo magnetic tracks on the same film—this system became widely used and is still relatively common today.

WIDE-FILM PROCESSES:

As early as 1930, there were experiments with photographing on film wider than the 35mm, to obtain a larger but still very sharp screen image. MGM used 70mm film for *Billy the Kid* that year, as did 20th Century-Fox with *The Big Trail*. The generally depressed economics of the time, together with the recent heavy expenses of sound installations, contributed to intermittent use of wide-film processes until after 1950, when television became increasingly popular.

In order to present an experience that could never be duplicated on the home screen, an elaborate system called Cinerama was first exhibited in 1951. This process had three cameras simultaneously photographing the left, center, and right parts of a subject. Three interlocked projectors ran the sections on a large, curved screen. Full stereophonic sound, recorded on another roll of film, ran in synchronization with the picture. Cinerama required specially modified theaters and became a roadshow presentation in a few large cities.

Most Cinerama productions were no more than travelogues. MGM, in cooperation with the Cinerama company, produced two narrative features in the three-camera process, *The Wonderful World of Brothers Grimm* and *How the West Was Won* in 1962. After the limited Cinerama showings, the three panels of film were combined optically to conventional 35mm for general theatrical release.

The Todd-AO Company, a collaboration between producer Michael Todd and the American Optical Company, perfected lenses and projection systems that could utilize 70mm film in both photography and projection, providing a larger screen image with superior clarity. It also allowed room on the print for six channels of stereophonic sound.

In the mid-fifties MGM's technical department, now under Douglas Shearer, took the large film process one step further and named its system "MGM Camera 65." (The camera negative was 65mm, but 70mm was needed for the sound tracks.) It used an anamorphic lens, similar to CinemaScope, which squeezed the image by 10 percent. But theaters had already spent heavily for CinemaScope lenses and screens, stereophonic sound, and in many cases 70mm projectors. MGM's system, used only on *Raintree County* (1957) and the remake of *Ben-Hur* (1959), did not gain acceptance.

"David, what have you got to offer? We've got the pictures."
A little more than a year later, the New York *Daily News*
quoted Schenck as saying that "so far television hasn't hurt
the box office. Good pictures do business as always." In fact,
movie attendance had declined close to 20 percent by then.
In addition, Hollywood's sale of eighty million movie tickets
a week at the end of the war would drop to thirty-five million
ten years later. As late as 1952, Schary, like Schenck,
did not believe that television would pose a major threat for
several years, even when colleagues at other studios were
telling him that his job at MGM was like taking over the
helm of the *Titanic*.

Rather than looking upon television as a gold mine of
opportunity, most studio executives viewed it as a system
that gave away for free a product that people always paid
good money to see in a theater. MGM was the longest holdout in refusing to sell or show its library of old films. The
studio also failed to exploit its series and B-pictures, which
were actually prototypes for television programming.
Lassie and *Dr. Kildare* did not appear on the small screen
until the late fifties and early sixties. Meanwhile, the broadcast companies went ahead and developed the new medium.
Deprived of films, they invented a golden age of innovative,
seat-of-the-pants live programming, using mainly talent
from radio, nightclubs, and theater. Like most studios, MGM
tried to prevent its contract players from appearing on television, creating a snobbish division in the entertainment
industry that persists to the present.

To draw viewers back to theaters, the major film companies turned to technological innovations that gave
audiences thrills they could not get from watching their
flickering black-and-white screens. Experiments in 3-D and
stereoscopic film—some dating back to the beginning of the
century—were updated and led to a number of productions
that studios gambled would relight the fire of the movie
craze, including MGM's 3-D version of *Kiss Me Kate*, Cole
Porter's musical version of *The Taming of the Shrew*.
Unfortunately, despite all the hoopla, no one could
perfect an inexpensive, comfortable 3-D process.
Theater projection of 3-D was very cumbersome, as it

*Leslie Caron as an orphan girl
who joins a carnival in* Lili
*(1953). Caron is nominated for
an Oscar, and Bronislau
Kaper's score wins one.*

1953

◆ MGM announces a "broad cooperative alliance" with NBC-TV in which the studio agrees to "make available its entire roster of talent for special appearances on NBC Television Shows."

◆ MGM releases *The Band Wagon*, a satire written by Betty Comden and Adolph Green based on themselves. Vincente Minnelli conceives the famous Mickey Spillane "Girl Hunt" ballet scene and films it in a brisk seven days. The rousing "That's Entertainment" is written for the picture.

◆ *Main Street to Broadway* boasts "in person" appearances by Tallulah Bankhead, Ethel Barrymore, and Lionel Barrymore. Though it's Lionel's last film, MGM honors his "life-time" contract, keeping him on salary until his death the following year.

◆ MGM's first film in CinemaScope, *Knights of the Round Table*, with Robert Taylor and Ava Gardner, is a blockbuster hit; as is the Cole Porter musical *Kiss Me Kate*, which features the dancing and, in one number, the choreography of a young Bob Fosse.

◆ Joan Crawford returns to MGM after ten years to make *Torch Song*.

Marlon Brando as Mark Antony in Julius Caesar. *Both Brando and the film are nominated for Oscars.*

296

TOP: *(Left to right) Ann Miller, Tommy Rall, Bobby Van, and Bob Fosse in* Kiss Me Kate *(1953).*

ABOVE: *A poster for* The Band Wagon *(1953) depicts Cyd Charisse and Fred Astaire in the film's climactic "Girl Hunt" ballet, a spoof of Mickey Spillane thrillers.*

required two projectors run in perfect synchronization, and viewers chafed at the headache-inducing eyeglasses they had to wear. Within a few years, the fad died as quickly as it had started.

Among the new wide-screen processes for projecting films was Cinerama. It used three projectors to throw a single image onto a vast curving screen. *This Is Cinerama* caused a sensation at New York's Broadway Theater when it premiered in September 1952. Its producers, however, had gone deeply into debt, and large investments were needed for the technical equipment to make film production pay off. The officers of the Cinerama Corporation, including broadcaster Lowell Thomas, searched for someone with experience in all aspects of the picture business. They approached Louis B. Mayer and invited him to be chairman of their board.

Mayer traveled to New York to see *This Is Cinerama*. After he viewed it, he was so enthusiastic that he compared the experience to the moment when *The Birth of a Nation* convinced him to become a producer. One of the conditions of the contract he signed was that Cinerama would buy the three literary properties he had been developing since leaving MGM, including the epic *Joseph and His Brethren*. The struggling corporation may have hoped its new chairman would dig into his deep pockets; in fact, he did not put any of his own money into the operation. But he did arrange loans and offer counsel and advice. Mayer settled his contract by late 1954, taking some losses in unpaid salary but probably making an overall profit with his stock options. Although Cinerama survived, it was used mainly for travelogues. Only a handful of feature films employed the process, including MGM's *How the West Was Won* in 1962.

The wide-screen process that really dominated the fifties, until Panavision came along in the mid-sixties, was

ABOVE: *A title card for* Kiss Me Kate *(1953).*
LEFT: *Ann Miller dances right in your lap—at least that's the implication in this trick photograph promoting the 3-D version of* Kiss Me Kate.

CinemaScope. Unlike Cinerama, CinemaScope needed only one camera with a special anamorphic lens for filming and only one projector for screening. The new wider screens may have encouraged the trend toward spectacles: so much space had to be filled with big events and larger-than-life characters. MGM licensed the process from 20th Century-Fox and then achieved commercial success with it in *Bad Day at Black Rock* and epics such as *Knights of the Round Table.*

But technology alone could not save Hollywood. By 1954, Hollywood realized it could no longer ignore television and began to eye it as a medium of advertising. That year, Walt Disney launched an hour-long weekly TV series, "Disneyland," primarily to promote his new theme park in California; a year later, Loew's made a deal with ABC for a half-hour program, "The MGM Parade." The studio's first clumsy entry into the field was a patchwork of shorts, backstage visits at Culver City, and clips from MGM's latest releases. Hosted by George Murphy, the program was not well received.

In Nicholas Schenck's eyes, this commercial failure confirmed his prejudices against the newfangled medium. Others felt that the executive, at seventy-four, was too conservative to adapt to a fast-changing industry that required bold decisions. Loew's board of directors came under increasing pressure from stockholders, who were alarmed by the company's growing debts and losses and even more so by its lack of direction. Finally, in late 1955, Schenck was eased upstairs into the position of chairman of the board. Arthur Loew, who had been successfully running the international operations, assumed control over his father's company. One of the first steps he took was to announce that "The MGM Parade" would be expanded to serialize some of the studio's classics, such as *Captains*

Courageous and *The Pirate*. Henceforth, Walter Pidgeon would introduce each episode.

By this time, several studios had made their film libraries available to television for flat sums. MGM, the last holdout, followed a more lucrative path of licensing its legendary hits. On the evening of November 3, 1956, in the middle of the Suez crisis and the Hungarian revolution, one third of America watched the first telecast of *The Wizard of Oz*, which CBS licensed for $250,000 as part of a deal for nine showings worth $1.7 million. The high ratings for *Oz* revolutionized Hollywood's attitude toward TV. MGM subsequently released for broadcast a package of seven hundred lesser-known features from the studio's library for $25 million. With the release of each old feature on television, many saw the famous logo for the first time; for others who had seen the movie previously on the big screen, the showings evoked nostalgic memories. Hollywood had found a way of taming the television monster; movies would become the main staple of home entertainment for the foreseeable future.

The new source of revenues, however, could not solve the deeper problems that beset management at MGM. A month before the *Oz* telecast, Arthur Loew grew tired of the power struggles with, and within, his board of directors and abruptly resigned. The confidence of the banking and the film communities, both of which held Loew in high regard, was shaken. One of Schenck's failures had been that he never named or trained a successor, and now he headed a search committee to find a new president. After two weeks, the board voted to install Joseph R. Vogel as president of Loew's Inc. and to create the position of honorary chairman for Schenck. Arthur Loew resumed his position as head of Loew's International and also took his place as chairman of the board.

Vogel was the compromise candidate agreed upon by the various factions on the board after each failed to get its own nominee elected. A rather nondescript organization man, he had come up through the ranks of Loew's exhibiting division. Starting as an usher, he trained as an accountant, then served as treasurer of a couple of smaller theaters before becoming manager of Loew's State in New York City in 1924. That was also the year Metro-Goldwyn-Mayer was founded. It took Vogel another twenty-one years to be named by Schenck as the general manager of all Loew's theaters. He was elected to the board in 1948, the year Dore Schary returned to MGM as production chief. Now, eight years later, the accountant in Vogel looked at the company's books and saw that the once-profitable studio was losing money. He soon decided that Schary would be the ideal scapegoat with which to explain the company's problems to the board, to the stockholders, and to the financial world.

Vogel summoned the studio chief to New York and asked him to resign. Schary preferred to be fired, though he settled his contract for $100,000 and another $900,000 in deferred salaries. Schary went on to achieve further success writing and producing plays for the Broadway stage, including two about his hero, Franklin D. Roosevelt. In a makeshift attempt to reassemble a management team, Joseph Vogel next appointed Benjamin Thau, the chief naysayer, to take over the badly demoralized studio on the West Coast. Veteran director Sidney Franklin accepted an associate position created to help Thau, an administrator, with artistic decisions.

Watching these machinations among his former associates and present enemies, Louis B. Mayer saw his chance to stage a comeback. It was during this period that he met Stanley Meyer, a coproducer of "Dragnet," who had become wealthy after selling his interest in the series. With the help of Joseph Tomlinson, who owned one of the largest blocks of Loew's common stock and who happened to be disgruntled at the way the company was being managed, Meyer led a campaign to bring back Mayer, either as president of Loew's or as a consultant to MGM. But at the age of seventy-two, Mayer was not his old self and hesitated at the very moment the members of the board began to wonder if indeed he might be the only one to restore MGM to its former greatness. His uncertainty gave Vogel a chance to mount an

Metro-Goldwyn-Mayer's
anniversary celebration of 1953.

299

effective counterattack from which Mayer could not recover. Although Tomlinson called his own faction on the board to a meeting in New York in order to name Mayer a director, the session was later declared illegal by a Delaware court. "I am here because I am lonely for Leo the Lion," a rather pathetic Mayer told the press after the meeting. In reality, the old lion was hurt by the unfavorable response from senior management, who felt that studio morale, badly damaged in the wake of Schary's departure, would be shattered further if Mayer were to take charge again. The emotional wound was quickly overshadowed by a deeper physical illness; the exhaustion he had been experiencing lately was discovered to be the result of leukemia.

On October 29, 1957, Louis B. Mayer died, attended by his second wife, Lorena, and second daughter, Irene. During his last days, he had hoped that his firstborn daughter, Edith (whom he had alienated after attacking her husband, William Goetz, for cohosting a Democratic fundraiser with Dore Schary), would come to see him, but she stayed away. In his will, he disinherited her and her children. After taking care of his immediate family, he left much of his $7.5 million estate to a vaguely defined Louis B. Mayer Foundation. Mayer had never been one to make charitable contributions. In fact, a business associate once approached Mayer on behalf of a good cause and was turned down. After being reminded that he could not take his wealth with him, Mayer, somewhat surprised, replied, "Then I'm not going."

Most of the studio executives and many stars, some no longer at MGM, came to the memorial service held at the Wilshire Boulevard Temple to say farewell to their old boss. Nicholas Schenck was not among them. Jeanette MacDonald sang "Sweet Mystery of Life," and Spencer Tracy read the eulogy, a collaborative effort by David Selznick and two of Mayer's favorite writers, Carey Wilson and John Lee Mahin. "MGM has got L. B. back again," said one joke that circulated after the funeral, as a final comment on the upheavals of the year. "Yes," was the reply, "but on its own terms."

A few months before Mayer's death, Loew's embattled directors had hired a management consultant firm to make a study of the company. They wanted to know what was wrong with MGM and what direction the studio should take. A man named C. R. MacBride was assigned this task and dispatched to the West Coast. He questioned Mayer, among others, on how MGM might be returned to its former greatness. The old mogul advised that the studio should concentrate its efforts on blockbusters as well as make deals with major independent producers. MacBride was impressed by Mayer's counsel, which predicted, more or less, the future course of the studio's existence as an independent entity. To anybody inside the industry, however, this advice was just common sense. It had been the policy of most of the major studios, and in order to stay competitive, Schenck and Schary should have pursued it long before.

Once Vogel and Thau felt secure in their positions, they announced a slate of projects—some already in the works, others in planning stages—in an attempt to assure the public that the MGM lion would roar again. Their choices emulated the production philosophies that had previously lifted the studio to the pinnacle of success, including Dore Schary's approach. In the mid-fifties, a number of Hollywood films were produced that dealt realistically with mature but

MASTERS OF MAKEUP

In the early days of movie-making, actors put on their own makeup, just as they had done for the stage. Some actors, such as the incredibly versatile Lon Chaney (Sr.), excelled at the task. But as movie production became more and more demanding, actors were better off in the hands of those who understood the visual requirements of lights, film, and camera.

British-born Cecil Holland is generally acknowledged as having founded the MGM makeup department in 1927. A successful stage and silent-screen actor himself, Holland enjoyed creating his own character makeup and had a flair for painting the faces of his fellow actors. He hand-painted more than 800 lines on Nigel De Brulier's face, transforming him into a Hindu holy man for *Son of India* (1931), and aged Helen Hayes for *The Sin of Madelon Claudet* (1932). That same year, Holland gave Lewis Stone a grenade-scarred face for *Grand Hotel*, made a mad monk of Lionel Barrymore for *Rasputin and the Empress*, and turned gentle Boris Karloff into the wicked namesake of *The Mask of Fu Manchu*.

TOP: *In* The Sin of Madelon Claudet *(1932),* Helen Hayes's *character goes through many changes—naive farm girl, kept woman, convict, prostitute, and old lady.*
ABOVE: *For* Broadway Melody of 1940, *Eleanor Powell's makeup, hair, costume, and nails are tended to—all at once!*

When Jack Dawn succeeded Holland, who left in 1934, the makeup department at MGM consisted of only two rooms and about four people. Dawn's assistant, William Tuttle, recalled: "Dawn was a perfectionist and an exacting man. He had big plans for a class operation." For starters, the work area was cleaned until it sparkled, and the employees were outfitted in white smocks. The men had to wear coats and ties under their smocks. But, according to veteran MGM makeup artist Charles Schram, Dawn was more than an administrator; he was also a fine sculptor and painter.

Schram, who learned his brushwork from both Dawn and Holland, was first hired to work with the former on *The Good Earth* (1937), for which Dawn also brought back Holland to help with the crucial job of turning Vienna-born Luise Rainer into the stoic Chinese peasant O-Lan. Dawn, who designed all the Chinese makeup, resorted to the extensive use of molds in making the gelatin eye tabs to cover the tear ducts, thus transforming Occidental eyes into Asian ones. (Such artificial devices for creating facial features are called *appliances*.)

The Good Earth was the first large-scale attempt to use molds in order to bring uniformity and consistency to appliances that heretofore had been re-created by hand each day. Hundreds of extras were also required to wear tight-fitting bald caps and queues made of highly flammable cellulose nitrate. Unfortunately, the caps shrank in the warm air, exposing skin that was not made up. So during the eleven months of shooting, the makeup personnel were kept hopping replacing bald pates.

As big as it was, The Good Earth was but one of several makeup projects—including the aging of Jeanette MacDonald for Maytime and the transformation of Charles Boyer into Napoleon for Conquest—tackled by MGM in 1937. (Dawn worked from Napoleon's actual death mask to build Boyer's appliances.) Not everyone appreciated such transformations. Spencer Tracy, for one, was embarrassed by the curls hairstylists gave him for the part of the Portuguese fisherman in Captains Courageous (also 1937). Joan Crawford did not help matters when she first saw Tracy's curls and hooted, "My God, it's Harpo Marx!"

Though preproduction for The Good Earth was well under way by the time Dawn came to MGM, he used this opportunity to recruit new talent, expanding his domain to include such makeup artists as Schram, Emile LaVigne, Jack Young, Eddie Polo, Jack Kevan, Kester Sweeney, and John Truii. Wig-maker Garland 'Skipper' Bryden was another stalwart. Lillian Rosine and Violette des Noyes, who applied body makeup to the actresses, were holdovers from the Holland era. They and many others would be needed for a colossal makeup job in the still-new medium of Technicolor for The Wizard of Oz (1939).

About forty extra makeup artists were hired for this fantasy, which required makeup for about 600 actors, including more than 120 Munchkins. During the twenty-two weeks of shooting, each of the principals had his or her own makeup artist, and between thirty and forty makeup people daily produced Munchkins at the rate of nearly fifty an hour. This efficiency was possible in part because of the assembly-line manufacturing of foam-rubber cheeks, noses, and other features. These appliances were far more durable than the gelatin-based ones. Building on others' work as well as on their own experience with molds, laboratory experts at MGM discovered ways of making foam-rubber pieces with thin edges that could be smoothly blended with real skin using spirit gum.

Even today, Oz's scarecrow gives audiences the illusion of a talking burlap bag

TOP: *MGM makeup master Jack Dawn puts finishing touches on a lifemask of Robert Morley. He will use the mask to design character makeup for the actor in* Marie Antoinette *(1938).*

ABOVE: *A makeup department worker displays mustaches, beards, and sideburns, including the one worn by Clark Gable in* Parnell *(1937).*

because the foam rubber was so subtly blended with Ray Bolger's face. The custom-tailored rubber bag, which covered all of Bolger's head except for his eyes, nose, and mouth took two hours to glue and paint. Another hour was required to remove it. After wearing as many as one hundred of these bags, Bolger found permanent lines etched on his chin and in the corners of his mouth.

Bill Tuttle officially became Dawn's second in command in 1942. By then, the department occupied a whole floor and had an elaborate setup of ten or fifteen stalls to make up some of the world's most beautiful women. A routine day began at 6:30 or 7:00 A.M., with makeup for actresses such as Ava Gardner and Lana Turner. It took Schram and other veteran artists around thirty minutes to make up each person, so they would work up three or four stars apiece. The rest of the schedule varied according to which films were in production and how many actors had to be prepared for screen tests, which was one of the chief duties of the makeup department. David Niven recalled his reaction to Tuttle's makeup for his first color test: "I had been painted a strange yellow ocher . . . and my eyes and lips had been made up like a Piccadilly tart—I felt ridiculous."

As Dawn's heyday waned in the late 1940s, his staff also started to diminish. Tuttle took over the department in 1950, and Charles Schram became his assistant shortly afterward. In this era, the MGM musical was briefly rejuvenated, causing bursts of activity for the makeup people. During the filming of *An American in Paris* (1951), Tuttle had as many as one-hundred hairdressers and makeup artists working for him. But as studio production spiraled downward, the makeup department lost its momentum.

A bright moment came in 1965, when the Academy of Motion Picture Arts and Sciences presented Tuttle with a Special Achievement Oscar in honor of his work on *Seven Faces of Dr. Lao.* It was the first such award to go to a makeup artist. Charles Schram retired in the same year, and promptly took up free-lancing. Tuttle retired four years later, after the makeup department folded, leaving a lustrous film legacy and a lot of industry artists who had cut their teeth at MGM.

Rare color frames from the 1950s show stars in makeup and costume being test shot to make sure they will photograph properly. (Clockwise from upper left) Howard Keel and

Keenan Wynn for Kiss Me Kate *(1953), Cyd Charisse for* Sombrero *(1952), and James Whitmore, Bobby Van, and Ann Miller for* Kiss Me Kate.

difficult subjects. In 1955, MGM made *The Blackboard Jungle*, an uncompromising portrayal of violence in urban schools directed by Richard Brooks. As soon as the studio announced its plans to produce Evan Hunter's best seller, the Motion Picture Association of America opposed it, but Dore Schary had been sold on the realistic treatment of a contemporary problem. The film starred Glenn Ford as an idealistic teacher who appeals to a young student, played by Sidney Poitier, to set an example among his delinquent friends. *The Blackboard Jungle* was also the first film to use rock-and-roll music ("Rock Around the Clock") on a sound track. With *Jailhouse Rock*, Elvis Presley launched a string of profitable films for MGM aimed even more directly at the youth market.

In 1958, Richard Brooks directed another hit based on a controversial subject. *Cat on a Hot Tin Roof* brought together a Pulitzer-Prize-winning play by Tennessee Williams with one of MGM's last great stars. Elizabeth Taylor was at the end of her studio contract when she made the film, which featured powerful screen performances by Taylor and Paul Newman, both of whom were nominated for Academy Awards, as well as by Burl Ives, who repeated his stage role as Big Daddy. Although the story's themes of impotence and homosexuality were censored, the ensuing controversy made it easier for later films such as *Suddenly Last Summer* to deal more openly with such subjects.

Hollywood usually managed to outfox the censors by packaging sex into biblical epics (which made the Reverend Malcolm Boyd defend *Cat on a Hot Tin Roof* as having more religion than *The Ten Commandments*). The Legion of

TOP: Seven Brides for Seven Brothers *(1954) draws raves for Michael Kidd's rambunctious, often hair-raising choreography. Recipient of five Oscar nominations, including one for best picture, it wins for its musical score.*
ABOVE: *In the film, Milly (Jane Powell) faces a mess made by the brothers.*

OPPOSITE: *Elvis Presley (center) in* Jailhouse Rock *(1957), the story of an ex-con who becomes a pop star. The title song alone sells over two million records in the first month of its release.*

1954

◆ Clark Gable ends his twenty-four-year-reign as the King of MGM in *Betrayed*. Moving on, he finds that freelance deals pay more than his annual $500,000 MGM salary.

◆ After fifteen years, Greer Garson also bids farewell to MGM with *Her Twelve Men*, costarring Robert Ryan.

◆ Although Van Johnson decides to leave as well after completing *The Last Time I Saw Paris*, he will return as a freelancer for several more films.

◆ *Seven Brides for Seven Brothers*, with Howard Keel and Jane Powell, is MGM's sensational and surprising hit of the year, due largely to the talented direction of Stanley Donen.

◆ *Brigadoon* does fairly well but falls short of expectation, as it is filmed in CinemaScope-AnscoColor. It is produced by Arthur Freed and directed by Vincente Minnelli.

◆ Edmund Purdom replaces a tempestuous Mario Lanza in *The Student Prince*, the stage operetta first filmed in 1927. MGM cancels his contract but then brings him back three years later.

◆ In the remake department, *Rose Marie* gets its third airing out, this time with Howard Keel and Ann Blyth.

Lucille Ball and Desi Arnaz in their honeymoon home, The Long Long Trailer.

305

BE A CLOWN

At one time or another, most of the great film clowns worked at MGM. Jack Benny hosted *The Hollywood Revue of 1929*, and later partnered with Ted Healy in *It's in the Air* (1935). The Three Stooges popped up in *Meet the Baron* (1933) and *Dancing Lady* (1933). The inimitible George Burns and Gracie Allen enlivened *Honolulu* (1938). Bud Abbott and Lou Costello starred in two brassy wartime musicals, then gave a tour of the MGM lot in *Abbott and Costello in Hollywood* (1945). And the normally misanthropic W. C. Fields was, in George Cukor's words, "born to play" Mr. Micawber in *David Copperfield* (1935). These performers were borrowed for their individual projects.

MGM had relatively few comedians under contract. Foremost in the stable was Buster Keaton. Between 1920 and 1928, he and his hand-picked crew turned out some thirty shorts and features. Filled with breathtaking stunts and intricate chases, these silent movies seem fresh even today. Keaton's resourcefulness and determination as a character, his mastery of sight gags and physical comedy, and his unsentimental directing had a profound impact on subsequent comedians.

Through a deal with his producer (and eventual brother-in-law) Joseph Schenck, most of Keaton's films were distributed by Metro and later by Metro-Goldwyn. In 1928, Schenck sold Keaton's studio and turned their contract over to his brother, Nicholas, at MGM. *The Cameraman* (1928) and *Spite Marriage* (1929), Keaton's first MGM films, were made with his own unit. Both captured the magic of his earlier work, and *The Cameraman* was used for decades to train MGM contract comics.

But under Thalberg's system of central authority, Keaton lost his unit and his autonomy. Producers Harry Rapf and Lawrence Weingarten cast him in a series of hastily assembled stage adaptations. These films made money, but lowered Keaton's standards and cheapened his character. He complained to Thalberg, who pointed out that his MGM

ABOVE: *Buster Keaton, the great stone face, looks to Lon Chaney, the man of a thousand faces, for makeup inspiration.*

BELOW: *Ted Healy, the Three Stooges, and director Robert Z. Leonard clown with Joan Crawford on the set of* Dancing Lady *(1933). (Left to right) Larry Fine, Healy (on top), Curly Howard, Leonard, and Moe Howard.*

films were more profitable than his silent masterpieces had been. Thalberg forbade Keaton from performing his own stunts (a point of honor with the comic), and rejected his ideas for movies, such as starring with Marie Dressler in a Western satire of *Grand Hotel*.

Keaton's crumbling marriage and rising alcoholism aided his downfall. By 1933, he was being teamed with Jimmy Durante in embarrassing efforts such as *What! No Beer?* After fighting with Mayer about parties in his studio bungalow, Keaton was suspended, then fired.

Over the next thirty years, he starred in low-budget shorts, worked as a gag writer (notably with Red Skelton), and had bits in films such as *In the Good Old Summertime* (1949). After the rediscovery of his silent films and the receipt of a special Oscar in 1959, Keaton's reputation reached new heights. Today, he is regarded as one of the premier talents in the history of film.

Like Keaton, the Marx Brothers started out in vaudeville, then conquered Broadway during the 1920s. Groucho's leering innuendos, Chico's tortured malapropisms, and Harpo's mute surrealism transcended the simplistic plots of their early films. But after five movies at Paramount, their irreverence and anarchy began to fail at the box office. Thalberg saw a solution: return them to their stage roots and restrict their zaniness within the confines of a straight romantic comedy. He hired Morrie Ryskind and George S. Kaufman to write a script, and allowed the Marxes to test the material on a nationwide tour. Helped by the hit song "Alone" and the presence of Margaret Dumont, *A Night at the Opera* (1935) became their biggest hit. Its crowded stateroom scene and its spirited attack on an opening performance of *Il Trovatore* are now comic legend.

Thalberg had found a winning formula for the Marxes, but he died before their next film, *A Day at the Races* (1937), was completed. Almost as buoyant as its predecessor, its highlight is a racetrack scene in which Chico pitches a complicated betting scheme to

Groucho. But without Thalberg's guidance, the vehicles became increasingly tired and predictable; fans also felt that the love subplots and popular songs injected into the stories diluted the Marxes' strengths. After two more mediocre movies, the brothers left the studio.

Red Skelton appeared in bit parts before starring in *Whistling in the Dark* (1941), a surprise hit that inspired two sequels. MGM groomed Skelton, placing him in supporting roles in musicals such as *Lady Be Good* (1941), and assigning Buster Keaton to hone his physical comedy skills. Skelton remade three Keaton features, reworking many of the silent star's sight gags for the sound era. By the late 1940s, Skelton was the most important comic star at MGM. He teamed twice with Esther Williams, and even sang a bit of the Oscar-winning "Baby, It's Cold Outside" in *Neptune's Daughter* (1949). He was surprisingly restrained and effective playing songwriter Harry Ruby to Fred Astaire's Bert Kalmar in *Three Little Words* (1950). In 1953, after *The Clown* (a maudlin reworking of *The Champ*) and the listless *Great Diamond Robbery*, Skelton left films for a long career on TV.

Lucille Ball came to MGM in 1943, after years of bit parts and supporting roles at other studios. In *Best Foot Forward* (1943), she gave a charmingly tongue-in-cheek performance as a publicity-obsessed movie star, then took the lead in *Du Barry Was a Lady* (1943). But subsequent roles were supporting ones, and it wasn't until she and Desi Arnaz developed *I Love Lucy* for TV that she became known as Hollywood's best female clown.

Other comedians included the silent team of George K. Arthur and Karl Dane, and the boyish William Haines, but MGM's style ran more to star-driven stories. The studio expected its stars, even Garbo, to work in comedy. Writers such as Donald Ogden Stewart, George Oppenheimer, Anita Loos, Frances Goodrich, and Albert Hackett wrote stories that were alternately brittle and frothy, penetrating and scatterbrained. The results helped broaden the appeal of stars such as Harlow, Gable, Tracy, and Loy. Farces, satires, and screwball comedies were rare at MGM, though Harlow did burlesque her sexpot persona in *Bombshell* (1933) and Joan Crawford indulged in some pratfalls in *Forsaking All Others* (1934). Typical MGM comedies—such as *Dinner at Eight* (1933) and *Libeled Lady* (1936)—tended toward upper-class characters and elegant settings.

ABOVE: *Louis XV (Red Skelton) thinks he and Madame Du Barry (Lucille Ball) are in the court of Louis XIV but will soon discover otherwise in* Du Barry Was a Lady *(1943). The two comedians will later reach their peaks in television.*

CENTER: *Jimmy Durante takes his patented swagger through the studio (circa 1934).*

BOTTOM: Hollywood Party *(1934) is a real oddity for MGM. Three directors work on the skits, but none receive screen credit. The musical mish-mash employs the comic talents of Jimmy Durante, Laurel and Hardy, Lupe Velez, Polly Moran, and a guest— Mickey Mouse—who strikes paydirt in the* Hot Chocolate Soldiers *cartoon segment from Walt Disney.*

1955

◆ *The Blackboard Jungle* sets a production speed record, going from script to release in three months. One of the biggest box-office successes of the year, the soundtrack introduces Bill Haley's "Rock Around the Clock" and launches the widespread popularity of rock music in film.

◆ *Guys and Dolls*, the only Samuel Goldwyn production distributed by MGM, hits box-office gold. Though it's two and a half hours long, the film packs them in at the theaters.

◆ MGM makes three biographical movies, each one about a female singing star: *Love Me or Leave Me* about entertainer Ruth Etting and her gangster husband; *I'll Cry Tomorrow* about alcoholic Lillian Roth; and *Interrupted Melody* about polio-stricken Marjorie Lawrence. All three are major hits.

◆ Lillian Gish returns to MGM for the first time in twenty-two years to appear in *The Cobweb*, produced by John Houseman.

◆ *Love Me or Leave Me* features two actors who have never worked for MGM before, James Cagney and Doris Day.

◆ *The King's Thief* is director Robert Z. Leonard's last MGM film, after thirty-one years with the studio.

‖ *Spencer Tracy in his Oscar-nominated performance in* Bad Day at Black Rock.

TOP: *The exuberant trash can dance from* It's Always Fair Weather *(1955). (Left to right) Michael Kidd, Gene Kelly, and Dan Dailey.*

ABOVE: *Susan Hayward receives an Oscar nomination for her portrayal of movie star Lillian Roth in* I'll Cry Tomorrow *(1955).*

OPPOSITE: *Maggie (Elizabeth Taylor) is impatient for the love of her husband, the emotionally tortured Brick (Paul Newman), in* Cat on a Hot Tin Roof *(1958), MGM's adaptation of a Tennessee Williams play. Both actors receive Oscar nominations.*

Decency and other guardians of public morality, however, were not solely concerned with a film's subject matter. A few years earlier, Brooks had directed Elizabeth Taylor in *The Last Time I Saw Paris*. During the filming, the studio became concerned that a dress the star was wearing revealed too much cleavage. The resident "bust inspector" was called to the set. This earnest-looking young woman actually climbed up a ladder to make a more thorough inspection, and then ruled against the dress. Brooks's reaction to her decision was so violent that the girl fled in tears and quit her job.

When Brooks worked with Elizabeth Taylor in *Cat on a Hot Tin Roof*, she was twenty-five years old and still in shock and mourning after the plane crash of her third husband, the great showman Mike Todd. Her sudden maturing as an actress during the making of the film may have been related to her intense personal grief. During the filming, there were times when it was difficult for her to get through some scenes without bursting into tears. There were even rumors that she came close to committing suicide. By the time the movie was in the editing stage, she had begun her celebrated affair with Eddie Fisher, who, in addition to having been Mike Todd's best friend, was still married to Debbie Reynolds. MGM demonstrated how far it had come from the proper days of L. B. Mayer by capitalizing on the growing scandal surrounding Taylor and Fisher and by publicizing her role in the picture as a woman who is trying to seduce an unwilling man. The studio's commercial instincts paid off: *Cat on a Hot Tin Roof* became one of the unlikeliest hits in MGM history. It won Taylor her second Oscar nomination and propelled her toward the pinnacle of stardom she has enjoyed since.

1956

◆ *High Society* is a huge moneymaker. All the songs but one are written by Cole Porter. "True Love" becomes a best-selling disc. Star Grace Kelly sings a few bars on it with costar Bing Crosby and receives royalties for years afterward.

◆ MGM has a well-timed coup with the release of *The Swan*, the story of royalty and romance starring soon-to-be Her Serene Princess Grace of Monaco, Grace Kelly. In celebration, MGM also produces a half-hour documentary called *The Wedding in Monaco*.

◆ Spencer Tracy walks off the set of *Tribute to a Bad Man* and leaves MGM, after twenty-one years with the studio. James Cagney replaces him.

◆ Playing fighter Rocky Graziano, Paul Newman achieves breakthrough stardom in *Somebody Up There Likes Me*.

◆ Marlon Brando displays his versatility, playing an Okinawan interpreter in the highly successful *Teahouse of the August Moon*.

Louis Armstrong and Grace Kelly appear in High Society, *MGM's biggest success of 1956.*

TOP: *Grace Kelly is filmed at poolside with Bing Crosby (left) and in a car with Frank Sinatra (right) in* High Society *(1956), a musical remake of* The Philadelphia Story *(1940).*

ABOVE: *Gene Kelly dances with an animated ballerina and with Carol Haney, whose image here will be drawn over by animators, in* Invitation to the Dance *(1956). The experimental film, which Kelly also directs, offers three stories in dance and has no dialogue.*

Another sign of changing mores can be traced in the evolution of *Gigi*, the last great musical collaboration between Arthur Freed and director Vincente Minnelli. Colette's novel had been brought to Freed's attention in the early fifties, at the same time Anita Loos was in the process of turning it into a stage play, but he was not interested enough to pursue the screen rights. After Freed saw the play in Los Angeles starring Audrey Hepburn, he learned that Anita Loos was next preparing a musical version of the same story. With renewed interest, Freed secured the film rights from Colette's widower and then paid off Loos and her partners so they would abandon plans for a Broadway show.

At this point in his career, Arthur Freed was no longer a staff producer at MGM. His new arrangement with the studio made him an independent producer and guaranteed him a percentage of the profits derived from the films he decided to make, subject to the approval of MGM's executives. They gave him a budget of $1.8 million, with an additional sum set aside for Audrey Hepburn, largely credited with making the play such a success. But Hepburn turned down the role, and Arthur Freed dispatched Alan Jay Lerner, working in Europe on the screenplay with composer Frederick Loewe, to recruit Leslie Caron, who had played Gigi in London. The lesser-known actress accepted at half of Hepburn's fee; even so, the final tally for the film would soar to almost $3.5 million, with the production extravagantly designed by Cecil Beaton and most of it shot on Paris locations.

Some costs were incurred after the previews revealed serious problems. Lerner and Loewe wanted twenty minutes taken out; Freed also felt the need for extensive reshooting. Retakes were easy enough when most of the actors were long-term employees, who merely had to be pulled for a few hours or days from another production. In

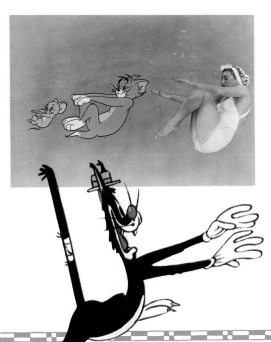

Joe Barbera and Bill Hanna together write the stories for the brilliant Tom and Jerry *series. Barbera then draws the story-boards, and Hanna times the film, makes the exposure sheets, and works with the animators. Later Hanna says: "I think the reason the series was so pop-ular was the slapstick comedy, the hard gags, and the little guy triumphing over the aggressor.* ABOVE: *A promotional poster.* CENTER: *Tom and Jerry join Esther Williams underwater in* Dangerous When Wet *(1953).* BOTTOM: *The lowlife alley cat from Tex Avery's best-known film,* King-Size Canary *(1947).*

I n the world of animation, MGM and Warner Bros. were the only studios to rival Disney. MGM entered the cartoon world in the early thirties, taking on the distribution of *Flip the Frog* by the brilliant Ub Iwerks, who had left Disney after working on Mickey Mouse . By the mid-thirties, MGM was commissioning shorts from Hugh Harman and Rudy Ising, who had already created *Merrie Melodies* and *Looney Tunes* for Warner. In 1937, MGM established its own animation department under the direction of Fred Quimby. Although MGM was among the last of the studios to become involved with animation, it quickly moved to the forefront.

In 1938, Harman and Ising worked exclusively for MGM, making *The Bear That Couldn't Sleep* and *Peace on Earth*, which gave the studio its first Oscar nomination for animation. MGM won an Oscar with *The Milky Way* in 1940, the same year William Hanna and Joseph Barbera made their first film together. That film, *Puss Gets the Boot*, not only won an Oscar nomination but also introduced the two characters soon to be known as Tom and Jerry (originally Tom was Jasper and Jerry was nameless). In their second film, *The Midnight Snack* (1941), they were officially christened, and their third, *The Night Before Christmas* (1941), took another Oscar nomination. The series continued for fifteen years, winning seven Oscars and three nominations, a run exceeded only by Disney during the thirties.

While Tom and Jerry were winning Oscars, Tex Avery picked up two nominations for *The Blitz Wolf* (1942), his first MGM film, and *Little Johnny Jet* (1953). Before working at MGM, Avery had developed Bugs Bunny and Elmer Fudd, and, although he never received another nomination, he was considered the funniest, most inventive animator in the business. Once at MGM, Avery created bold, wildly funny, even risqué cartoons. Released during the war years, his *Red Hot Riding Hood* raised so many eyebrows that the Hays Office complained and ultimately deleted some of the wolf's takes.

Tex Avery left MGM in 1954, Fred Quimby retired in 1955, and Hanna and Barbera left shortly thereafter. By 1957, MGM had closed its animation unit, and so became one of the first of the studios to stop producing cartoons.

LEO THE LION

Goldwyn Pictures was incorporated on December 19, 1916. To commemorate his new company, Sam Goldfish (later Goldwyn) asked advertising man Philip Goodman to design a distinctive trademark. Goodman assigned a new employee, Howard Dietz, to the task.

Dietz chose the image of Leo the Lion—perhaps because his college magazine used a lion insignia, or perhaps because the Goldwyn offices overlooked the entrance to the New York Public Library, which was graced with two reclining marble lions. Whatever his inspiration, Leo the Lion appeared in full-body profile, surrounded by a crest of film proclaiming in Latin, *Ars Gratia Artis*, which means "Art for Art's Sake."

The first live Leo was brought to America from the Sudan in 1917, by a Mr. Phifer, the owner of an animal farm in Gilette, Pennsylvannia. The lion was used to promote films and then was brought to the Goldwyn Company, where his image prefaced all the movies Goldwyn released after 1921. Once the company merged with Metro Pictures and Louis B. Mayer in 1924, Dietz replaced the logo's full-body profile with a that of a full-faced lion. By 1927, Dietz arranged for MGM to get its own live "Leo the Lion." The kingly animal came from Walter Beckwith, trainer at the Los Angeles Selig Zoo.

On May 8, 1928, a photograph was printed showing a lion named Pluto being sound recorded (on the newly invented sound machines) for

TOP: *An early Technicolor version of the logo (circa 1938).*
ABOVE: *The original Goldwyn Pictures logo, designed by Howard Dietz.*
BELOW: *Greta Garbo nervously poses alongside MGM trademark Leo the Lion (circa 1926).*

the MGM trademark. The animal's best angles and moods were studied and screen tested. Finally, after many takes, Louis B. Mayer decided on two fast roars, a pause, then a third roar. Goldwyn's first lion, the photographic Leo who could roar on command, was eventually retired to a Philadelphia zoo in 1934. A decade later, the great-grandson of the original Leo posed for a new MGM trademark, and during the 1950s, MGM updated the trademark a few more times, in 3-D and in CinemaScope, as well as rerecording the lion's roar in stereophonic sound.

When MGM's movies were leased to television in the 1960s, Leo appeared in countless homes, in a newly designed logo, where he was shown full-faced, with a montage background of lion faces. MGM sent Leo to the MGM Grand Hotel in Las Vegas in 1974, to promote its new picture, *That's Entertainment*, and during the early 1980s, the corporate logo was again redesigned, using a highly stylized "lion head" motif.

In the seventy-five years since his first appearance, Leo the Lion has become one of the most recognizable trademarks in film history. In all his various incarnations and modernizations, Leo has continued to fulfill his original intent. On screen, a roaring Leo proclaims that something majestic is about to appear. Like the marble lions that still adorn New York City's public library, MGM's Leo remains forever imperial.

◆ Elvis Presley has his breakthrough film appearance in *Jailhouse Rock*. The title song sells two million copies.

◆ MGM introduces its new wide-film process Camera 65 in *Raintree County*. Production had been halted for two months after Montgomery Clift was severely injured in a car crash. The film cost $6 million, a record for an MGM movie shot in the United States.

◆ *Les Girls* is Gene Kelly's last MGM screen appearance until the 1974 documentary *That's Entertainment*. It also features the last film score written by Cole Porter.

◆ MGM remembers Garbo in *Silk Stockings*, a musical remake of *Ninotchka*, starring Cyd Charisse and Fred Astaire.

◆ MGM shows a loss for the first time in its history, going $455,000 into the red, $5.6 million down from 1956, with gross receipts down $18 million at $154.3 million. The contract player system also dwindles from 598 actors under contract to the major studios in 1947 to a current roster of 253.

Elizabeth Taylor and Montgomery Clift in Raintree County, *a Civil War drama that MGM hopes will outgross* Gone with the Wind. *Taylor gets an Oscar nomination, but the film makes only a small profit.*

the new Hollywood, however, contracts specified exactly how long an actor would be available and at what price. MGM management balked at the additional $300,000 needed and only gave in when Lerner and Loewe were concerned enough first to put up their own money, in return for ten percent participation in the profits, and then to offer to buy the negative outright. Joseph Vogel, who flew out to the West Coast to settle the crisis, claimed to have been deeply impressed by Lerner and Loewe's commitment and especially by their *My Fair Lady*, then in the middle of its triumphant run on Broadway.

And it was on Broadway, at the Royale Theatre, that *Gigi* finally was given its gala premiere. Afterward, in the old Broadway tradition, Freed, director Vincente Minnelli, and their friends went to Sardi's and waited for Bosley Crowther's review in *The New York Times*, which began: "There won't be much point in anybody trying to produce a film of *My Fair Lady* for a while, because Arthur Freed has virtually done it with *Gigi*." The following April the picture won an unprecedented nine Academy Awards; during the ceremonies, Tony Martin dried up as he tried to sing the lyrics for the winner in the best song category. He crooned, "Gigi, la-la-la-la-do-do-do-do, la-la-la la-do-do-do-do, la-la-la-la." Alan Jay Lerner remarked tersely afterward, "It was very avant-garde."

Gigi earned the studio more than fifteen million dollars, one of the highest grosses in its history. The film was licensed for another two million dollars to NBC television in 1970, the year Arthur Freed finally left MGM. Although he produced three more films and tried to get a dozen other

A sports reporter (Gregory Peck) and a dress designer (Lauren Bacall) marry but don't always see eye to eye in Designing Woman *(1957), a comedy for which George Wells wins an Oscar for his original screenplay.*

THE EVOLUTION OF A MUSICAL

ABOVE: *Poster art for 1958's best picture winner,* Gigi.
BELOW: *A Cecil Beaton costume sketch for Gigi as a young girl.*

DECEMBER 1951: Writer/producer Joe Fields holds a financial interest in the screen rights to *Gigi*, Colette's semiscandalous novella about a young girl raised to be a courtesan. He meets with Arthur Freed to discuss turning it into a musical. Freed screens the French film version, calls it a "nice little film," and forgets about it.

NOVEMBER 1953: Freed sees the Los Angeles stopover of Anita Loos's production of *Gigi*, starring Audrey Hepburn. He likes it, but director Vincente Minnelli, along for consultation, hates it. Undaunted, Freed submits the novella to the Motion Picture Code Office for a censorship report. Objections begin with: All the characters in this story participate, or did participate, or intended to participate, in a man-mistress relationship..."

LATE 1954: Anita Loos wires Freed that she's now working on a Broadway musical version of *Gigi*, and wants to see the censorship report. Now he's really interested. He mollifies the Production Code office and then kills the Broadway musical version by paying $87,000 to a disgruntled Loos and producer Gilbert Miller.

FEBRUARY 1956: From rehearsal, *My Fair Lady* moves to Philadelphia for that crazed pre-opening condition between chaos and bedlam called "out of town." Freed arrives, unexpectedly, to remind Alan Jay Lerner that, since Lerner has only completed two out of the three films of his three-film contract, he might consider *Gigi* to fulfill his obligations. Both Freed and Vincente Minnelli, who's been persuaded to direct, want Lerner on the film. Lerner, completely absorbed in *My Fair Lady*, nods politely and promptly files *Gigi* away.

AUGUST 1956: Now famous as the lyricist/librettist of one of the most phenomenal Broadway musicals in history, Lerner returns to Hollywood and MGM with two demands regarding *Gigi*: (1) *If* he can build up the part of Gaston's uncle, Honoré Lachaille, every effort should be made to get Maurice Chevalier for the role. (2) *If* he develops the screenplay, Cecil Beaton will design the costumes and sets. Freed and Minnelli agree. But who will compose the music? Lerner avoids their question and departs for New York.

AUTUMN 1956: Lerner returns to Hollywood with the first draft of the script. He is vaguely aware that, by following Freed's suggestions, he has written something similar to *My Fair Lady*, but the producer tells him, "Stop trying to be different. You don't have to be different to be good. To be good is different enough." And then, what about Frederick Loewe for composer? Lerner shrugs and departs for New York.

MARCH 1957: Lerner has spent the winter trying to persuade Fritz Loewe to write the score, but Fritz hates writing for films—or writing at all. He would rather rest, travel, and play *chemin-de-fer*. Finally, with Minnelli, Lerner evolves a plan: *Gigi must* be shot in Paris, and this is also where the score should be composed. Paris—with its out-of-Hollywood ambiance, its inspiration, *and* its *chemin-de-fer* tables. Loewe accepts the assignment, leaves for Paris, and there, with Lerner, begins to compose the songs.

LATE MARCH 1957: Lerner is sent to London to snare Audrey Hepburn for the lead (she turns it down), to get Leslie Caron for the lead (she accepts, though Lerner is disturbed; her delightful French accent has become pure British), to sign Dirk Bogarde for the role of Gaston (he's unavailable; Louis Jourdan is cast). Last, but not least, Lerner is sent to Marne-la-Coquette, to interest Maurice Chevalier in playing Honoré Lachaille (he accepts!).

APRIL 1957: Minnelli and Freed arrive in Paris. The director and Cecil Beaton immediately begin to scout for locations. With growing excitement, Minnelli decides to emulate the great caricaturist Sem for the Palais de Glace and Maxim's scenes; Constantin Guys for the opening sequence in the Bois de Boulogne; Boudin for the later scenes on the beach at Trouville. Beaton retreats to London to prepare costume sketches. Minnelli continues to explore and sometimes wants to rebuild Paris, which creates problems of State Department dimensions: convincing the official who oversees the Palais de Glace that no damage will be caused by redoing the main floor; cajoling the curator of the Musée Jacquemart-André into thinking that shooting it as the interior of Gaston's house is an honor and will not harm its priceless contents; convincing the owners of Maxim's that closing their doors for four days of shooting in August is a wise decision.

SPRING 1957: A heat wave descends upon Paris, where air-conditioning is considered a barbarity. At Lerner's suite on the top floor of the Georges V, Howard Dietz and his wife, Lucinda Ballard, along with Arthur Freed, Cecil Beaton, Vincente Minnelli, and Freed's assistant, Lela Simone, hear the first performance

of the Lerner–Loewe score. Dietz shakes Freed's hand and says, "Arthur, this will be the most charming flop you've ever made."

JULY–AUGUST 1957: The rest of the crew arrives in Paris, which is still sweltering. Songs are prerecorded, to André Previn's piano accompaniment. Shooting begins. The hottest spring in years has now become one of the century's hottest summers. The opening and closing sequences are set up in the Bois de Boulogne. Cocottes, strapped into corsets, faint dead away. Fake trees collapse. Costumes wilt. And Maurice Chevalier, the legend, to whom all defer, creates anxiety. Will he cooperate? He has been known to chew up and spit out directors he does not like. The morning after the first day of shooting, Minnelli receives a note from Chevalier: "If I were a sissy I would be in love with you."

MID-AUGUST 1957: Location shots continue: the sun scorching the glass roof of the Palais de Glace, makes lovely configurations on the ice rink below, but also melts the ice. Furthermore, nobody has asked Jacques Bergerac, who plays Zsa Zsa Gabor's skating instructor, if he can skate. But this is Paris. Anything is possible. Bergerac can't skate, but he can be pho-

TOP: *Leslie Caron as Gigi, a Parisienne tomboy who initially resists the idea of becoming a lady.*

ABOVE: *Gigi, as a young girl, with Gaston (Louis Jourdan) at the famous Palais de Glace.*

tographed from the waist up. Shooting now moves to Maxim's, whose mirrors pose a problem to cinematographer Joseph Ruttenberg. He solves it by having black scrolls painted on some of them. And so, despite the crowds and the heat, the Maxim's scenes are a triumph of fun, a series of paintings joyously pirated from earlier works by Sem, with their beak-nosed *grisettes* intact, enhanced by the out-of-context, Renoiresque cocottes, ripe and rosy despite the discomfort beneath their corsets.

LATE AUGUST 1957: Shooting proceeds, and of course there is much of *My Fair Lady* in *Gigi*, enough for critics to dub the latter *Eliza Goes to Paris*: there is, for instance, the Ascot set transplanted to Maxim's; the breathless ball-gown transformation of *Gigi*; the musical recognition scene, talked and sung by Gaston very similarly to Henry Higgins when he became accustomed to Eliza Doolittle's face. Even Minnelli borrows from himself, directing Leslie Caron to sing "Say a Prayer" to a cat on a bed, much as Judy Garland sang "Have Yourself a Merry Little Christmas" to Margaret O'Brien in *Meet Me in St. Louis* (1944). But the echoes are overlooked because the rushes arriving in Hollywood are better than good.

END OF AUGUST 1957: Shooting winds down. Minnelli is bitten by a swan in the Jardin de Bagatelle; unpredictable weather cancels location shots in Trouville, and MGM executive Benny Thau phones from Hollywood: the picture is already nearly a half million dollars over budget. Come home.

SEPTEMBER 13, 1957: Shooting resumes in Hollywood. The beach at Venice becomes the beach at Trouville; "I Remember It Well," with Chevalier and Hermione Gingold, is shot on Stage 11 in Culver City; and, nearby, the interior of *Gigi* and Mamita's apartment is recreated for "The Night They Invented Champagne," a new song that requires the choreographic talents of Chuck Walters to bring it off. André Previn conducts and records Conrad Salinger's

RIGHT: *Leslie Caron and Louis Jourdan share a laugh during a break.*
BELOW: *Caron and Jourdan on location at Venice Beach.*

BELOW: *One of the skills Gigi learns is how to choose a cigar for a gentleman.*

orchestrations, and postrecords Leslie Caron's numbers, with Betty Wand singing for Caron. Cecil Beaton, horrified, surveys it all and later confides to colleagues and interviewers: "All the scenes that were taken in Hollywood were very damaging...suddenly it looked like Hollywood instead of France."

JANUARY 20, 1958: More trouble. The first preview occurs at the Granada Theatre in Santa Barbara. The audience loves it; the composer and lyricist/librettist hate it. "That's not the film we wrote," complain Lerner and Loewe, and it's showdown time in Culver City. They want multiple, expensive changes: smaller orchestrations, different editing, different shots, slower tempos in "The Parisians" as well as a rerecording of Louis Jourdan's soliloquy. MGM refuses. *Gigi* is already over budget. Lerner and Loewe are adamant and propose to put up their own money. The changes are finally agreed to, but without Minnelli directing. He's already off to London to begin *The Reluctant Debutante*. And without Cecil Beaton, who must return to London, but leaves a list of written complaints about the color balance. (Freed changes the word "complaints" to "suggestions" in the designer's memo.) And without Lela Simone, who, under constant pressure, finally resigns.

MAY 15, 1958: *Gigi* opens to cheers in New York City. Its success is unstoppable. The awards rush in: four *Downbeat* encomiums, including "The Best Musical Motion Picture of 1958," and "Best Original Song," the Golden Globe Award as "The Best Musical of 1958," and the Photoplay Award for "The Most Popular Picture of the Year." In addition, *Gigi* wins nine Academy Awards, including best picture, and Maurice Chevalier wins a special award. *Gigi* is not *Eliza Goes to Paris,* after all.

Freed and Minnelli will make one more musical together: *Bells are Ringing.* But that pale transplantation of a Broadway show will be a mere coda to their careers. The *real* finale, the last of the great MGM musicals, is—and will always remain—*Gigi.*

TOP: *Gigi has become a lady. Bosley Crowther of* The New York Times *writes in his review, "There won't be much point in anybody trying to produce* My Fair Lady *for a while, because Arthur Freed has virtually done it with* Gigi.
CENTER: *Jourdan, Caron, and Maurice Chevalier on the set.*
BOTTOM: *A Cecil Beaton sketch for some of his Oscarwinning costumes.*

projects off the ground, including *My Fair Lady* and *Camelot*, nothing would match either the achievements or the difficulties of *Gigi*. He left MGM, without much regret, to devote more of his extraordinary energies to his hobbies: antiques and growing orchids.

Gigi may have ended the great period of MGM musicals, but the studio continued to exploit its past triumphs and now returned to the epic that had first helped to put it on the map in 1925. When he first took the helm at Loew's in the fall of 1957, Joseph Vogel announced his plans to remake *Ben-Hur*. The idea of undertaking such a mammoth project had been kicked around MGM since the beginning of the decade, when the studio was buoyed by the success of *King Solomon's Mines* and *Quo Vadis?*. Sam Zimbalist, who had worked on the old *Ben-Hur* as a cutter and meanwhile become a specialist in producing such epics, managed to nurse the new *Ben-Hur* production through the turbulent changes of management. Vogel saw immense risk in committing more than $7 million to a single project; the company had never invested that much in a film. But it was during this period that some spectaculars racked up immense profits: *Around the World in Eighty Days* earned Mike Todd $23 million in domestic grosses, while Paramount took in almost $40 million with De Mille's remake of *The Ten Commandments*. Tempting as such figures were, Vogel was also aware that *Raintree County*, MGM's most recent attempt to replicate the success of *Gone with the Wind*, had barely made back the $6 million it had cost. But Benny Thau, who had gained all his experience in MGM's heyday, especially during his long years as Mayer's assistant and later executive vice-president, knew that all creative decisions were a gamble and that to win big, you had to risk big.

By the time Mayer's takeover bid had failed and Schary had departed, Zimbalist had gone through several distinguished writers, including Maxwell Anderson, S. N. Behrman, and Gore Vidal, in an attempt to get a good script. After director William Wyler replaced an ailing Sidney Franklin, the English verse dramatist Christopher Fry was brought in to do the screenplay. He sat on the set, writing throughout the entire shoot, only to be denied credit for his efforts by the Screen Writers Guild. When the movie was finally released, Karl Tunberg was credited as the sole screenwriter.

Like Zimbalist, Wyler had worked on the silent version of *Ben-Hur* as an assistant to Fred Niblo. Since then, Wyler had acquired a reputation for his expensive methods of shooting countless retakes. When he was asked to take over the direction, Wyler refused the job at first, primarily because large-scale religious epics were outside the range of his experience and because he was just finishing *The Big*

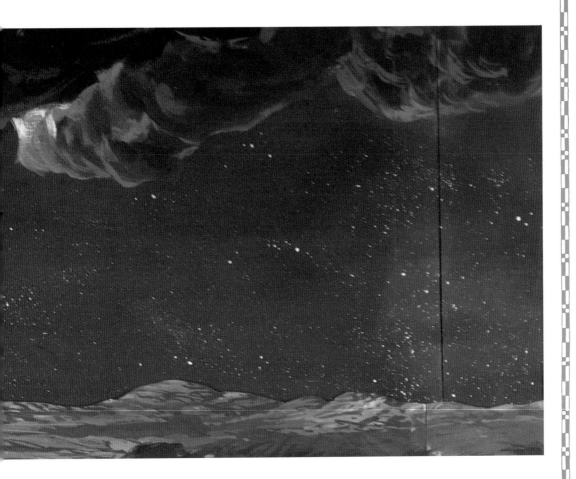

An art study by Edward Carfagno for a matte shot in the beginning sequence of Ben-Hur (1959) in which the Magi follow the Star of Bethlehem to the Nativity.

Country, an ambitious western that left him feeling exhausted. But Zimbalist persuaded the director that he was needed to inject intimacy into the epic, and Wyler later said that he undertook the project to "see if I know how to make a picture like this."

In 1925, in an effort to control costs, Mayer and Thalberg had brought back the production of *Ben-Hur* from Italy to Culver City. Now, conditions were different. For the new version, Thau negotiated to have the film shot entirely at Cinecittà studios, near Rome. In the poststudio era, MGM no longer had the resources or long-term contracts to accommodate a huge project like *Ben-Hur* on the lot. Unions had driven costs up and the epics out of Hollywood. Foreign labor was cheaper to hire, and Loew's still had resources trapped in Italy. Filming on location in Europe also avoided close supervision by the studio.

"Merely colossal," which was Arthur Mayer's description of Hollywood and its aspirations, reached one of its defining moments with the production of *Ben-Hur*. Six hundred sets were built; the Circus Maximus, needed for the film's chariot race, occupied eighteen acres; a man-made lake was created for the sea battles. When an ad was placed in a local newspaper calling for bearded men to act as extras, almost five thousand hirsute Romans showed up, resulting in a riot; apparently, many of them had been growing beards

1958

◆ *Gigi* is the biggest grossing film of Arthur Freed's career, bringing in $15 million in world rentals and winning a whopping nine Academy Awards. The day after the awards, receptionists at MGM are instructed to answer the phone, "M-Gigi-M."

◆ *Cat on a Hot Tin Roof* is the year's top moneymaker, as well as the tenth biggest moneymaker in MGM history. As Maggie the Cat, Elizabeth Taylor radically changes her screen image.

◆ Maggie Smith debuts in *Nowhere To Go* and signs a joint Ealing-MGM contract.

◆ *Nowhere to Go* is Bessie Love's first MGM film in twenty-eight years.

◆ The studio releases one last Andy Hardy film, *Andy Hardy Comes Home.*

◆ James Jones's *Some Came Running* is adapted for the big screen, and stars Jones's choice for the role of the homecoming GI, Frank Sinatra.

◆ Although Donald O'Connor campaigns for the role, Russ Tamblyn is cast as the lead in *Tom Thumb*, directed by George Pal.

Maurice Chevalier, in his masked ball costume for Gigi, *clowns with Hermione Gingold, in her nightwear costume.*

1959

◆ *Ben-Hur* is produced for
$15 million and brings in $80
million in worldwide rentals. It
receives a record twelve Oscar
nominations, including best
picture, director, actor, and
costumes, and wins eleven,
only losing for best screenplay
(Adapted From Another
Medium) to *Room at the Top*.

◆ *North by Northwest* is
Alfred Hitchcock's first MGM
film and Cary Grant's fourth
and final one for the director.
MGM wanted Cyd Charisse to
costar, but Hitchcock, always
preferring a blonde, insisted on
Eva Marie Saint. The U.S.
Department of the Interior
wouldn't allow the use of Mt.
Rushmore, saying it would be
"patent desecration," so the
studio built mock-ups of the
faces for close-up shots.

◆ *The Big Operator*, a remake
of Dore Schary's *Joe Smith,
American*, stars Mickey Rooney
in a different kind of role: a
sadistic gang-leader.

◆ Cecil B. De Mille dies at the
age of seventy-seven.

◆ MGM is the last film company to divest itself from its
theater chain. The studio then
hits a profit of $7,698,952, the
highest since 1951.

Ben-Hur, *with its total of eleven
Academy Awards, breaks* Gigi's
*1958 record for most Oscars
won by one film.*

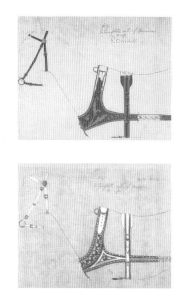

ABOVE: *Two of Carfagno's harness designs for horses in the
chariot race. Each racer's horse
has a leather harness of a different style and/or color. At
top is a Roman theme, and at
bottom is the white design
for the harness worn by Ben-
Hur's horse.*

for months in anticipation. More than a million props were
assembled for the production. When Wyler wanted a
Hebrew parchment, he had an expert in Jerusalem tran-
scribe actual words from the Dead Sea Scrolls. Charlton
Heston, who played the leading role after Marlon Brando,
Rock Hudson, and Burt Lancaster all turned it down,
recalled the director's passion for authenticity. "When Wyler
wanted to show rats leaving a sinking ship," the actor told a
reporter from the *Los Angeles Examiner*, "propmen
hunted rats all over Rome and trapped a lot of them.
But an animal lover in the prop department overfed the rats
before they were used, and when the galley sank the
contented rats just took it in stride, staying with the
ship until it sank, and then swimming leisurely away from it.
The scene was no good."

Heston, who had previously worked with Wyler in *The
Big Country*, found him a slave driver. "Doing a film for
Wyler," he said in summary of his experience, "is like getting
the works in a Turkish bath. You darn near drown but you
come out smelling like a rose." Along with mounting
costs—the original $7 million escalated to $15 million—the
human toll also rose. Henry Henigson, production manager
for MGM in Europe, was ordered by doctors to take a rest. In
November 1958, Sam Zimbalist collapsed and died of a heart
attack; J. J. Cohn, an original member of Goldwyn Pictures,
was sent out to supervise. Part of the stress and delays came

from an extraordinary publicity bonanza; more than five hundred reporters visited the set, demanding interviews with the stars or Wyler. Cinecittà became a major Roman tourist attraction, with celebrities of all kinds and 25,000 tourists dropping by to watch the filming.

MGM's publicity department fed endless bits of trivial information to those who could not secure interviews. "Many women in Italy gave their hair for *Ben-Hur*," said one release. "More than four hundred pounds were assembled at Cinecittà Studios to be made into wigs and beards required by the thousands of people taking part in the production." After the shooting was over, Wyler and his team spent almost a year cutting a million feet of film down to four hours. Miklos Rozsa, the composer who had scored *Quo Vadis?*, also worked for a year on scoring the music. MGM, worried about its huge investment, launched its largest advertising campaign to date, along with merchandising tie-ins, including Roman helmets, breastplates, and scooter chariots; the studio even signed an agreement licensing tiaras and hair ornaments worn by Roman women.

The picture was finally launched in 1959, with top ticket prices at an unprecedented $3.50. It became one of the great blockbusters. For a few years, it ranked as the second top-grossing film of all time. *Ben-Hur* brought in $66 million to MGM in ten years. Despite its popular success and sheer grandeur, William Wyler was embarrassed when *cinéastes* found it inferior to his other great movies. "I don't think it is more pretentious than the story dictates," he told the editor of *Cinema*.

MGM did not just benefit financially from *Ben-Hur*. The film garnered eleven Academy Awards, a record, and a host of other prizes. By the time it was released, Sam Zimbalist was dead and Benjamin Thau had retired. The new production chief, Sol C. Siegel, who took over in April 1958, had had little involvement with *Ben-Hur* and left Joseph Vogel to accept the kudos, which he eagerly claimed in a foreword to the special souvenir program: "I believe I have seen every important motion picture made in the last forty years and in my opinion *Ben-Hur* may well set a new standard for years to come. It is not only a notable contribution to the art of motion pictures, but it is my sincere belief that it approaches the ultimate in dramatic entertainment in any medium."

Ben-Hur was, perhaps, the last flowering of the studio system, as typified by MGM at its highest level. The people who made it wanted this phantom of a glorious past to become a symbol for a new beginning. But the times required a much bolder vision than simply looking back. Most critics found the silent version of *Ben-Hur* superior. Yet, *Ben-Hur* did reflect something about both the past and the future. Soon the grandeur of Metro-Goldwyn-Mayer, like that of Rome, would pass away.

The chariot race is on! Bosley Crowther writes in his New York Times *review: "There has seldom been anything in movies to compare with this picture's chariot race. It is a* stunning complex of mighty setting, thrilling action by horses and men, panoramic observation and overwhelming dramatic use of sound."

EPILOGUE

More than three decades have passed since *Ben-Hur* was released in 1959, a period almost as long as the golden era of MGM, which has been chronicled in these pages. Empires do not yield easily to oblivion, and their lingering decline often inflicts vast suffering on their subjects. MGM has proven no exception. Although the magic of those three letters survives, the mighty lion has been shorn of his mane and much else besides.

In the 1960s, the overwhelming financial success of *Ben-Hur* steered the studio even more firmly toward its past. In addition to producing a new version of *King of Kings*—one of the last silent epics made in 1927 by Cecil B. De Mille—and profitably re-releasing *Gone with the Wind,* MGM also picked up distribution rights for cheaply-made spectacles by such filmmakers as Sergio Leone. The wave of epics reached its culmination in the middle of the decade with David Lean's *Doctor Zhivago*, which won five Oscars in 1965 and eventually surpassed *Ben-Hur* as the second-highest grossing film in MGM history. However, the studio was scarcely involved in its production, which took place on European locations far away from Culver City.

Although MGM continued to produce or distribute between twenty and thirty pictures a year, the company's fortunes became hostage year after year to the success or failure of such blockbusters. With the departure of Sol Siegel and Joseph Vogel in 1962 and 1963 respectively, the link to the past, going back to Marcus Loew, was finally broken. The stability and continuity of management that had pulled the studio through past crises had disappeared. The new executives who came and went through MGM's had their roots in advertising and consumer companies, like Seagram's and General Mills, and little or no firsthand experience in filmmaking. By 1969, with losses mounting and the company's stock falling, battles on the board and proxy fights among shareholders increased; MGM finally became vulnerable to a takeover bid by a financier who set in motion the dismantling of the factory of dreams.

The son of Armenian immigrants, Kirk Kerkorian had performed handyman jobs at various film studios, including MGM, in his youth. By the time he became the majority shareholder in the company, the reclusive millionaire had built an empire that included an airline and several hotels in Las Vegas. With no background in filmmaking, Kerkorian chose James T. Aubrey, a former president of CBS, to run MGM. Known variously as "Jungle Jim" or "the Smiling Cobra," Aubrey was a legend for his ruthless corporate style and lusty womanizing, which supposedly provided the model for the character of Robin Stone in Jacqueline Susann's best-selling novel, *The Love Machine*. At a stockholders' meeting in January 1970, he announced that half of MGM's remaining staff would be dismissed. He then cancelled several major film projects and began interfering in the rest. As a result, Aubrey alienated many powerful figures in the creative community, some of whom sued the studio, while others would boycott it for years to come.

Operating as though they were wheeling and dealing properties on a giant board of the Monopoly game, the new owners closed MGM's London studios, which had turned out a number of stylish and profitable films during the sixties, and sold the company's overseas movie theaters that had been retained after divestiture of its chain at home. The famous backlots were sold to developers, stripped of the permanent outdoor sets, and townhouses went up around the lake where *Huckleberry Finn* and *Show Boat* were filmed. The site of *Raintree County* was turned into the Raintree condominiums. The MGM kingdom had shrunk back to forty-two acres.

In May 1970, thousands of props, costumes, and memorabilia accumulated from almost half a century of filmmaking went on the auction block in the largest rummage sale in history. A local auctioneer paid $1.5 million for 150,000 costumes, many of them museum pieces, and more than 12,000 props, including original eighteenth-century French furniture assembled for such movies as *Marie Antoinette*. Writing in *Newsweek*, Karl Fleming described the experience "as if an old friend's wedding ring, Sunday suit and fishing rod were being sold to settle debts." During the eighteen days of the auctions, stars scrambled to bid on mementos from their films. Debbie Reynolds snapped up as much as she could in hopes of establishing a Hollywood film museum (recently she sold back some of her collection to Kirk Kerkorian). Items such as the brass bed from *The Unsinkable Molly Brown* and the Time Machine used in the film of the same name were quickly sold to the highest bidder. A restaurant owner from Sacramento, California, paid $4,000 for a chariot used in the 1959 version of *Ben-Hur*. Three years later, during the height of the 1973 gasoline shortage, he was arrested for driving it on a freeway.

The sale of assets continued, as Kerkorian and Aubrey concentrated the business on real estate, gambling, and airlines. MGM's profitable music publishing companies were sold to raise funds. The studio's stamp of quality was applied to obtain bank loans and to lure tourists to Las Vegas. Film stars were on hand for the ground-breaking ceremonies of the world's largest hotel, the MGM Grand. Its suites were to be named after famous characters in MGM films and its banquet rooms were to reflect themes from celebrated MGM movies. These decorating plans were scrubbed in the interest of lower taste; however, the hotel's gift shop was stocked with movie memorabilia overlooked by the auctioneers. That is how Jack Haley, Jr., son of the actor who played in Tin Man in *The Wizard of Oz*, acquired the shooting script of *Mrs. Miniver*, complete with William Wyler's handwritten notes, for twelve dollars. Several MGM executives suggested that either the remaining treasures should be donated to archives or held until they could be used more effectively as tax write-offs. They were ignored and the looting continued.

There was more of the past left to exploit. In May 1974, MGM celebrated its golden anniversary with a gala premiere of *That's Entertainment*, an anthology that selected the best moments and numbers from the great MGM musicals, with narration provided by some of the original participants. Although *That's Entertainment Part Two*, failed to repeat the enormous success of the first tribute, these nostalgic confections packaged and popularized for another generation the essence of the MGM style—romanticism, innocence, zest, energy, and glitter, taken at times to self-parodying excess.

Meanwhile, new production amounted to no more than three or four medium-budget pictures a year, too small an output to justify the vast global network that had been developed originally to promote and launch one movie a week. Kerkorian turned to Arthur Krim, the respected lawyer running United Artists, which became MGM's domestic distributor. Another deal for overseas distribution was set up with Cinema International Corporation, which was owned by MCA and Paramount. MGM limped along for the rest of the decade, while Kerkorian opened a second MGM Grand Hotel in Reno and tried unsuccessfully to take over Columbia Pictures. He did, however, acquire United Artists in May 1981 for $380 million, considered a colossal overpayment at the time. UA had been weakened by the debacle of Michael Cimino's infamous *Heaven's Gate*, but it also owned such lucrative franchises as the *James Bond* and *Rocky* series, not to mention a film library of some 900 movies. Even in its parlous state, UA was still wrapped in the mystique of its famous founders. Together the five letters MGM/UA spelled prestige, and for the first time in years, the two companies faced fairly bright prospects.

But, unfortunately, there was no stable management at either company. Top executives would bring in their own expensive teams, embark on a new schedule of projects, and leave (or be forced to leave) before the films could be completed and marketed. In 1985, Kerkorian recruited Alan Ladd, Jr., a man well liked and respected in both the creative and financial community, to be president and chief operating officer of a united MGM and UA . But at the same time, the secretive financier was also trying to unload the debt-burdened company. He found a buyer in Ted Turner, the Atlanta-based media tycoon who had recently been rebuffed when he attempted to take over CBS; now the entrepreneur bought MGM/UA for a staggering $1.5 billion, assuming another $500 million of the company's debt.

But it was a deal Turner could not afford, so Kirk Kerkorian agreed to buy back UA for $480 million, as well as other property, including the MGM logo, for another $300 million. Then Turner sold what remained of the MGM lot in Culver City to Lorimar-Telepictures, the company that grew rich with such television series as *Dallas*, *Falcon Crest*, and *The Waltons*. A couple of years later, Lorimar was bought out by Warner Bros., which, in turn, was acquired by Time Inc. With merger mania reaching a climax in Hollywood, Sony bought Columbia Pictures in 1989. At the same time, it hired Peter Guber and Jon Peters from Warners to run the company. Warners, which had a number of projects in development with the two producers, sued Sony, and when the dust settled, Columbia ended up with the MGM lot in Culver City. The famous MGM lab, considered for decades the finest in the business, had been included in the Lorimar deal, but was eventually sold to Technicolor.

The remnants of the enterprise known as MGM moved into a modern building, resembling a ziggurat, near the old lot. By June 1986, Ted Turner had sold MGM's television operations to United Artists and had ended up with what he always wanted—the richest film library in the world, including its crown jewel, *Gone with the Wind*. Told repeatedly that he had paid far too much for old movies, the owner of Turner Broadcasting System once explained his decision to a reporter: "How can you go broke, buying the Rembrandts of the programming business when you are a programmer?" Since the purchase, the Turner Entertainment Company has enlarged the library, which now includes most films made by Warner Bros. before 1950, and the RKO film library in the domestic U.S. market, some 3,300 theatrical motion pictures in all. In addition, Turner owns and licenses 2,000 shorts and cartoons, and 2,000 hours of television programs. The company has brought back into circulation many famous and obscure Metro-Goldwyn-Mayer movies on television, videocassettes, and occasionally on the big screen; the fiftieth anniversaries of *Gone with the Wind*, *The Wizard of Oz*, and *Citizen Kane* were recently celebrated with new prints and major theatrical releases.

Turner's most controversial decision has been the "colorization" of some of the old black-and-white films. Directors and stars have protested against the "sacrilege." Others counterargue that the colorized versions are more accessible to new generations who have only known color movies and television, and they contend that film buffs can still view the black-and-white versions on their own video cassette players.

In the meantime, Kirk Kerkorian found himself in the strange position of having sold MGM/UA and yet still owning it. Both companies continued to produce films, some of which proved critical and commercial successes. During his tenure at MGM, Alan Ladd, Jr., was responsible for such offbeat hits as *Moonstruck* and *A Fish Called Wanda*. United Artists came through with an unexpected success in *Rain Man*. But with Kerkorian showing no interest in filmmaking, most of the top executives left. Finally in November 1990, twenty-one years after he first bought control of MGM, Kerkorian sold his film companies yet again, but this time for an astonishing $1.3 billion—minus the real estate and film library. He also retained limited rights to the name and logo, which are used in connection with the Grand hotels and airline. MGM, for so long the industry leader, had less than 3 percent of the box office in the domestic market.

The new buyer was Pathé Communications, a European film company with roots going back even further than Metro's, the oldest of the component parts of MGM. Its logo, the crowing rooster, has long been famous, especially on newsreels shown in theaters before the days of television news. By the spring of 1991, Alan Ladd, Jr., was back in charge of MGM/Pathé Communications, which—although in serious financial straits—is still producing and releasing motion pictures and television programs.

The film business runs on the fuel of extravagant optimism, and some dream, no doubt, about a new golden age now that the lion is lying down with the rooster. Perhaps this latest chapter in the studio's unfinished story may become just another cautionary tale not to be found in Aesop. "The very substance of the ambitious is merely the shadow of a dream," Guildenstern told Hamlet. The dream for which tycoons gambled their hard cash turned out to be "but a shadow's shadow": symbols, initials in a name, and miles of celluloid. For lovers of movies, however, MGM's legacy of great films will always endure, and the land of Oz beckons to them each time the lion roars.

SELECTED BIBLIOGRAPHY

Astaire, Fred. *Steps in Time*. New York: Harper and Brothers, 1959.

Aylesworth, Thomas G. *Broadway to Hollywood*. New York: Bison Books, 1985.

Bainbridge, John. *Garbo*. Garden City, N.J.: Doubleday, 1955.

Bandy, Mary Lea (ed.). *The Dawn of Sound*. New York: The Museum of Modern Art, 1989.

Bart, Peter. *Fade Out: The Calamitous Final Days of MGM*. New York: William Morrow and Co., 1990.

Bego, Mark. *The Best of Modern Screen*. New York: St. Martin's Press, 1986.

Behlmer, Rudy (ed.). *Memo from David O. Selznick*. Hollywood: Samuel French, 1989.

Behrman, S. N. *People in a Diary*. Boston: Little, Brown & Co., 1972.

Bergman, Andrew. *We're in the Money: Depression America and Its Films*. New York: New York University Press, 1971.

Betts, Ernest. *Inside Pictures*. London: The Cresset Press, 1960.

Brownlow, Kevin. *The Parade's Gone By . . .* New York: Alfred A. Knopf, 1969.

Cannom, Robert C. *Van Dyke and the Mythical City Hollywood*. Culver City: Murray & Gee, 1948.

Carey, Gary. *All the Stars in Heaven: Louis B. Mayer's MGM*. New York: E. P. Dutton, 1981.

Chierichetti, David. *Hollywood Costume Design*. New York: Harmony Books, 1975.

Crowther, Bosley. *Hollywood Rajah: The Life and Times of Louis B. Mayer*. New York: Holt, Rinehart and Winston, 1960.

———. *The Lion's Share: The Story of an Entertainment Empire*. New York: E. P. Dutton, 1957.

Dardis, Tom. *Keaton: The Man Who Wouldn't Lie Down*. New York: Charles Scribner's Sons, 1979.

Day, Beth. *This Was Hollywood*. Garden City, N.Y.: Doubleday, 1960.

Eames, John Douglas. *The MGM Story*. New York: Portland House, 1990.

Eastman, John. *Retakes: Behind the Scenes of 500 Classic Movies*. New York: Ballantine Books, 1989.

Fenton, Robert W. *The Big Swingers*. Englewood Cliffs, N.J.: Prentice Hall Press, 1967.

Finch, Christopher. *Rainbow: The Stormy Life of Judy Garland*. New York: Grosset & Dunlap, 1975.

Finch, Christopher; and Linda Rosenkrantz. *Gone Hollywood: The Movie Colony in the Golden Age*. New York: Doubleday, 1976.

Finler, Joel W. *The Hollywood Story*. New York: Crown Publishers, 1988.

Flamini, Roland. *Scarlett, Rhett and a Cast of Thousands*. New York: Macmillan Publishing Co., 1975.

Fordin, Hugh. *The World of Entertainment! Hollywood's Greatest Musicals*. Garden City, N.Y.: Doubleday, 1975.

Fricke, John; Jay Scarfone, and William Stillman. *The Wizard of Oz: The Official 50th Anniversary Pictorial History*. New York: Warner Books, 1989.

Friedrich, Otto. *City of Nets*. New York: Harper & Row, 1986.

Gabler, Neal. *An Empire of Their Own: How the Jews Invented Hollywood*. New York: Crown, 1988.

Gardner, Gerald. *The Censorship Papers: Movie Censorship Letters from the Hays Office, 1934 to 1968*. New York: Dodd, Mead & Company, 1987.

Geist, Kenneth L. *Pictures Will Talk: The Life and Films of Joseph L. Mankiewicz*. New York: Da Capo Press, 1978.

Gish, Lillian; and Anne Pinchot. *The Movies, Mr. Griffith, and Me*. Englewood Cliffs, N.J.: Prentice Hall Press, 1969.

Goodman, Ezra. *The Fifty-Year Decline and Fall of Hollywood*. New York: Simon & Schuster, 1961.

Grady, Billy. *The Irish Peacock: The Confessions of a Legendary Talent Agent*. New Rochelle, N.Y.: Arlington House, 1972.

Granlund, Nils T. *Blondes, Brunettes and Bullets*. New York: David McKay, 1957.

Green, Abel; and Joe Laurie, Jr. *Show Biz: From Vaude to Video*. New York: Henry Holt & Co., 1951.

Green, Stanley. *Encyclopedia of the Musical Film*. New York: Oxford University Press, 1981.

Hagen, John Milton. *Holly-would!* New Rochelle, N.Y.: Arlington House, 1974.

Halliwell, Leslie. *The Filmgoer's Companion, Sixth Edition*. New York: Avon Books, 1978.

———. *Halliwell's Film Guide, Fourth Edition*. New York: Charles Scribner's Sons, 1983.

Harmetz, Aljean. *The Making of the Wizard of Oz*. New York: Alfred A. Knopf, 1977.

Harvey, Stephen. *Directed by Vincente Minnelli*. New York: The Museum of Modern Art/Harper & Row, 1989.

Hecht, Ben. *Charlie: The Improbable Life and Times of Charles MacArthur*. New York: Harper & Brothers, 1957.

———. *A Child of the Century*. New York: Simon & Schuster, 1954.

Hemming, Roy. *The Melody Lingers On: The Great Songwriters and Their Movie Musicals*. New York: Newmarket Press, 1986.

Heston, Charlton. *The Actor's Life: Journals 1956-1976*. New York: E. P. Dutton, 1978.

Houseman, John. *Front & Center*. New York: Simon & Schuster, 1979.

Kanin, Garson. *Together Again! Stories of the Great Hollywood Teams*. Garden City, N.Y.: Doubleday, 1981.

Kanin, Garson. *Tracy & Hepburn*. New York: Viking, 1971.

Katz, Ephraim. *The Film Encyclopedia*. New York: G. P. Putnam's Sons, 1979.

Kobal, John. *Gotta Sing Gotta Dance*. London: Hamlyn Publishing, 1971.

———. *People Will Talk*. New York: Alfred A. Knopf, 1985.

Koppes, Clayton R.; and Gregory D. Black. *Hollywood Goes to War*. New York: The Free Press, 1987.

Koszarksi, Richard. *Hollywood Directors 1914-1940*. London: Oxford University Press, 1976.

Kotsilibas-Davis, James; and Myrna Loy. *Myrna Loy: Being and Becoming*. New York: Alfred A. Knopf, 1987.

Lahr, John. *Notes on a Cowardly Lion*. New York: Alfred A. Knopf, 1969.

Lambert, Gavin. *On Cukor*. New York: Putnam, 1972.

———. *Norma Shearer*. New York: Alfred A. Knopf, 1990.

Lasky, Jr., Jesse L.; with Pat Silver. *Love Scene: The Story of Laurence Olivier and Vivien Leigh*. New York: Crowell, 1978.

———; with Pat Silver. *Whatever Happened to Hollywood?* New York: Funk & Wagnalls, 1975.

Latham, Aaron. *Crazy Sundays: F. Scott Fitzgerald in Hollywood*. New York: Viking, 1971.

Lerner, Alan Jay. *The Street Where I Live*. New York: W. W. Norton, 1980.

LeRoy, Mervyn; told to Dick Kleiner. *Take One*. New York: Hawthorn, 1974.

Lescarboura, Austin C. *Behind the Motion-Picture Screen*. New York: Scientific American Publishing Company, 1919.

Likeness, George. *The Oscar People*. Mendota, Ill.: The Wayside Press, 1965.

Loos, Anita. *Cast of Thousands*. New York: Grosset & Dunlap, 1977.

———. *Kiss Hollywood Good-by*. New York: Viking, 1974.

———. *The Talmadge Girls, a Memoir*. New York: Viking, 1978.

Madsen, Axel. *William Wyler*. New York: Crowell, 1973.

Maeder, Edward (ed.). *Hollywood and History: Costume Design in Film*. Los Angeles: County Museum of Art, 1987.

Maltin, Leonard. *Selected Short Subjects: From Spanky to the Three Stooges*. New York: Da Capo Press, 1972.

——— (ed.). *Leonard Maltin's TV Movies and Video Guide*, 1991 Edition. New York: Penguin Books USA, 1990.

Marion, Frances. *Off with Their Heads! A Serio-Comic Tale of Hollywood*. New York: Macmillan, 1972.

Martin, Pete. *Hollywood without Make-up*. Philadelphia: J. B. Lippincott, 1948.

Marx, Harpo; with Rowland Barber. *Harpo Speaks!* New York: Avon Books, 1961.

Marx, Samuel. *A Gaudy Spree: Literary Hollywood When the West Was Fun*. New York: Franklin Watts, 1987.

———. *Mayer and Thalberg: The Make-Believe Saints*. New York: Random House, 1975.

Mast, Gerald. *Can't Help Singin': The American Musical on Stage and Screen*. Woodstock, N.Y.: The Overlook Press, 1987.

———. *Howard Hawks, Storyteller*. Oxford: Oxford University Press, 1982.

Mattfield, Julius. *Variety Music Cavalcade*. Englewood Cliffs, N.J.: Prentice Hall, 1962.

May, Lary. *Screening Out the Past*. New York: Oxford University Press, 1980.

McGilligan, Pat. *Backstory: Interviews with Screenwriters of Hollywood's Golden Age*. Berkeley: University of California Press, 1986.

McShane, Frank. *The Life of Raymond Chandler*. New York: E. P. Dutton, 1976.

Miller, Don. *"B" Movies*. New York: Curtis Books, 1973.

Minnelli, Vincente; with Hector Arce. *I Remember It Well*. Garden City, N.Y.: Doubleday, 1974.

Minney, R. J. *Hollywood by Starlight*. London: Chapman and Hall, 1935.

Montgomery, Elizabeth Miles. *The Best of MGM*. New York: Bison Books, 1986.

Mordden, Ethan. *The Hollywood Studios: House Style in the Golden Age of the Movies*. New York: Alfred A. Knopf, 1988.

———. *Movie Star*. New York: St. Martin's Press, 1983.

Morsberger, Robert E.; and Katharine M. Morsberger. *Lew Wallace: Militant Romantic*. New York: McGraw-Hill, 1980.

The Motion Picture Guide. Chicago: Cinebooks, 1986.

Niven, David. *The Moon's a Balloon: An Autobiography*. New York: G. P. Putnam's Sons, 1972.

Norman, Barry. *The Story of Hollywood*. New York: New American Library, 1988.

Parish, James Robert; and Ronald L. Bowers. *The MGM Stock Company: The Golden Era*. New Rochelle, N.Y.: Arlington House, 1973.

Pasternak, Joe; told to David Chandler. *Easy the Hard Way*. New York: Putnam, 1956.

Pennington, Lucinda W.; and William K. Baxter. *A Past To Remember: The History of Culver City*. Culver City: City of Culver City, 1976.

Porges, Irwin. *Edgar Rice Burroughs: The Man Who Created Tarzan*. Salt Lake City: Brigham University Press, 1975.

Rosenberg, Bernard; and Harry Silverstein. *The Real Tinsel*. New York: Macmillan, 1970.

Ross, Lillian. *Picture*. New York: Rinehart and Co., 1952.

St. Johns, Adela Rogers. *Love, Laughter and Tears: My Hollywood Story*. Garden City, N.Y.: Doubleday, 1978.

Schary, Dore. *Heyday*. Boston: Little, Brown & Co., 1979.

———; told to Charles Palmer. *Case History of a Movie*. New York: Random House, 1950.

Schatz, Thomas. *The Genius of the System: Hollywood Filmmaking in the Studio Era*. New York: Pantheon Books, 1988.

Schwartz, Nancy Lynn. *The Hollywood Writers Wars*. New York: Alfred A. Knopf, 1982.

Selznick, Irene Mayer. *A Private View*. New York: Alfred A. Knopf, 1983.

Sennett, Ted. *Lunatics and Lovers*. New York: Limelight Editions, 1985.

Shale, Richard (compiler). *Academy Awards*. New York: Frederick Ungar Publishing Co., 1982.

Sharaff, Irene. *Broadway & Hollywood*. New York: Van Nostrand Reinhold, 1976.

Silver, Alain; and Elizabeth Ward (eds.). *Film Noir*. Woodstock, N.Y.: The Overlook Press, 1979.

Sklar, Robert. *Movie-Made America*. New York: Vintage Books, 1975.

Spehr, Paul C. *The Movies Begin*. Dobbs Ferry, N.Y.: Morgan Press, 1977.

Stallings, Penny; with Howard Mandelbaum. *Flesh and Fantasy*. New York: St. Martin's Press, 1978.

Stenn, David. *Clara Bow Runnin' Wild*. New York: Penguin Books, 1988.

Suid, Lawrence H. *Guts and Glory: Great American War Films*. Reading, Mass.: Addison-Wesley Publishing Co., 1978.

Swindell, Larry. *Spencer Tracy: A Biography*. New York: New American Library, 1969.

Thomas, Bob. *Thalberg: Life and Legend*. Garden City, N.Y.: Doubleday, 1969.

Trumbo, Dalton (ed. Helen Manfull). *Additional Dialogue: Letters of Dalton Trumbo, 1942-1962*. New York: M. Evans, 1970.

Variety Film Reviews. New York: Garland Publishing, 1983.

Vidor, King. *A Tree Is a Tree*. New York: Harcourt, Brace, Jovanovich, 1953.

Walker, Stanley. *Stardom*. New York: Stein & Day, 1970.

Wayne, Jane Ellen. *Crawford's Men*. New York: Prentice Hall, 1988.

Wanamaker, Marc (ed.). *The Hollywood Reporter Star Profiles*. London: Octopus Books, 1984.

——— (ed.). *Gable's Women*. New York: Prentice Hall, 1987.

White, Mark. *You Must Remember This . . . Popular Songwriters 1900-1980*. New York: Scribners, 1985.

Wilkerson, Tichi; and Marcia Borie. *The Hollywood Reporter: The Golden Years*. New York: Coward-McCann, 1984.

Wood, Michael. *America in the Movies*. New York: Dell Publishing Co., 1975.

INDEX

A showing of The Big Parade *(1925).*

North by Northwest *(1959)*.

Kathryn Grayson.

Melvyn Douglas.

William Powell.

Elizabeth Taylor.

Rosalind Russell.

Irving Thalberg.

Louis B. and Margaret Mayer.

Norma Shearer.

N

Joan Crawford.

O

Franchot Tone.

P

Robert Young.

Set for The Wizard of Oz (1939).